Alumni
Continuing
Education

Alumni Continuing Education

Steven L. Calvert

National University Continuing Education Association

American Council on Education • Macmillan Publishing Company
NEW YORK

Collier Macmillan Publishers
LONDON

Copyright © 1987 by American Council on Education and Macmillan Publishing
            Company
            A Division of Macmillan, Inc.

The American Council on Education/Macmillan Series on Higher Education

Macmillan Publishing Company
866 Third Avenue, New York, N.Y. 10022

Collier Macmillan Canada, Inc.

Library of Congress Catalog Card Number: 87-5722

Printed in the United States of America

printing number
1 2 3 4 5 6 7 8 9 10

Library of Congress Cataloging-in-Publication Data

Calvert, Steven L.
  Alumni continuing education.

  (American Council on Education/Macmillan series
in higher education)
  Bibliography: p.
  Includes index.
  1. Continuing education—United States. 2. Universi-
ties and colleges—United States—Alumni. I. Title.
II. Series.
LC5251.C28   c1987   374'.973   87-5722
ISBN 0-02-905171-1

To **J. Michael McGean,** whose intelligence, perseverance, and extraordinary vision into the true nature of alumni relations made possible Dartmouth's Alumni College since 1964, and whose generosity and patient teaching made possible this book, and its author's profession.

CONTENTS

What Is Alumni Continuing Education? What Is (and
Is Not) the Purpose of Alumni Continuing Education?
An Introduction to Alumni Relations and Continuing
Education. Alumni Relations. Continuing Education.
The Birth of Alumni Continuing Education. 1956–1966:
A Critical Decade Initiates the Modern Alumni Con-
tinuing Education Era.

The Alumni Speak Out. Responsibility for Alumni
Continuing Education. Differences at Public and Private, Large and Small, Young and Old Institutions.
Advantages of Alumni Continuing Education. Advantages to University Leaders. The President and Alumni
Continuing Education. Advantages to the Alumni Office. Advantages to Continuing Education. The New
Professionalism. Advantages to the Faculty. Advantages to the Undergraduates. Advantages to the Admissions Offices. Advantages to the Fundraising Of-

Alumni College Relatives. Elderhostel. Chautauqua Institution. The Aspen Institute. Alumni Family Hall. Family Camps. Writing Workshops. Computer Alumni Colleges, Alumni Language Programs, and Other Specialty Alumni Colleges. Institute, Professional, and Technical School Summer Programs. Executive Programs in the Humanities. Religious Schools' Summer Programs.

Summer Educational Opportunities, Williams Style. A Final Word about Alumni Colleges.

A Definition of Alumni Seminars. The Purposes of Alumni Seminars. Planning Schedules and Cycles for Alumni Seminars. Alumni Seminar Finances. Who Comes to Alumni Seminars? Organization and Staffing for Alumni Seminars. Cooperative Alumni Seminars. Themes for Alumni Seminars. Examples of Alumni Seminar Formats. On-Campus Alumni Seminars. On-Campus Programs Related to Alumni Seminars. On-Campus Seminars Within Other Events. Seminar Days on the Campus. Turn About: the Alumni Teach the Faculty. Evening Seminars on the Campus. The On-Campus Mealtime Seminar Series. Alumnae and Women's On-Campus Seminars, Series, and Weekends. On-Campus Weekend Seminars. Reunion Seminars. The Unique Educational Opportunity of the Alumni Class Reunion. The Dean of Reunions. Reunion Seminars by Academic Department. Off-Campus Alumni Seminars. The Off-Campus Football Saturday Seminar. The Off-Campus Evening Seminar. The Off-Campus Seminar with Cultural Event. The Off-Campus Seminar Series. The Off-Campus Saturday Seminar. The Off-Campus Alumni Conference. Weekend Alumni Seminars.

Programs Related to Alumni Seminars. Continuum. The National Issues Forum. M.I.T.'s Enterprise Forums. Alumni Club (Chapter) Seminars. Club Seminar Handbooks. Sample Alumni Seminar Schedules.

The Future of Alumni Seminars.

The Purposes of Alumni Colleges Abroad. Planning
Schedules and Cycles. Cooperative Alumni Colleges
Abroad. Financing Alumni Colleges Abroad. Organization and Staffing. Legal Risks (IRS, U.S. Postal Service). Participants. Topics. The Importance of Education on Alumni Colleges Abroad.

Print Media Educational Programs for Alumni. Edu-
cational Programs Using Electronic Media. Special
Programs. Alumni Teaching. Alumni Auditing. Alum-
ni-in-the-College. Alumni Continuing Education for
Credit. Parents Programs. Educational Programs for
High Schoolers, Undergraduates, Retired Alumni, and
Others. Career and Continuing Education Counseling.

Guidelines from Adult Development and Learning
Theories. Choosing Curriculum Before Faculty. The
Strength of the Liberal Arts in Alumni Continuing Ed-
ucation Programs. The Importance of Interdisciplinary
Programs for Adult Learners. How to Teach Adult
Learners in Alumni Continuing Education. The Depth
Charge Principle. Curricula Aimed at Specific Age
Groups of Alumni. The Classroom for All Ages.

Successful Topics for Alumni Continuing Education
Programs. Topics for Short programs (Half-Day, Eve-
ning, or One-Day). Topics for Weekend Programs
(Three and Four Days). Topics for Weekday or Week-
end Series (2–8 Half-Day or Evening Programs). Topics
for Alumni Colleges (One Week or Longer), Topics/
Destinations for Alumni Colleges Abroad. Domestic
Travel Programs.

The Faculty. Hiring the Faculty. Paying the Faculty.
Curriculum Planning. Offering Credit, CEUs, and
Certificates of Participation.

Financing Alumni Continuing Education: The Big Picture. Alumni Continuing Education's Value-Added Effect on Development. Four Views of the Alumni Continuing Education Budget. The Annual Budget. Institutional Funding as an Investment in Alumni and Public Relations. Outside Funding. The Long-Term Effects on Fundraising. Summarizing the Views on Funding Alumni Continuing Education. Developing Budgets for Specific Alumni Continuing Education Programs. An Alumni College Budget. Price Sensitivity of Different Program Types. An Alumni Seminar Budget. Budgeting an Alumni College Abroad. Faculty Honoraria. Academic Materials. Promotional Materials. Staff Costs. Revenue and Reimbursements. An Overall Alumni Continuing Education Budget.

Toward a Coherent Lifelong Relationship Between Adults and Universities. What is the Role of Volunteer Adults in the Education of Undergraduate and Graduate Students? How Might Alumni Relations Better Represent the Qualities and Needs of the University to Alumni, and Alumni Opinions and Needs to the University? How Might the Fundraising Profession Better Serve the Needs of University and Patron Alike? How Might Continuing Education Be Redesigned to Provide Lifelong Continuity and to Use the Educational Resources Implicit in an Adult's Life Experience? How Might Enhanced Professionalism in Alumni Relations and Continuing Education Improve the Relationship Between Adults and Universities? Where Do College and University Responsibilities End? The Baby Boom

Effect. University Responsibility for American Higher Education.

Applying Alumni Continuing Education. University Life for a Future Alumnus. Four Proposed Additions to the Relationship Between Adults and Universities. Reshape Student Life to Develop Lifelong Learners. Teach Lifelong Learning Skills to Undergraduates and Alumni: 1. Offer an undergraduate course on adult education. 2. Teach adult education in extracurricular settings. 3. Provide catch-up adult education courses. 4. Create a lifelong learning center. Develop a Coherent Lifelong Relationship Between Adults and Universities. Alumni Sharing.

Conclusion.

FOREWORD

Years ago, many a commencement speaker told the story of the young graduate who rushed down the steps from the platform, waving his diploma and shouting, "Educated, by gosh!" That, of course, was before any widespread awareness of alumni continuing education permeated the academic community. Actually, such diffusion has yet to occur although the notion is spreading, and hopefully this volume will hasten the flow of the idea.

The recognition and acceptance of a responsibility for the continuing education of its alumni may signal a college or university's entrance into modern times. The G.I. Bill of World War II taught many faculty members that adults could be stimulating and better-than-average students, a point which Steven Calvert makes on behalf of alumni continuing education. Some of the post-war faculty also discovered that part-time students could learn as well as those who were enrolled full-time. The continuing education of the alumni adds another extension to a continuing education movement which established a base in the 1920s and '30s and really gained strength in the 1940s and '50s.

The United States truly will become a learning society if our colleges and universities can and will establish an intellectual relationship with their matriculants, not from the cradle to the grave but from matriculation until "the inquiring mind" has lost its curiosity. How many alumni may be receptive, and for what reasons many may fail to respond, only time will tell, but, after all, every professor wonders about the same two questions when he faces each new class.

In any event, the possible rewards are well worth the effort. The idea works, as Calvert's long list of successful ventures indicates. Every institution of higher education has the capability if it has the will. With this volume as both stimulant and guide, it may be that increasing numbers of academic communities will invite their "old grads" back to a continuing academic fellowship with seats on the intellectual fifty-yard line.

Ernest E. McMahon, Ph.D.

St. Michaels, Maryland
December 1, 1986

PREFACE

Increasing numbers of individuals are winning college degrees, but the degree is no longer considered preparation for a lifetime. Shortly after entering the work force, today's new alumni are apt to find themselves headed back to a university classroom. The rapid pace of technological change makes it critical for the American work force to absorb innovations and adapt its skills to new technologies. Apart from the economic reasons for maintaining occupational skills, there are important individual and social reasons that prompt more and more college graduates to invest in continuing higher education in an information society. It is this new reality that led the National University Continuing Education Association (NUCEA) and the Council for the Advancement and Support of Education (CASE) to sponsor the publication of *Alumni Continuing Education*.

In *Alumni Continuing Education* Steven L. Calvert challenges colleges and universities to accept responsibility for the lifelong education of alumni. Implicit in this charge is a recognition of the importance of continuous learning in an information society. Paralleling this is the declining interest in social and athletic events, once considered sufficient to sustain the interest of the alumni upon whose support higher education institutions depend. Thus, Calvert argues, it is important for institutions to convince their students and alumni to conceive of their undergraduate alma mater as a permanent "intellectual home."

The book traces the hundred-year history of alumni continuing education and discusses how the fields of continuing education and alumni relations each have contributed to this enterprise. Written especially for university leaders, continuing higher education and alumni professionals, and alumni association volunteers, *Alumni Continuing Education* offers practical guidelines for organizing and planning a higher education institution's lifelong education program for alumni. Also, the book describes a wide range of model alumni continuing education programs appropriate to different institutional types, public or independent, large or small, old or new.

What Calvert quite simply suggests is that it is time for colleges and universities to rethink their programs for alumni in light of the lifelong educational needs of their alumni. Expanding numbers of well-educated adults are seeking continuing higher education opportunities. Responding to the demands of alumni throughout their lives can serve to strengthen ties between higher education institutions and their alumni and thus bring enhanced benefits both to the alma mater and to its alumni.

KAY J. KOHL
Executive Director
NUCEA

GARY QUEHL
President
CASE

ACKNOWLEDGMENTS

If ever there were a collaborative effort, this was it. This book began at Dartmouth College's Minary Conference Center on Squam Lake in New Hampshire's White Mountains in September 1978. Minary (as this annual gathering of alumni college directors came to be known since its beginning in the late 1960s) still brings together many of the most knowledgeable professionals in alumni continuing education. These vice-presidents, alumni directors, and their line officers gave so much advice about alumni continuing education to colleagues around the country that it became clear a book would be more effective. The early book outlines grew out of close work with Sallie K. Riggs, then of Brown University (now at Brandeis), James Quitslund of Harvard, and G. Michael McHugh, then at Cornell. (McHugh, now a private tour operator and consultant, had called for the first Minary meeting in 1969.) They have been collaborators for over ten years.

Eventually, in the late fall of 1985, Virginia Carter Smith, vice president at the Council for Advancement and Support of Education (CASE) in Washington, D.C., formally requested a book. The earlier partners agreed to supply expertise and the

project was launched. In addition, dozens of professionals at
other schools, experienced in alumni continuing education,
have contributed material and invaluable advice. Many of them
are listed in the Appendix, which will serve both as acknowledgment and as a further resource for readers. I thank these
colleagues not only for help with this book, but for support,
mentoring, and friendship.

To Milton Stern, who gave careful attention to early stages
of the book's preparation, helped shape its ideas, and gave both
encouragement and wise counsel in the form of unabashed critical assistance, my thanks for attending the book's birth and
early childhood. If books have champions, Milton championed
this one.

For pioneering work in alumni continuing education and a
willingness to be quoted and depended upon, I want to acknowledge the leadership of Ernest E. McMahon and thank
him for the Foreword. His 1960 monograph, "New Directions
for Alumni: Continuing Education for the College Graduate,"
brought the subject alive for me and many others. We also owe
great debts to Lowell Eklund, whose experimental Oakland Plan
at Oakland University in the 1960s still stands as our best attempt at alumni continuing education on a large scale; and to
Linda Carl, whose 1978 CASE monograph, "The Alumni College Movement," added much empirical evidence to our understanding of the subject.

Special thanks go to Kay J. Kohl, executive director of
the National University Continuing Education Association
(NUCEA) in Washington, D.C., without whose judicious vision,
patience, and educational efforts on the author's behalf this
book could not have reached continuing education professionals
through NUCEA's relationship with both the American Council
on Education (ACE) and Macmillan Publishing Company. My
thanks to James J. Murray at ACE for his helpfulness. At Macmillan, my sincerest thanks go to executive editor Lloyd Chilton
for his unfailing good nature, confidence, and optimism; and
to Elly Dickason for her considerable contribution to a readable
text and for carrying the manuscript through to publication.

For their timely help and advice with the manuscript, I wish to thank Eustace D. Theodore and Catherine Spinelli at Yale University, Robert A. Reichley at Brown University, Sallie K. Riggs at Brandeis University, Lowell Eklund at Oakland University, J. Michael McGean and Professor Charles T. Wood at Dartmouth College, James C. Votruba at the State University of New York at Binghamton, and also Linda Carl and Cyril Houle. Virginia Carter Smith and Kay J. Kohl did much more than read the final manuscript; they gave the book its final form.

At Dartmouth College, I also owe thanks for patience, technical assistance, and hard work to my staff assistant, Lorraine Marcotte, who not only held the Alumni Continuing Education program together while the book was being written, but who proofread the text twice and developed considerable computer expertise in order to keep book and office on schedule. Thanks also to Patricia Downing, office manager in alumni affairs for two decades, who taught Lorraine and me how to run the Alumni College and who also helped prepare the manuscript and page proofs; and to Karen Parker for careful proofreading.

To Robert A. Reichley, vice president for university relations at Brown University and chair of the CASE Board of Trustees in 1986–87, who has been a long-distance mentor and inveterate Minary participant, go the thanks and the admiration of an apprentice and friend.

And, most sincerely of all, I have the pleasure of putting into print the names of three individuals who made the book possible through love and understanding, and by adjusting daily lives to the clicking Macintosh computer in the upstairs study: my wife, Patti, and daughters Tiffany Charlotte and Elizabeth Lynn. They have more than my thanks; they have my love.

Part One

Seventy-Five Years of Continuing Education for Alumni

CHAPTER 1

WHAT IS ALUMNI CONTINUING EDUCATION?

In 1863, the Xavier Alumni Sodality brought together the graduates of all Roman Catholic colleges "to promote the study of good books and to foster a taste for the sciences and arts" (Knowles, 1962, p. 23). The Association of Collegiate Alumnae was founded in 1882, also for the specific purpose of continuing education:

> Its purpose was to engage in practical education work, and its membership was restricted to women who had received degrees from approved colleges, universities, or scientific schools. The program of the association included the raising of standards of higher education for women; the organization of study groups, for which a national staff provided study guides; and the sponsorship of such community activities as classes for illiterates, concerts, recreational services, war services, and many others [Knowles, 1962, p. 61].

Today, after more than a century, fostered by continuing education and alumni relations, alumni continuing education stands ready to play an important role in enriching the future relationship between adults and their colleges and universities

3

of all kinds—large and small, public and private, all around the country.

This book will make the experience of that hundred-year history, and of hundreds of institutions that currently offer alumni continuing education programs, more readily accessible than it has been. Institutions that have recently discovered alumni continuing education, and institutions wishing to expand existing programs, should find this book a helpful resource, but the field is growing quickly and readers may also want to contact some of the many professionals listed in the Appendix.

What is Alumni Continuing Education?

Alumni continuing education is an overall program for continuing the relationship between alumni and the university. This definition assumes that the relationship will be intellectual, cultural, social, and recreational, perhaps even in that order, about as it was when the alumni were undergraduates. It assumes that the relationship will be reciprocal, and that it will exhibit continuity from the acceptance of high school applicants until the symbolic end in alumni magazine obituaries.

We can read the three-word phrase, alumni continuing education, in several ways. In one sense, it describes a special kind of education (continuing, and for alumni). Or, we can read the phrase as a sentence (subject–transitive verb–object), describing college graduates who are continuing their education.

By way of further definition, it is worth looking at each word in the phrase, alumni continuing education. For example, alumni continuing education is almost never for alumni only. It is usually designed primarily for alumni, but nonalumni are welcome as participants. This makes sense in a field deriving in part from alumni or university relations. Spouses are often nonalumni, and welcome; so are parents and other relatives of alumni or undergraduates. And every college or university has its otherwise unaffiliated friends. As a practical matter, then, it is hard to imagine excluding anyone from alumni continuing education programs.

Most alumni continuing education programs are short-term and offer no credit, but they are continuing in the same ways that all good education is continuing. Some program formats provide for continuity through advance or follow-up study, others depend upon the programs themselves to spark further work by participants.

For many participants who become regulars, even in programs that take place once a year for a few days, the lasting effects can be substantial. In this sense, alumni continuing education is real education, even when some of the attraction for participants comes from social, cultural, or recreational aspects of the programs.

In defining alumni continuing education, we need to be flexible, for we are describing a field that is still taking shape. When Linda Carl, then a doctoral candidate and running the University of Illinois's alumni college at Urbana-Champaign, wrote her Council for Advancement and Support of Education (CASE) monograph in 1978, she called it "The Alumni College Movement." While Carl acknowledged that colleges and universities had developed a great variety of educational programs to bring alumni and faculty back together, she nevertheless concentrated her survey on one particular kind of program, which she called an alumni college. She defined an alumni college as "a five- to seven-day residential experience for adults, focused on the noncredit study of the liberal arts, sponsored by an institution of higher education" (p. 1). Today, the original alumni college concept has inspired so many other kinds of educational programs for alumni that we now need the rubric, alumni continuing education, for the whole field, and we reserve the term "alumni college" for one specific program type.

This is an important distinction. As the alumni college movement has become an alumni continuing education movement, we have gained the advantage of seeing the alumni college as one of the most difficult of alumni continuing education formats for most institutions to mount. Therefore, colleges and universities can think today with a broader perspective about what program formats to use when initiating or expanding alumni continuing education. They need no longer feel obligated to start with a full-blown, on-campus, week-long summer alumni college in order to get into the movement. Indeed, an alumni college may be, for many institutions, exactly the wrong place to begin. Instead, these institutions might begin by adding educational aspects to reunions or the alumni travel program, or by sending a faculty member instead of a coach to the alumni club's annual dinner. The alumni college can come along when the institution and the alumni are ready.

More will be said later about on-campus summer alumni colleges, but regarding definitions it is worth noting that even alumni colleges as Carl defines them may not be called alumni colleges. In *The Future of Adult Education*, Fred Harvey Harrington calls them "vacation workshops for alumni" (p. 3). As Carl reported in 1978,

> *When the alumni college is not sponsored by an alumni association, it is sometimes called a vacation college. The Office of Summer Sessions at the University of Oregon, The Office of Continuing Education at American University, and the Office of Continuing Education and the alumni association at the University of Rhode Island sponsor vacation colleges. On the other hand, the Summerweek of Ohio Wesleyan is sponsored solely by the alumni association, and Cornell's Alumni College is sponsored by the Office of Public Affairs Education Program. In short, name alone may give you a clue as to the sponsor—but it also may not [p. 20].*

Some universities call their alumni college the "alumni university."

Even some professional schools have begun alumni continuing education programs. Topics often amount to professional updates in the fields of business management, accounting, law, and medicine. If this variation takes hold, it will be in addition to (not competing with) existing professional education which provides credentials, and could be partly motivated by the alumni relations needs of the sponsoring school. In other words, it would have the same relationship to continuing professional education (professional education for credential purposes) that alumni continuing education has to continuing education-sometimes cooperative, sometimes complementary, sometimes entirely distinct, but usually short-term, noncredit, and never in direct competition for the same adult market. We may soon want a new term, like professional alumni continuing education, for this kind of program, in order to identify the sponsor as a professional school and the market as professional school alumni. The University of Pennsylvania's Wharton School of business management has taken on this relatively new educational responsibility.

What Is (and Is Not) the Purpose of Alumni Continuing Education?

A university serves many purposes, and alumni continuing education can support many of them. This flexibility can lead to some confusion about the purposes of alumni continuing education. The primary purpose is twofold: to provide educational programs for the alumni, and through that contact to develop interested, informed, involved, and supportive alumni.

On the other hand, it is natural to assume that, if the alumni office sponsors an alumni college, the institution's ulterior motive is to help the fundraising office. This is partly true, but only in the sense that alumni continuing education raises money just as other arms of the university raise money—by showcasing university excellence, which in turn inspires support of many kinds from the university's publics. At the same time, an alumni college is not normally designed to make a profit.

Readers not entirely familiar with alumni relations may need to know that at most colleges and universities the alumni and development (or fundraising) offices work hand-in-glove but have separate functions. The distinction can be made this way: the alumni office houses the "friendraisers," the development office the "fundraisers." The alumni office's business is to keep alumni and others involved with the university, on the theory that the more involved they are, the more generously they will respond later when asked to provide their alma mater with volunteer and financial assistance. Alumni continuing education, while it may pay for itself, should not have to do so when it is designed as a key program in the alumni office. Like any other alumni program, its purpose will be to keep alumni involved in the business of the university. Since that business is education (teaching and learning), alumni continuing education will actually serve this purpose better than most other alumni programs; but it will not necessarily make a profit, any more than reunion programs or the alumni council.

In the area of student services, continuing education and alumni continuing education overlap to some degree. All good programs strive for high-quality service and satisfied customers. But alumni continuing education treats participants like alumni, which should mean very special treatment, sometimes but not always beyond normal attention to students' needs. Continuing education offices that run some of the finest liberal arts and other programs for executives, for example, provide the highest quality service and take great care about student comforts and needs. If there is a difference in this regard, it is that alumni continuing education must strive in every program to match continuing education's highest level of service. The standard is to dedicate an administrator full-time to an alumni continuing education program while it is in session. Few other continuing education programs can afford this luxury, because they are not simultaneously in business to provide education and effective public or alumni relations.

In "A Report on the Continuing Education Program of the Tufts Alumni Council," Fred P. Nickless, Jr., pointed out that an administrator gave refunds "clearly contrary to publicized policy." This refund flexibility typifies an alumni continuing education director's concerns over the happiness of alumni who come back to the campus for a reunion. We all wish that all our students will be perfectly happy; but alumni relations programs—including alumni continuing education programs—must ensure it.

To answer another question commonly asked, alumni continuing education should not compete with the continuing education office. The purposes and motivations of these offices are different, and should be kept in mind. At institutions where continuing education already offers fine short-term noncredit programs, the alumni office may only need to offer marketing access to the alumni mailing list, or in some other way throw in with the continuing education office to provide alumni continuing education. With its short-term, noncredit focus, alumni continuing education can benefit continuing education by giving adults a non-threatening taste of education at midlife that can lead to further participation in continuing education's programs.

An Introduction to Alumni Relations and Continuing Education

Alumni continuing education issues from two parent professions—*alumni* relations and *continuing education*—and was a twinkle in both parents' eyes very early in their lives. For example, we know about the Xavier Alumni Sodality from the continuing education side—that is, from a history of the Roman Catholic Church and adult education. On the alumni relations side, the second meeting of the Association of Alumni Secretaries in 1913 included discussion about educational programs for alumni. Therefore, for readers unfamiliar with alumni relations or continuing education, a brief orientation into these parent fields will enrich our definition of alumni continuing education and serve as a useful background for the rest of this book.

ALUMNI RELATIONS

Robert G. Forman, executive director of the University of Michigan Alumni Association, described the history, purpose, and possible future of alumni relations in 1979. At the time, Forman was volunteer chair-elect of the Council for Advancement and Support of Education (CASE), the professional organization created in 1974 when the American Alumni Council and the American College Public Relations Association merged.

Alumni relations began as a peculiarly American phenomenon. Alumni involvement (as alumni) in their alma maters was almost entirely absent in European universities. Forman traces alumni relations in this country back to 1792, when Yale College first organized its alumni classes. The first general alumni associations started at private small colleges and universities in the Northeast: Williams was first in 1821, followed over the next thirty years by Amherst and then most of the schools that later formed the Ivy League, before the idea moved farther south and west.

Early professionals, called alumni secretaries, kept graduates' addresses and other records. A few alumni secretaries keep the historical title; most now use titles such as director of alumni relations, or director of alumni affairs.

Today, alumni organizations exhibit nearly as much diversity as the colleges and universities they support:

> One of the peculiarities of alumni relations, and perhaps one of the reasons that it seems difficult to define the field properly, is the fact that no two alumni organizations are alike.
>
> I strongly support the concept of the independent alumni association. Others, from equally valid points of view, suggest that the best approach is the totally integrated and dependent association housed within the university's overall organization. Most alumni associations are hybrids of these two approaches. . . .
>
> What they all have in common are two simple objectives: to develop ways to enable alumni to serve their university and to carry out programs and activities that serve alumni. Our real professional challenge is to keep these two objectives in proper perspective and make them mutually supportive.
>
> Today's programs would be unrecognizable to many of our early professionals. We employ individuals whose academic training and work experience cover a variety of backgrounds. To manage an alumni relations program properly, we need advice from specialists in marketing and sales, group dynamics, camp administration, travel consulting, interpersonal communications, and other fields.
>
> Alumni relations reaches every aspect of the university community. A well-rounded program involves alumni in fund raising, government

relations, decision-making, faculty selection, student relations, student recruitment, scholarship and financial aid, visiting [committees], club organization, reunion activities, merchandising, insurance, and other areas. Some associations' gross income is many millions of dollars, counting receipts from travel, camps, and merchandise [Forman, 1979, p. 8].

The Association of Alumni Secretaries first met in Columbus, Ohio, on February 22, 1913. Participants gave papers on alumni publications, class reunions, and the relation of alumni organizations to university governing boards. The second meeting, which included a discussion about alumni continuing education, followed just eight months later.

Since those first meetings prior to World War I, the alumni relations profession has gone through two developmental stages and now enters a third, according to Forman. During the first stage, professionals organized their alumni, themselves, and the early body of knowledge that defined the new profession. The second stage saw the development of programs to link alumni to alma mater and honed alumni directors' professional techniques. Forman sees a third stage already underway, in which alumni relations is moving into the mainstream of higher education administration, helping to define the mission, goals, and activities of our colleges and universities.

Continuing Education

Whereas the alumni movement has been almost entirely an American institution, the roots of university continuing education in this country can be found in Britain where mid-nineteenth-century Mechanics' Institutes provided worker education and where lecture clubs served a middle-class clientele.

Also critical to American university continuing education was the Morrill Act of 1862. It created the land-grant colleges to teach agriculture and the mechanic arts along with other scientific and classical subjects. These new institutions placed the emphasis on making higher education accessible to all with ability, without regard to financial means, and on developing cooperative relationships with federal and state governments. From the beginning, the state and land-grant universities assumed a public service obligation "to disseminate knowledge widely and to apply the results of campus research for the benefit of the people." It was this commitment which led to the development of university extension services whose very mandate was to reach out into the community in an effort to improve the life of the citizens of all ages through learning.

By drawing upon various studies of the extension movement, especially that of Lowell Eklund, it is possible to trace the history of American university continuing education prior to 1915:

pre-1776........ Library-related night schools and juntos inspired by Benjamin Franklin

1785–1790...... Brown University lectures for the public

1808............. Yale University science courses for the public

1816............. Rutgers lectures on chemical philosophy for the public

1820s .... Lyceum cooperative study group movement

1836............. Lowell Institute for public lectures established at Harvard University

1839............. Teachers Institutes in Connecticut

1852............. University of Michigan agricultural courses for non-matriculated students

1868............. Kansas State College farmers' institute

1873............. Chautauqua rural-based summer schools

1876............. Johns Hopkins University "academic lectures" and "lesson courses" provided to the public

1879............. University of Kansas lectures and off-campus programs organized

1880............. University of Utah off-campus classes

1886............. Drafting lessons in wood and metal work offered to public by Pennsylvania State

1888............. University of Wisconsin farmers' institute and teachers' summer school

1891............. University of California Extension established

1891............. Extension and correspondence courses offered on credit basis by University of Wyoming

1892............. University of Chicago opened its doors and offered lecture courses to adults from the outset

1892............. Extension programs for teachers begun at University of Nebraska

1895............. Department of correspondence studies and speakers bureau established at University of North Dakota

1902............. University of Alabama extension services begun

1904............. University of Oklahoma lecture bureau founded

1908............. Georgia Tech Night School founded at Georgia Institute of Technology

1909............. University of Texas extension department established

1910............. University of Missouri extension division created

1910............. University of Pittsburgh extension program begun

1910............. Off-campus organized instruction for university credit offered by Ohio University

1913............. University of Minnesota general extension division established

1913............ University of Iowa division of extension and
      university service organized

1913............ Engineering extension begun at Iowa State
      University

Industrialization and urbanization, immigration and labor
unions, soon changed the face of America and generated an
enormous demand for continuing higher education. University
extension programs and night schools began to proliferate.
These new divisions sought to meet not only the educational
needs of adults in an increasingly industrialized economy, but
also attempted to offer classes at locations and times that would
be convenient to adult students.

Early in 1915, twenty-two higher education institutions—
some public and some independent—formed the National University Extension Association (NUEA), which some decades
later would be re-named National University Continuing Education Association (NUCEA). NUEA's charter members included: Columbia University, Indiana University, Iowa State
College, The Pennsylvania State College, Harvard University,
the State University of Iowa, and the Universities of California,
Chicago, Colorado, Idaho, Kansas, Michigan, Minnesota, Missouri, North Carolina, Oklahoma, Pennsylvania, Pittsburgh,
South Carolina, South Dakota, Virginia, and Wisconsin.

Cyril O. Houle suggests that the crucial period for American
continuing education really began about 1919, when the Carnegie Foundation got behind the idea financially. English adult
education had taken a relatively elitist tone from the rigid social
structure of that nation in the nineteenth century. Transferred
to this side of the Atlantic, however, the reverse took place:
even America's finest institutions gradually took responsibility
for the practical educational needs of agriculture and the other
vocations throughout the nation.

Still, American colleges and universities, remembering their
English roots, continued to serve the less practical but equally
important intellectual needs of the people. As one example,
Malcolm Knowles (1962) points to the public lectures on natural
science that Yale Professor Benjamin Silliman took around the

country for thirty years after 1930. This might have made Silliman the Johnny Appleseed of American continuing higher education (and Yale the birthplace of both continuing education and of alumni relations in this country), except that Silliman spoke to "ladies and gentlemen" by subscription. It took the Land Grant College (Morrill) Act of 1862 to bring the practical teaching of agriculture to the American farmer.

During the period 1915–1929, Charles A. Wedemeyer says (*Spectator*, pp. 9–12) that the leaders of British and American thought about education (including Alfred North Whitehead, John Dewey, William James, and Frank Ward) advocated a more practical focus for continuing higher education. William Rainey Harper "established extension as a major division in Rockefeller's new University of Chicago" in 1892. The Smith-Lever Act of 1914 put the federal government behind agricultural extension, and the Smith-Hughes Vocational Education Act of 1917 funded training in other vocations.

Ernest E. McMahon reports (*Spectator*, pp. 13–15) that the period 1929–1941, dominated by the Great Depression, saw "the rise of the evening college and the extension center and the founding of the Association of University Evening Colleges, now the Association for Continuing Higher Education" (*Spectator*, p. 14). During this period the universities further focused their role as a provider of services to the general adult population.

After World War II, continuing education expanded rapidly to keep up with G.I. Bill adults returning to the classroom (Paul H. Sheats and Lynda T. Smith, *Spectator*, pp. 16–18). Then came a crucial period of assessment, for both continuing education and alumni relations. Interestingly, the Ford Foundation's Fund for Adult Education helped to fund two landmark studies for these two professions. On the continuing education side, it was the Morton Study, which in 1953 became the first thorough study of university extension in the United States. That Study found that "education has become a continuous need throughout life." On the alumni relations side, the Fund for Adult Education co-sponsored with the American Alumni Council the Shoreham Conference in 1958 which looked specifically at continuing education for alumni of America's colleges and universities.

From this point, continuing education played an increasingly important role in higher education. The Kellogg and other centers for continuing education were built at some eighty universities around the country. Professionalism developed steadily, and by the 1980s, 85 percent of the deans and directors holding membership in the National University Continuing Education Association (formerly the NUEA) held terminal degrees (the Ph.D. or equivalent), not to mention backgrounds in curriculum development, marketing and entrepreneurship, financial management, counseling, and other skills required to serve the needs of part-time nontraditional adult students. The profession also began to differentiate among the terms *adult education* (for pre-postsecondary adult learning), *extension* (still more agriculturally or at least vocationally based), and *continuing education* (for adults in postsecondary study), as the field divided into more specialized functional areas, including part-time for-credit programs, professional education, liberal and general studies, community development and services, conferences and institutes, instructional telecommunications, and alumni continuing education.

The Birth of Alumni Continuing Education

The early histories of continuing education and alumni relations set the scene for the birth of alumni continuing education. It is important to understand that most early alumni continuing education programs came out of the alumni offices at private colleges and universities in the Northeast, starting soon after 1916. These were already mature institutions whose alumni bodies included retirement-aged men and women with the time and money to attend recreational alumni colleges and seminars. Nearly all of these early sponsors of alumni continuing education were private institutions who depended upon the generosity of alumni for their survival. They were therefore the institutions who developed strong alumni programs well back in the nineteenth century. By World War I, many of these colleges and universities already had some experience with small education programs for alumni and were poised for bigger things.

Three periods stand out in the history of alumni continuing education: 1916, when statements in 1916 by Dartmouth and Amherst colleges' presidents argued for substantial intellectual involvement by alumni in their alma maters; 1928–1930, when the first substantial commitments were made for alumni continuing education at Lafayette College and the University of Michigan; and the decade 1956–1966, which launched the modern alumni continuing education era.

Ernest E. McMahon's 1960 monograph, "New Directions for Alumni: Continuing Education for the College Graduate," traces the history of alumni continuing education back to Ernest Martin Hopkins's 1916 inaugural address at Dartmouth College. Here is the crucial passage:

> *If the college, then, has conviction that its influence is worth seeking at the expense of four vital years in the formative period of life, is it not logically compelled to search for some method of giving access to this influence to its graduates in their subsequent years? . . .*
>
> *. . . the College has no less an opportunity to be of service to its men in their old age than in their youth, if only it can establish the procedure by which it can periodically throughout their lives give them opportunity to replenish their intellectual reserves* [Dartmouth Alumni Magazine, *Volume IX, 1916–17, p. 16*].

McMahon was well-qualified to judge the beginnings of alumni continuting education: he had served Rutgers as alumni director, and then as dean of University College and of the University Extension Division. McMahon takes his cue about Hopkins from Wilfred B. Shaw's paper, "Recent Progress in Alumni Education," which McMahon found in the 1930 *Report of the Seventeenth Annual Conference* of the American Alumni Council (Ithaca, p. 42).

Hopkins did not invent the idea of continuing education for alumni. The Xavier Alumni Sodality preceded him by fifty-three years. Whether or not Hopkins knew of that particular program, he must have been aware of an early interest in alumni continuing education. His words echo important parts of a letter (quoted below) that Dr. William E. Channing wrote to Harvard president Josiah Quincy in 1835:

> The education of the people seems to me more and more to be the object to which the college should be directed. This institution has always existed, and exists now, for the people. It trains young men, not so much for themselves, as that they may be qualified to render services to the community; and perhaps they render no higher service than by spreading their own intelligence and giving a higher tone to the public mind. Can not the college do more for this end? I hope it may. If it can furnish a course of philosophical instruction, which can be pursued by a greater number than now pass through college; if it can extend the demand for this higher education by supplying this means, and if it can give a rank to those who enjoy this advantage, it will render inestimable service to the community.
>
> Perhaps the most important inquiry for the friends of the college is, How can it become a popular institution, an object of public interest, without narrowing at all its present course of instruction? Its well being requires that the community should look to it as their friend and benefactor [quoted in Knowles, 1962, pp. 32–33; emphasis added].

The turn of the phrase, and the powerful questioning mode with little attempt to answer, make it hard to believe Hopkins did not know of the Channing letter.

Later on (not long before Hopkins's 1916 address), at the Association of Alumni Secretaries's second annual meeting in 1913, Yale University's Edwin Rogers Embree described

> a unique extension work unknown to western institutions, trying to work out a plan for the continuous development of the individual. The A.M. is given to Yale A.B.'s in absentia for a course of reading at least three years after the A.B. . . . . It is a stimulus for definite work in certain lines. Many take it in English. A thesis or examination is required. It has kept the graduates interested [quoted in McMahon, 1960, p. 7].

McMahon goes on:

> Embree further stated that the Yale Review, "a scholarly and literary review of the times," tied the intellectual interest of the alumni to the university. He also reported on the organization of advisory committees for the university departments as a means of fostering alumni interest in the academic work of Yale.

Hopkins must also have been cognizant of continuing education gaining strength and getting organized through federal action. The 1914 Smith-Lever Act had put the federal government behind university extension, and the NUEA formally adopted its constitution on April 13, 1916 (see Knowles, 1962, p. 160). During the following summer Hopkins would have been writing the alumni education section of his October inaugural address.

Then, at the 150th anniversary celebration of Rutgers College just eight days after Hopkins's address, Amherst College's president Alexander Meiklejohn called for an entirely new definition of a college community:

> . . . I should like to mention one of the phases of college life in which the lack of correlation is clearly and painfully evident. It is that of the relations between the college and its graduates. Here . . . we have hardly begun to think of the principles and purposes involved. . . .
>
> [The real test of a graduate's loyalty is that] of membership in a college community. If the college has given itself up to the pursuit of knowledge and appreciation philosophic, literary, scientific, humanistic, no man who has ceased from that pursuit is in any genuine sense a member of the college community. I sometimes think that the only real test of our teaching is that of the extent to which pupils continue to study our subjects after they leave us.
>
> . . . I am dreaming of the college community as a body of thousands of men—teachers, graduates, undergraduates—all of whom are engaged in the same intellectual operation, in the same great enterprise of the mind [quoted in McMahon, 1960, p. 6].

The Great War may have contributed to the sense of educational urgency expressed by these first alumni continuing education leaders. Alan Knox, describing "change events" in his *Adult Development and Learning* (1977), and Carol B. Aslanian and Henry M. Brickell (*Americans in Transition: Life Changes as Reasons for Adult Learning*, 1980), refining the notion that transition events in adult lives can trigger continuing education activity, suggest that adults often use educational activity as a way to handle stress. Why not apply the theory to whole nations? Could not the trauma of a world war send an entire nation into a learning mode? That seems to be John W. Gardner's point in this passage from *Self-Renewal* (1961):

It was a characteristic experience during the Second World War that men and women who had been forced to break the pattern of their lives often discovered within themselves resources and abilities they had not known to exist. How ironic that it should take war and disaster to bring about self-renewal on a large scale! It is an expensive way to accomplish it [p. 10].

The periods around the Civil War, two World Wars, and the Korean and Vietnam Wars coincide with expansionary periods in continuing education. This pattern holds for alumni continuing education as well. For example, during the winter of 1918–1919, Dartmouth's president Hopkins sent a weekly series of evening lectures on war and peace issues seventy-five miles through the wilderness to alumni and other interested adults in Manchester, New Hampshire—the rough equivalent today of sending one's first off-campus alumni lectures halfway across the country. Meiklejohn's Amherst was not far behind, offering alumni reading courses that McMahon believes were the first educational programs developed by an alumni association (McMahon, 1960, p. 8).

By 1928, between wars but on the eve of a national economic crisis, there was enough alumni continuing education activity for a survey:

The first national survey of continuing educational programs for alumni was made in 1928 by Daniel L. Grant of the University of North Carolina among both member institutions of the American Alumni Council and non-members. In an AAC membership of approximately 250, plus 164 responding non-members, there were forty-nine institutions which reported past, present, or planned alumni education programs. Without attempting to eliminate duplicates resulting from multiple activities, his findings may be summarized as follows: twenty-five reported reading lists for alumni; seventeen conducted short courses, institutes, or clinics; twenty-five planned either to increase existing programs or to initiate such activity [McMahon, 1960, p. 12].

Then, in 1928–1929, two very different institutions—Lafayette, a small private, eastern college, and the large, midwestern University of Michigan—shifted alumni continuing education into a higher gear. Michigan's *Encyclopedia* tells the story:

The Bureau of Alumni Relations is an agency developed by the University of Michigan to stimulate and maintain a co-operative relationship between the institution and its alumni on the basis of their educational and intellectual interests. It is designed as a means of continuing into postcollege years the educational experience and interests of the undergraduate period.

The history of the Bureau began with a plan for a postcollegiate, or alumni, educational venture to be denominated the "Alumni University." . . .

In October, 1928, the Regents appropriated $24,000 for a two-year period "for the expenses of carrying on extension work through alumni fellows and other activities of the movement known as the Alumni University." . . .

Upon the establishment of the Bureau of Alumni Relations in 1929, one of the first projects to be planned was a week of lectures and classes for such alumni as desired to return to the University for a period of recreative study under conditions similar to those of their student days. Such a project had been tried with great success by President William Mather Lewis at Lafayette College the previous year, under the name of the Alumni College. This was attended by Wilfred B. Shaw, at that time with the American Association for Adult Education, and on his return to Ann Arbor as Director of Alumni Relations he made plans for a similar project, the first to be held in a large institution.

. . . [The June program offered ten courses, with] five lectures in each course. In addition, there were special programs in the evenings, including a reception in the William L. Clements Library, lectures, and plays in the Lydia Mendelssohn Theater. The attendance at this first session was seventy-two.

. . . The fee of ten dollars and the duration of the series for six days have limited the enrollment somewhat as compared with the attendance at similar enterprises in some other institutions [pp. 337, 340–41].

In 1929 the Carnegie Corporation funded Michigan's first alumni club seminars—the same Carnegie Corporation that had helped import continuing education from England ten years earlier.

The Michigan, Lafayette, Amherst, Dartmouth, and other examples before 1930 teach us six important lessons about the birth of alumni continuing education. First, presidential leadership by Lafayette's Lewis, Michigan's Clarence Cook Little, Dartmouth's Hopkins, and Amherst's Meiklejohn was crucial in every case. Second, alumni relations at Dartmouth and at Michigan began with continuing education in mind. Little was very explicit about it. Hopkins went further, simultaneously creating the alumni association, the alumni magazine, and alumni continuing education. Third, demonstrating their seriousness of purpose in establishing alumni relations upon an educational foundation, presidents at Michigan and Dartmouth brought back from the outside world men who had given prior important service to their institutions—Wilfred B. Shaw and Ernest Martin Hopkins; no minor officer was asked to take on the new responsibilities. Fourth, like many successful innovations alumni continuing education required and received significant initial investments. In 1928, Michigan's $24,000 represented a serious commitment to alumni education, and the regents backed the new program despite a depression. Fifth, Shaw did not need to change the alumni continuing education concept when he transplanted it from Lafayette (a small private college) to Michigan (a large university). He only changed the name: Lafayette College coined the term "Alumni College," while Michigan used "Alumni University." Clearly, the idea had merit no matter what kind of institution wanted to establish strong ties with its alumni. And sixth, while Linda Carl saw in her 1978 survey a new era for the alumni college starting in 1958 (at the University of Michigan and elsewhere), there is continuity in the alumni movement reaching back to these earlier programs at Michigan and Lafayette, Vassar's 1924 residential alumnae forum, and Cornell's 1935 "Alumni Institute." The intent of all these programs—their length, formats, curricula, and even their concerns about price and marketing among alumni—anticipates precisely the characteristics of the modern alumni continuing education era after 1956.

1956–1966: A Critical Decade Initiates the Modern Alumni Continuing Education Era

Alumni continuing education programs grew rather slowly and sporadically before 1966. Between 1956 and 1966, however, the foundations were laid for unprecedented growth in alumni continuing education. That growth continues today.

The modern alumni continuing education era began in 1956 at the Shoreham Conference in Washington, D.C. That conference was co-sponsored by the two parent fields of continuing education and alumni relations—specifically, the Fund for Adult Education and the American Alumni Council. Based on working papers that analyzed a survey of 700 institutions, the Shoreham Conference both confirmed and heightened a growing interest in alumni continuing education across the country, judging by the surge in the birth rate of new alumni colleges that took place in all kinds of institutions, all around the country, over the next decade. One may fairly draw this conclusion from Linda Carl's table of alumni college births (a good but not complete sampling through 1977), taken here from her "Alumni College Movement." A few of these schools had prior experience with smaller alumni continuing education programs, and Michigan's "Alumni University" some thirty years earlier seems to have fit even our modern definition of an alumni college.

YEAR OF FIRST ALUMNI COLLEGE

1958	University of Colorado*
1959	
1960	
1961	Brown University
1962	
1963	University of Oregon
1964	Dartmouth College Princeton University
1965	Syracuse University
1966	Stanford University
1967	
1968	Cornell University
1969	
1970	

1971   Harvard University
        Pomona College
        University of Pennsylvania

1972   Brown University [second start]
        The Principia
        University of Rochester
        Wellesley College

1973   Hobart and William Smith Colleges
        The Johns Hopkins University
        St. Mary's College of Maryland
        University of Vermont

1974   Five College Consortium (Amherst, Hampshire, Mt. Hol-
        yoke, Smith, University of Massachusetts)

1975   University of California/Berkeley
        University of Kansas
        University of Michigan*
        Pennsylvania State University*

1976   American University
        Carleton College
        University of Chicago
        Pennsylvania State University*
        University of Illinois at Urbana-Champaign
        Ohio State University
        Whitman College
        College of Wooster

1977   University of Connecticut
        University of Notre Dame
        Ohio Wesleyan University
        University of Washington
        Yale University
        Bowling Green State University

*Carl was unable to determine with certainty when the University of Michigan and Pennsylvania State University started modern alumni colleges, but suspected that both began before 1960. Therefore, Colorado may not have been first. [From Carl, p. 14].

Two other factors seem to have contributed to this first surge of alumni continuing education activity after the Shoreham

Conference. One was Ernest E. McMahon's "New Directions for Alumni: Continuing Education for the College Graduate," which went far beyond an assessment of the state of the art. McMahon's monograph, published by the Chicago-based Center for the Study of Liberal Education for Adults (the Center was supported by the same Fund for Adult Education that had co-sponsored the Shoreham Conference), urged a new educational vision in which continuing education and alumni relations might work hand-in-glove to produce the kind of adult involvement in education and other university affairs that visionaries of that period believed would be necessary to the future health of higher education and of the nation at large.

The other factor was the Oakland Plan for continuing education, the brain-child of Lowell Eklund. During the late 1950s and early 1960s, while the first modern alumni colleges were still on the drawing boards around the country using such models as the Aspen Institute (founded in 1949 to serve the nondenominational continuing education needs of adults outside the university environment), Eklund was formulating his plan for alumni continuing education at the new Oakland University in Rochester, Michigan. Heavily funded by the Kellogg Foundation beginning in 1963, the Oakland Plan was part of Oakland University from that institution's founding in 1959. It would become the most ambitious approach to alumni continuing education to date.

Eklund, who became president of the National University Extension Association in 1974–1975, implemented the Oakland Plan as dean of continuing education at Oakland. His goal was access for graduates to "true learning not a frothy, perfunctory showpiece of social activity aimed more at strengthening the old college ties than at cultural enlightenment and professional improvement" (1964, p. 17). Building upon the long history of mostly social programming in alumni relations, Eklund derived great strength from Cyril Houle's prediction that "sooner or later, some college or university will undertake in a systematic fashion, to plan a lifetime program of education. It will give to young people those basic and structural elements which best set the pattern for their later life. It will then offer a program of continued study for its alumni . . ." (Houle, 1948; quoted in Eklund, "The Alumni University," 1961).

The Oakland Plan addressed one of continuing education's most difficult challenges—the development and implementation of an entirely new educational model. Because Oakland was established as an experimental institution, it had the opportunity to design organizational structures which could ensure institutional responsiveness to the needs of part-time adult students. To quote Eklund, the novel characteristics of this plan were "greater systematization and intensification of opportunities for learning—opportunities which currently exist but are usually available and undertaken on a very transitory basis."

The Oakland Plan focused upon two other ideas of importance to the worlds of continuing education and alumni relations. One was the concept of "alumni sharing," where universities would provide services for each other's alumni. Eklund did not have to invent either the term or the idea out of whole cloth. In some sense the Xavier Alumni Sodality had shared alumni almost one hundred years earlier; and McMahon anticipated this feature of the Oakland Plan by quoting John S. Diekhoff's 1957 article, "The Alumni University," which called for alumni sharing in continuing education. Eklund proposed the concept among ten large midwestern universities, and they came close to implementing it before Kellogg funding ran out. It was, however, back under discussion, this time in the Ivy League, in the spring of 1987.

Eklund's other important concept was undergraduate orientation to lifelong education. The idea was to motivate undergraduates by "frequent and explicit reminders of the importance of continuing education." That is, the university intended to make sure that students learned how to learn before they became lifelong members of the university's intellectual community.

The Oakland Plan ran out of steam when it ran out of Kellogg funding, but it remains our best attempt to date at alumni continuing education of truly substantial proportions. Two things remain important about Eklund's Oakland Plan. First, the plan's influence is still felt around the country, and from time to time pieces are resurrected at other institutions. And second, Eklund saw that alumni relations and other university functions like career advising are intimately, perhaps ultimately, related to continuing education. Indeed, at Oakland, the alumni and career advising offices reported to Eklund as dean of continuing education—an arrangement nearly identical to that recommended by McMahon.

As we move on now to describe the great variety of alumni continuing education programs sponsored by continuing education and alumni relations offices at all kinds of institutions around the country, and then as we think ahead to the contribution alumni continuing education might make to the future of American higher education, it will be important to keep in mind what happened during this crucial decade, 1956–1966. With the Cold War producing a technological and educational race for space that dominated international events, two professions coming of age—continuing education and alumni relations—located a plot of common ground, assessed their responsibilities and their potential to provide continuing education to college and university alumni, and generated the first handful of modern alumni colleges. Thus began a new era, not only for alumni colleges, but for the whole variety of alumni continuing education programs that shall be explored next.

CHAPTER 2

REDEFINING THE UNIVERSITY COMMUNITY:

The Importance of Alumni Continuing Education

The educational leaders who have championed alumni continuing education over the last 125 years shared a vision in which adults—especially an institution's own alumni—enjoyed a lifelong relationship to alma mater, to the benefit of the institution and the individual. Before World War II, college and university presidents kept this vision alive through sheer power of vision. The alumni were not quite ready: if they shared the vision, their voices are nearly silent in university records of these early years.

Things changed soon after World War II, however. Surveys uncovered strong alumni interest in lifelong education focused upon alma mater. A world that went through several major social or economic upheavals in a lifetime forced continuing education into the consciousness of the alumni, who turned first to alma mater.

This chapter will show that the importance of alumni continuing education lies first in its immediate benefits to many arms of the university, and to the alumni and other adults. But its importance lies also in alumni continuing education's contribution toward a new definition of adult membership in the university community.

Before we explore the importance of alumni continuing education, however, the alumni themselves should have their say, because the rapid growth of these programs—especially since 1958—derives as much from alumni interest as from the philosophies of a few college presidents seventy-five years ago.

The Alumni Speak Out

We have come a long way since the Shoreham Conference in 1956, and while educators in the fields of continuing education and alumni relations deserve much of the credit for that progress, much credit belongs also to the alumni themselves. Several alumni studies contributed energy and direction in those early years after Shoreham. In 1958, a committee of Dartmouth alumni thoroughly studied alumni relations and then called for more educational activity. The committee suggested that "the time is passing when busy alumni will get together enthusiastically to listen to sports reports, to perpetuate their boyhoods through sentimental reminiscence, to wear the old school tie and yell the old school yell" (*Committee on Alumni Relations Report*, p. 1). Four years later J. Michael McGean, who had participated at Shoreham and staffed the Dartmouth report, started an alumni college that operates to this day. Brown University alumni issued a similar report three years later in 1961.

Then in 1970, as a result of late-1960s social and educational pressure on all American institutions, an alumni commission charged by then President Kingman Brewster and appointed by the Yale Corporation studied that university's role in education and society. With its other findings, the commission sent Yale a powerfully worded call for alumni continuing education.

Yale responded with an equal seriousness of purpose: its alumni college opened in 1977. Six years later, Yale President A. Bartlett Giamatti appointed Eustace D. Theodore, a dean and member of the Yale faculty, as executive director of the Association of Yale Alumni—an appointment of great significance to alumni continuing education at Yale and elsewhere. Theodore's philosophy of alumni relations echoes Amherst's President Alexander Meiklejohn's 1916 address at Rutgers College about the nature of the university community, and carries forward Yale's own commitment, which began with alumni reading lists in 1912:

> *Education for alumni must be part of every alumni affairs program, not simply one aspect of a specific program called "continuing eduction." Reunions, club meetings, association gatherings, one-day seminars, the opportunity to return for an extended period of time to the formal classroom, all must be part of alumni affairs; each must have at its center a process which brings faculty and alumni together so that those entrusted with the task of education can share the recent developments with those who continue to be engaged and interested in the process of learning.*
>
> *If commencement is only the beginning of one's educational experience, then alumni affairs must orient itself toward helping extend the educational relationship begun as an undergraduate or graduate student. The university cannot simply assert the importance of education and then leave alumni to fend for themselves. If universities neglect this important alumni need, alumni affection will be redirected toward institutions that support their desire for continued learning [Letter from Eustace D. Theodore to Steven L. Calvert, May 25, 1986].*

During the 1970s other schools discovered that alumni wanted education from their alumni associations. What Linda Carl referred to as the "alumni college movement" made its way across the country during the next seven years, spreading to large and small private and public institutions, including Pomona College (1971), The Principia and the University of Rochester (1972), Hobart and William Smith Colleges, Johns Hopkins University, St. Mary's College of Maryland, and the

University of Vermont (1973), and as many as twenty more before Carl ended her survey in 1977.

As continuing education and alumni relations became more sophisticated during the 1970s, schools more frequently surveyed their markets before providing services like alumni continuing education. Most of these surveys tell us the same thing, seemingly without regard for the type of school doing the survey: alumni want education from their alumni associations more than they want any other service.

Sue B. Dueitt's 1975 study of Tufts alumni "concluded that alumni generally have higher expectations than are presently being realized," and that "much work needs to be done in alumni continuing education and leadership training to bring the concept of lifelong learning into reality for more alumni" (quoted in Morgal, 1979, p. 12). John D'Ambrosio used the Dueitt questionnaire to survey the sixty-four State University of New York campuses in 1978. Alumni were asked what they wanted from the University, and their interests were compared with what they were actually getting. The returns suggested that "alumni associations should place their priorities for expansion in ten areas where the largest discrepancies between the actual and ideal goal ratings were found to exist." Two of those areas were off-campus learning and alumni continuing education.

The movement continues in the 1980s. At Iowa State University, James Hopson, executive director of the Alumni Association, surveyed a large random sample of alumni in 1980, and found that nearly two-thirds (62.5 percent) felt the alumni association should provide educational programs, compared with 50.5 percent in favor of alumni club programs, 47.4 percent for reunions, 42.6 percent for cultural events sponsored by the association, and only 26.1 percent who thought the association should spend time assisting the athletic programs of the university.

Confronted with these kinds of survey results, colleges and universities are responding with a greater variety of alumni continuing education programs than ever before. Many institutions now offer a range of on- and off-campus, long- and short-term programs, from reunion and homecoming seminars to outreach education at alumni clubs and even abroad, where alumni travel programs have begun to focus heavily on educational goals through faculty participation.

Alumni Responsibility for Alumni Continuing Education

As continuing education becomes more important to adult lives, alumni may be expected to become more vocal supporters of alumni continuing education's role in their relationship to alma mater. Some institutions will respond quickly and effectively; others may welcome the early involvement of volunteer alumni and share with them the responsibility for starting up these programs.

Institutions should not hesitate to use volunteers in these programs. On the alumni relations side, volunteers have always played important programmatic roles, and alumni continuing education should be no different. Normally, faculty members will develop the academic content for programs, but alumni volunteers may help by suggesting topics, and can provide much of the organizational support and promotional and other expertise. They may even be the ones who study the field and guide program proposals through institutional channels. Thus, alumni volunteers often have been essential to the development of an institution's alumni continuing education program.

Differences at Public and Private, Large and Small, Young and Old Institutions

While the general concept of alumni continuing education offers advantages for every kind of college and university, the differences between public and private, large and small, young and old institutions will determine which programs work best.

Consider the differences between large universities and small colleges. Large institutions have larger staffs, and more alumni, and so they can more easily start and sustain alumni continuing education programs. Very small colleges with small staffs and few alumni need to be more inventive in staffing new programs (volunteers can help), and have to be careful to sponsor programs that will attract sufficient numbers of alumni.

Young institutions (Marymount College in Palos Verdes, California, and Spring Hill College in Mobile, Alabama, for example) may not have enough alumni to attempt more than reunion seminars at first, especially if one officer runs their alumni programs and annual fundraising. Other colleges and universities, temporarily experiencing declining enrollments, may need to concentrate their alumni involvement on finding next year's freshmen.* Finally, young institutions have only young alumni, who as a group nationally show the least interest in short-term, noncredit alumni continuing education programs. Thus, the newer institutions may need to postpone on-campus alumni colleges until their alumni bodies expand and grow older.

Public and private institutions often differ as to the alumni continuing education programs that work best. Private colleges and universities with dispersed alumni bodies may find that weekend or evening seminars in the field, and longer summer alumni colleges (worth traveling long distances to attend) work best for them, while public universities, whose alumni live closer to the campus, may be able to focus on campus-based programs. Frequently, public institutions have substantial continuing education divisions that offer both credit and noncredit courses, and under these circumstances the best strategy may call for collaboration between the continuing education and the alumni offices.

Public universities once paid less attention to alumni relations than private colleges. State government appropriations made fundraising from private sources (including alumni) less important than it is today with shrinking government support of higher education and escalating higher education costs. Today, public and private institutions both treat alumni relations seriously, and as state universities' alumni operations become

*Idaho State University, which held five vacation colleges in the 1970s, found itself in this situation in the mid-1980s.

more sophisticated, they will include more alumni continuing education.

At public universities and particularly at land-grant institutions, the continuing education office focuses on in-state students and therefore serve the continuing education needs of many other institutions' alumni. The convenience of a nearby state university makes it far less likely that alumni of other institutions will travel long distances or put up with difficult distance-learning arrangements merely for the sake of continuing their education with undergraduate alma mater. This fact will limit the continuing education activity with old alma mater. Still, many college graduates wish to remain in close touch with their undergraduate institutions, and will participate in alumni continuing education if it is made reasonably accessible. This includes alumni colleges abroad (where location is not linked to any campus), reunion seminars, and alumni club seminars near graduates' home towns.

This strong attachment of many adults to their undergraduate institutions makes it practical for any school to offer at least some forms of alumni continuing education, for the same reason that fundraising historically has proven more successful for undergraduate institutions than for graduate schools. Iowa State University's 1980 alumni survey confirmed this strong undergraduate attachment. Furthermore, there appear to be "no significant differences between the proportions of alumni giving to ISU who obtain all degrees from ISU and those who obtain graduate degrees from other institutions." In fact, "students who matriculated but did not graduate gave more generously to the university than the average." Conversely, just to prove the point, for alumni "who obtained bachelor degrees from other institutions, the proportions giving to ISU are smaller than for any other degree categories."

Such lifelong devotion to one's undergraduate institution raises the possibility that Lowell Eklund's "alumni sharing" concept might eventually work, if properly and patiently developed. Indeed, in 1986–1987, several schools in the Ivy League began discussing how alumni of all participating institutions who lived near the campus of one of the schools would receive invitations co-signed by both alumni directors to participate in any alumni continuing education programs at the nearby sponsor. Being an alumnus of one school would qualify one for specified educational privileges at any of the others. Such an arrangement would solve the affiliation versus location dilemma inherent in many of alumni continuing education's offerings.

Finally, some schools have not heard of or seriously considered alumni continuing education. A few others have tried it and failed, but as the twenty-first century approaches, and baby-boom adults reach mid-life, sheer demographics will make another attempt at alumni continuing education worth the effort.

Advantages of Alumni Continuing Education

Alumni continuing education's importance derives partly from the many benefits it offers a sponsoring college or university, as well as its alumni and other participants. A reader building the case for alumni continuing education will be well-armed with these benefits in mind. Let us look first at advantages for the institution as a whole, from the point of view of its leaders, and then explore the further benefits.

ADVANTAGES TO UNIVERSITY LEADERS

Alumni continuing education can help institutional leaders to face two important challenges in the coming years. One is the external challenge by what Nell Eurich calls the "corporate classroom," through which corporations spent something like $60 billion in 1985 on the education of adults—more than all of higher education combined. The internal challenge stems from four of higher education's fears about itself.

In the May 7, 1979 *Chronicle of Higher Education*, Carter A. Daniel of Rutgers University published a commencement address that contained this withering criticism of higher education:

College has spoiled you by reading papers that don't deserve to be read, listening to comments that don't deserve a hearing, paying attention even to the lazy, ill-informed and rude. We had to do it, for the sake of education. But nobody will ever do it again. College has deprived you of adequate preparation for the next 50 years. It has failed you by being easy, free, forgiving, attentive, comfortable, interesting, unchallenging fun. Good luck tomorrow.

This passage defines four of the greatest fears in higher education:

1. College and university students don't actually learn anything,
2. Therefore, they become untrustworthy alumni
3. and inept, inadequately educated citizens;
4. because the dedicated but disappointed faculty is finished with them.

Like Daniel, Cyril Houle (who did much of his work at the University of Chicago) worries that faculty and students are through with each other after college. In *The Inquiring Mind* he suggests why:

Those who would like to encourage the growth of continuing education must apparently face the fact that many of the attitudes and values of American society are directly and specifically opposed to the idea of life-long learning and that this opposition has a vehemence and spread of impact which is not apparent to those who do not feel it directly themselves. The enemy is not apathy, as many would like to believe, but outright opposition, and opposition from places where it counts most— from the family, associates, and friends who surround the person who feels an inclination toward learning [p. 46].

Such fears partly explain why "deschoolers" like Ivan Illich ("for most men the right to learn is curtailed by the obligation to attend school," Illich, 1971, p. vii) seek to dismantle the whole educational system. With all those fears and all that distrust (they seem to be saying), how shall we achieve anything like Emerson's community of scholars, or in common parlance, the "learning society"?

These views are helpful in attracting attention to problems in higher education, but they are too pessimistic. Our colleges and universities produce most of our leaders these days, including some the faculty admire. Many students learn well enough to enter graduate school and then join the very faculties which Houle and Daniel fear might have been through with the alumni. And many alumni (admittedly not always the vocal ones) stay tuned to higher education, and to alma mater, and they support improvement, even when this means changes that might distress the stereotypical alumnus. In short, we are doing better than Carter Daniel suggests.

But no matter how well we are doing today, college and university leaders must improve the imperfect relationship between adults and universities. The alternative is to yield to external challenges from the corporate world, proprietary schools, the YMCA, and other providers that seem to be taking over higher education's business (see Nell P. Eurich, *Corporate Classrooms: The Learning Business,* 1985).

In focusing attention on these challenges, higher education leaders will want always to keep in mind what colleges and universities are for. Despite their differences, most institutions claim the same fundamental mission: to make a better world by better educating citizens.

From now on, this mission will mean more than educating adolescents. As recently as the turn of this century, educating adolescents served us reasonably well: adults lived their whole lives in essentially the same world in which they were educated. Today, adults live through five or six different worlds, worlds so radically changed by advancing knowledge that without continuing education they can be left behind by their own cultures. When we add the demographic facts with which we have all become familiar, it becomes clear that adult learners will soon outnumber the younger members of our universities.

A new definition of adults' roles in universities based in part upon alumni continuing education holds great potential for calming the four greatest fears in higher education, especially if those adults are alumni. Having alumni back in the classroom will not guarantee that these former students learned and are learning, but it does increase the chances. The contact between alumni and the faculty can allay fears and demolish stereotypes on both sides. And, most important, through continuing education, alumni can become better informed citizens, providing the university with its greatest effect for good in the world. This is not to say that alma mater must provide all the continuing education for every graduate, but that each university must share with its alumni the responsibility for making American adults true and purposeful lifelong learners.

At the other end of the undergraduate experience, alumni continuing education can enrich the way in which adults and universities think about a "commencement." The term commencement holds ironic overtones: for many students, it signifies not a commencement at all but an end to a specific educational experience. Today, we must begin thinking of these rites of passage more literally as continuation exercises at which younger members of the university community are congratulated on having learned how to learn as we welcome them to the rest of their university lives.

To the extent that "commencement" still means "starting the rest of your lives," presidents in their commencement addresses could emphasize that nothing has really changed. The question that applies equally to undergraduates and to alumni is, "What is the relationship between your intellectual life and the rest of your life?" We should therefore make it clear to undergraduates that their jobs are the curriculum, but that education comes from everywhere around them—in their residence halls, fraternities, and sororities; from teachers and mentors outside the classroom; from art galleries, theaters, and libraries; and from interaction with the larger community surrounding the university itself. To encourage this kind of holistic thinking about the lifelong relationship between education and work, some colleges and universities encourage students to create mini-universities of noncredit, extracurricular learning. If we have provided this rich educational environment for our adolescent students and have taught them how to use it, we will be able to say at their continuation exercises, "Go, work and learn exactly as you have done here at alma mater."

Colleges and universities can use this model of working and learning when dealing with several institutional challenges that have become increasingly important since the 1960s. For example, many colleges and universities, wrestling with the relationship between classroom life and the rest of students' lives, wonder whether residential life and even athletics can be made more effectively a part of the educational experience of going to college. Treated as isolated problems, these residential life and athletic challenges can be exceedingly difficult. One ends merely by coercing the best students to lead seminars in dormitories, or by calling coaches faculty members. If, on the other hand, institutions can say to the entire college community that one's whole life, inside the university or out, depends upon learning everywhere one can (not just in the university classroom) and throughout one's life, then students, faculty, residence masters, and the greater college community can participate in an intellectual life outside the classroom that makes perfect sense and indeed gives a more or less permanent shape to human life itself.

College athletics can benefit from this lifelong perspective. As James A. Michener points out in *Sports in America*, we do the nation a disservice by focusing our university athletics on the quasi-professional performances of a very few students in those sports which few individuals can play after age thirty-five. One unfortunate result is a devaluation of physical education for the rest of the student body. Physical education should be an important part of a rich educational experience for young people in which they learn the place of physical activity in a healthy life and acquire the skills to participate in carry-over sports. We have a good place to begin. The fitness craze shows that Americans are interested in healthy bodies; some even understand the relationship between healthy bodies and healthy lives. If colleges shifted more effort into teaching physical fitness as an important part of life, we might produce healthier adults less vulnerable to risky health crazes (from dieting to marathoning) and even moderate the vicarious and parochial boosterism that can distort the true purposes of the university's undergraduate athletic programs.

Alumni continuing education offers other specific benefits to the university. For example, most institutions find that continuing education in general, and alumni continuing education in particular, can provide significant additional revenue from the use of otherwise vacant facilities and underutilized staff during the summers, on weekday evenings, and on weekends. By taking advantage of underutilized faculty, lecture and residence halls, and food service, short-term noncredit educational programs can comfortably fit into the cracks. The result can be extra revenue, sometimes well into six figures annually, from alumni continuing education programs alone. Chapter 9 will look more closely at typical program budgets. Here the point is that, even when individual program budgets do not show net revenues, they generate significant incomes, especially in the university's housing and food service departments.

Finally, the community outreach, community service benefits of alumni continuing education programs can be enormous, according to Sallie Riggs, vice-president for communications and public relations at Brandeis University, and for fifteen years a national leader in alumni continuing education while at Brown University. This is not surprising if we think how hard it would be to exclude the general community. The spouses of alumni are welcome in these programs, as are the families of alumni and employees of the institution and their families. So, despite program design and marketing aimed at alumni, the audience for alumni continuing education looks a lot like the general educated public.

THE PRESIDENT AND ALUMNI CONTINUING EDUCATION

Throughout the history of alumni continuing education, presidential leadership has proven critical to success at many institutions. Enlightened self-interest seems to have motivated many of the presidents who envisioned and then instituted these programs for their graduates. For example, in 1959, Brown University President Henry Merritt Wriston inaugurated one of the first modern alumni colleges, in part because he believed the program could help him explain university changes to the alumni:

> We set up an alumni college . . . to acquaint alumni with the current faculty members, to give them first-hand contact and help them believe later members of the teaching faculty were "up to standards." . . . Its effect was greatly to facilitate alumni acceptance of change, and reduce frictions that retard new programs [text provided by Sallie K. Riggs].

Today's college and university presidents can take confidence and inspiration from their earlier counterparts who saw the benefits of taking alumni seriously as members of their intellectual community, and the risks of failing to do so.

The University of Michigan: An Encyclopedic Survey, a university history published in 1942, credits President Clarence Cook Little with having developed a vision of alumni relations, and an organization to carry it out, during the 1920s:

> The program of the Alumni Association during the Little administration is marked most notably by the institution of the Michigan Alumni Ten-Year Program and by what was called the "Alumni University." Little subscribed heartily to the idea that the University is decidedly not through with a student as soon as it has conferred a degree upon him, and the Alumni University which was proposed and explained by him was a device to provide for continuing individual interests on the part of alumni. . . . This idea was publicly proclaimed at a dinner sponsored by the Ann Arbor University of Michigan Club and held January 21, 1928, at the Michigan Union. Representatives from nearly all the alumni centers throughout the country attended this dinner, and the plan was well received. . . . Both the Alumni University and the Michigan Alumni Ten-Year Program . . . resulted in the eventual establishment of the Bureau of Alumni Relations, as part of the University's program. . . .
>
> President . . . Little . . . advocated a broad program in continuing educational effort based on a co-operative movement on the part of both the University and the alumni, to which he gave the name of the Alumni University.
>
> Upon the establishment of the Bureau of Alumni Relations in 1929, one of the first projects to be planned was a week of lectures and classes for such alumni as desired to return to the University for a period of recreative study under conditions similar to those of their student days. Such a project had been tried with great success by President William

Mather Lewis at Lafayette College the previous year under the name of the Alumni College. This was attended by Wilfred B. Shaw, at that time with the American Association for Adult Education, and on his return to Ann Arbor as Director of Alumni Relations he made plans for a similar project, the first to be held in a large institution [pp. 94, 340].

Little provided three important kinds of leadership, then, to get alumni continuing education started over half a century ago at the University of Michigan. First of all, probably aware of the efforts of Presidents Hopkins, Meiklejohn, and Lewis at Dartmouth, Amherst, and Williams, he personally gave the ideas form and power at his own university. Second, he made the idea available to all alumni in a public speech before establishing any specific programs. And third, he found a highly qualified academic in Wilfred Shaw to run his brandnew Bureau of Alumni Relations.

This kind of presidential leadership is even more critical today than it was fifty years ago. Hopkins, Meiklejohn, Lewis, and Little were to a great degree inventing alumni relations from scratch, defining the alumni relationship as they went along. They bucked no existing trends or programs, no long and sturdy traditions. Hopkins of Dartmouth started an alumni council and was its first president; he started the alumni magazine and was its first editor—both before taking the presidency. Two years into his presidency in 1918–1919 he created the first alumni seminars off campus. By contrast, today most presidents have inherited alumni programs with long histories but often without much vision or effort at linking alumni with the intellectual life of the university. For this reason, presidential leadership is more desperately needed. In university politics, course correction can be harder than initial navigation.

We cannot know precisely how we ever got off track in the first place. It makes very little sense, looking back. Perhaps it was because, until the middle of this century, alumni had little interest in continuing education of any kind. Their degrees served them reasonably well for a lifetime. Because the relationship was lopsided (colleges and universities needed them, but not the reverse), the result seems to have been a tradition

of alumni programming that provided enjoyable but nonintel-
lectual contact.

This will no longer do. Today's college and university resources are too precious to spend so many of them (people,
dollars, programs) on activities barely related to education. Even
the Internal Revenue Service and the United States Postal Service are running out of patience with universities operating tax-
exempt, tax-supported alumni services that have nothing to do
with education. The federal government merely acts with con-
sistency here. Fred Harvery Harrington reminds us that Title
One, the Continuing Education and Community Service section
of the 1965 Higher Education Act (which originally provided
$10 million annually to support continuing education and com-
munity service programs) barred the use of federal funds for
"purely recreational or social activities" (Harrington, 1977, p.
105).

As presidents contemplate how to get from where they are
with alumni relations and continuing education to where they
want to be, they may not choose Ernest E. McMahon's vision
in its entirety, but they still may keep it in mind:

> The Alumni Secretary as Educator
>   . . . the alumni secretary or director is seldom selected for his ability
> to establish and direct continuing education programs. In fact, the
> Shoreham Conference [the 1958 Washington conference of the American
> Alumni Council that discussed the place of alumni education in alumni
> relations] took cognizance of his frequent lack of status as an educator.
> While such an opinion may be unfair, it does exist. The alumni officer
> has many demands upon his time other than planning educational pro-
> grams. His experience is likely to include little such planning. He is a
> fund-raiser, an editor, a record-keeper, a direct-mail expert, an after-
> dinner speaker, a number of things, but not an educator of adults.
>   It is not a digression from the theme of the alumni college to speculate
> that acceptance by the university of a responsibility for alumni education
> may change the job specifications for the alumni secretary. Although
> many an alumni official has almost single-handedly launched a
> thriving alumni college, such enterprise is not quite the same as
> developing and maintaining a place for the alumni in the college
> community. The isolated alumni college, which may be only a half-
> day or day of lectures and symposia, may require only promotional abil-

ity; the development of a broad, continuing education program requires promotional ability plus other skills or insights.

From fairly extensive observation, it seems likely that most alumni officials can meet the demands of the added specification. However, both they and their institutions may need a new orientation which, in view of the early discussions of the Association of Alumni Secretaries, will be for many colleges only a reorientation. It will be necessary to do as Dartmouth did [in their 1958 alumni relations study, part of which was written by Hemingway biographer Carlos Baker '32 about alumni continuing education] and involve alumni leaders in educational planning. This will mean that the alumni official will become an educational officer to the extent that many other academic administrators are educational officers. Such a change in emphasis can only strengthen the value of the alumni office to the institution [McMahon, pp. 41–42; emphasis added].

In return for all the advantages that alumni continuing education offers a president and other institutional leaders, the programs can use some presidential assistance in return. No other officer can so plainly see the mutually beneficial aspects of alumni continuing education as a concept capable of unifying the institution's efforts in alumni and public relations, continuing education, fundraising, and to a lesser degree admissions, athletics, and undergraduate deaning. The president is the focal point for trustee, regent, or legislative leadership on one side, and for all institutional activity on the other; therefore, his or her support—and ideally, direct action—will determine the success of alumni continuing education.

Among the most important things the president can do for alumni continuing education is to serve as its chief spokesperson and cheerleader within and outside the university's walls. President Little served Michigan's early program in this role. During his Yale presidency, so did A. Bartlett Giamatti:

The relationship between a graduate and an institution of higher education must be based on the same motive that brought the individual and institution together in the first instance, a desire to bring focus to the process of learning. Alumni relations must be placed in the hands of someone who understands the importance of education as a central organizing principle of alumni affairs. Whenever possible, alumni affairs

officers should have academic experience, a background which includes
collegiate teaching. The process of bringing faculty and alumni together
to stimulate an enduring educational relationship must be at the center
of alumni affairs activities if the energy and enthusiasm of alumni in-
volvement is to be maintained over the years [statement provided to
Steven L. Calvert on May 25, 1986].

Making progress toward the goals of alumni continuing education without drastically and suddenly redesigning the existing alumni program will require presidential leadership and
the cooperation of several offices that report to him or her. Rad-
ical change in an existing alumni program has not worked where
it has been tried; too many alumni, and the alumni staff, have
built their relationships with the university on the basis of the
existing program, and the new goal should be to augment these
relationships, not to change them entirely.

Therefore, two intermediate steps may be advisable. First,
under presidential leadership, the alumni office can be allied
with the continuing education unit (department, division, or
office). Such arrangements exist, to the advantage of both offices, since they may share a need to move closer to the center
of the institution in the minds of their colleagues around the
campus.

Normally in this alliance, the continuing education professionals do what they do best, which is to design the educational
packages, hire the faculty, and set tuition. The alumni office
then goes into action where its strengths lie, promoting the
program to the friendliest audience available (the alumni) and
making sure that amenities accompanying the educational program meet alumni relations standards. Linda Carl suggests that
the alumni office act as an educational broker as often as possible, promoting in addition to its own alumni continuing education programs any educational, cultural, or other events
sponsored anywhere around the university that alumni would
enjoy and from which learning could result.

The second intermediate step is to appoint a director of
alumni continuing education. This person, who would concentrate on alumni continuing education programming, would join
a growing group of professionals around the country, and report

either to the alumni director or to the dean of continuing education, or both.

Once a college or university has developed a sophisticated alumni continuing education program with its own director, it may be ready to do what Yale, Johns Hopkins, the University of New Hampshire, and several other schools have done: appoint an academic (a Ph.D. with teaching experience) as alumni director. Such an appointment, especially by the president, goes a long way toward reorienting the relationship of alumni to the university with a minimum of upheaval among the loyal old guard. Such an appointee should have alumni relations sensitivities, in addition to the wide range of abilities and experience Fred Harvey Harrington wants in any continuing higher education leader:

> Apart from the president's role, the central administration of every college or university, and every higher education system, needs at least one high-level spokesperson for adult education. This may or may not be the individual who carried the adult education word to the president. Either way, the job description should specify ability to speak up, maintain outside contacts, and negotiate with and persuade government officials, cooperating agencies, private donors, and a great variety of prospective clients. Inside, in addition to administrative chores, this man or woman should relate well to fund raisers, business officers, academic deans, and all sorts of professors. Particularly important is a satisfactory tie to the admissions and registration offices. (pp. 176–77)

An alumni continuing education professional may in addition work closely with the undergraduate faculty and their deans of residential life.

ADVANTAGES TO THE ALUMNI OFFICE

Alumni continuing education offers what Brown University's Robert A. Reichley calls an "organizing principle" of alumni relations. It can help to define an overall institutional vision of the lifelong relationship between adults and universities characterized by a balance among the intellectual, cultural, social, and recreational lives of all members of the academic community. At times the relationship will be primarily educational; at other times it will be more service-oriented, with alumni giving to the university through student recruitment, volunteer leadership, consultation, patronage, and more. According to this vision, the success of alumni relations lies in the overall value to the institution of a relationship that is mutually beneficial, full of giving and taking on both sides, and in the end very important to the lives of individual and institution alike. The difference from most alumni relations programs today lies in a new vision, recognizing that, when the university gives, in this lifelong give-and-take relationship with its alumni, what it gives best is education. Few alumni offices have overseen that part of the relationship in the past. This is the most important reason why alumni offices have led a risky existence on the fringe of university life. Alumni continuing education legitimizes alumni relations by putting the profession in touch with the heart of the institution, which is its intellectual life.

As an organizing principle, alumni continuing education programs can strengthen everything else the alumni office does. According to Sallie Riggs,

> These sessions are designed for alumni with the long-range objective of involving them in the activities of their alma mater. The purpose of the program is two-fold: to provide a service to the participants; and to create a body of alumni with a greater understanding of the institution through their involvement in the basic purpose of that institution, the educational process [Statement provided by Sallie Riggs].

Adding faculty participation to a class reunion, or faculty presentations to a program that introduces potential benefactors to the institution today, tells alumni they are taken seriously as participants in the central business of the institution. If the university takes alumni club or chapter programs on the road, educational programs have a power to attract alumni participation that is matched only by presidential appearances. Indeed, an educational program for alumni can become more successful than the sponsoring alumni club itself.

Faculty essays, articles, and book reviews in alumni magazines send an important message to all alumni, inviting them into the academic life of the university. In this way alumni continuing education tempts a whole group of alumni (who do not read sports reports, class notes, or letters to the editor) to open the magazine and think seriously about alma mater each time an issue arrives in the mail.

One alumnus claims he stopped reading his alumni magazine when, due to editorial changes, he felt that it stopped connecting him to the intellectual life of his undergraduate college. For any president who understands the effects of good alumni relations on all parts of a university, there is real pain here: think what this situation cost the neglected school in terms of accidental interest the alumnus might have found in the next alumni magazine issue, of his financial support, of his potential activities in recruiting, and more. We are reminded of Mark Singer's "Alumni Magazines: The Editors Reach Out," an essay in *The Nation* back in October of 1974. Singer said that "an alumni magazine should be a vehicle for continuing education; the publication that functions as a house organ is bound to estrange its audience from the intellectual life of the institution" (p. 306).

There are even two legal advantages to alumni offices in taking alumni continuing education seriously. One involves the Internal Revenue Service, the other the United States Postal Service.

Several years ago the IRS successfully challenged the University of North Carolina's practice of earning tax-exempt revenues from its alumni travel program. The IRS argued in court that the travel programs were not educational in any usual sense for which the university held tax-exempt status. The travel program was judged to be "business unrelated" to the tax-exempt purposes of the university, and all revenues were deemed taxable. According to a lawyer retained by the Council for Advancement and Support of Education (CASE), alumni offices wishing to justify tax-exempt revenues from alumni travel programs must establish significant educational activity in those programs. No IRS case since North Carolina's has proven how much education is enough to justify tax-exempt alumni travel program revenues, but clearly universities must now make alumni travel programs truly educational, or report income and pay taxes.

The U.S. Postal Service, on the other hand, in 1986 and 1987 sponsored congressional investigations aimed specifically at preventing travel agents and universities from promoting alumni travel programs through the "cooperative" mailing of brochures. Here the issue was not whether alumni travel programs are educational enough (although making them educational should help a university's status with the USPS). The issue for the USPS was whether program brochures advertised the educational purposes for which universities hold third-class nonprofit mailing permits. Since third-class postal rates result in millions of dollars of "revenue forgone" at a time when the federal government needs to cut budgets dramatically, the USPS is not interested in subsidizing what it sees as the lucrative travel business. Therefore, colleges and universities, and especially their alumni offices, will be on much firmer ground if they offer truly academic travel programs to their alumni in brochures they are willing to defend before the USPS as their own (and not their travel agents').

There is symbolic as well as practical educational value in alumni continuing education's contribution to alumni relations, according to Robert Fure, Washington and Lee University's director of alumni continuing education:

> We are . . . aware of the symbolic value of these programs in this area of alumni relations: the very fact that the University is reaching out to the minds of its extended family—and not merely to their pocketbooks—conveys an important message that many alumni appreciate, even though they may not find time to attend the programs [Letter to Steven L. Calvert, May 1, 1986].

This symbolic value gives alumni continuing education more power to enrich alumni relationships than would be the case if the programs affected only actual participants.

Few alumni relations offices work this way, yet. Some shifts in emphasis will have to be made, but we know that alumni will welcome the change. Richard D. Morgal's "A Study of Four

University Alumni Associations: Implications for Adult Lifelong Learning" shows that most alumni do not know what their alumni association is doing; when informed, they value current alumni association goals less than the association does (that is, less than its professional directors do); and a majority wants more continuing education than the alumni association now offers (pp. iii, 41–44). Sallie Riggs's analysis of Brown University's alumni Summer Colleges discovered that "95 percent of those attending had not been involved in other alumni activities. And between 65 and 95 percent of those attending our off-campus seminars were not members of the local Brown club or otherwise involved in alumni activities" (material provided to Steven L. Calvert). The same kinds of statistics appear in reports from other institutions (see Riggs, 1979, p. 20). Alumni want to be taken seriously as part of the intellectual community they once joined as adolescents. Stephen Barrett, executive director of Brigham Young University's Alumni Association, says: "[w]e found in a random survey that most of our graduates want the alumni association to expand the continuing program rather than offer more cultural events and job placement services. Your graduates may hold the same views" (1976, p. 18). In short, alumni continuing education enriches alumni relations by bringing in adults who will not participate in other alumni events—athletic, social, even cultural.

Alumni continuing education is also beginning to attract a new kind of professional into the alumni office. In 1978, Sallie Riggs suggested that the opportunity to work with the best of the university's faculty on attractive academic programs amounted to a new fringe benefit for alumni officers and staff members. Some alumni directors believe this can improve the quality of the professionals who join their staffs, as well as the professionalism of those who stay in alumni relations.

A number of prominent institutions now fill the post of alumni director with a faculty member. The appointments have initiated a shift of alumni relations toward continuing education, thus adding credibility to the alumni office on campus and with many alumni. These schools may be the first to realize the quarter-century-old dream of Ernest E. McMahon, former alumni secretary and former dean, University College and University Extension Division at Rutgers, The State University of New Jersey, as expressed on the last pages of his "New Directions for Alumni" monograph (1960):

> It is impossible to study the development of an activity like that of educating college alumni without thinking ahead to what the future may-or might-hold for the alumni college and the alumni. . . .
>   Alumni education may be the means of meeting the conflicting demands of breadth and specialization [in the curriculum]. . . .
>
> The New Alumni Organization
>   Any such development will change the function and nature of the alumni organization. If full recognition of the alumni college materializes, it is easy to envision the new situation. The new head of alumni activities will not be the director of alumni relations (a title which indicates a trace of public relations for a very special public) nor the alumni secretary (a vestigal title reminiscent of the record-keeping days). The new head will be the Dean of Alumni College. . . .
>   . . . The emergence of the Dean of Alumni College may become one of the routine accomplishments of the Space Age [pp. 51–52].

These new alumni directors have accepted the challenge to maintain a well-rounded intellectual, cultural, social, and recreational relationship between alumni and alma mater. For them, alumni continuing education provides a new elasticity in an up-to-date definition of alumni relations, and gives the alumni office an expanded purpose, a broader range of programs, and a greater role in advancing higher education.

As a final example of alumni continuing education's contribution to the alumni office, consider the class reunion, an event most schools already offer alumni. At their best, alumni reunions could recapture the fully rounded, carefully balanced university life, but at many schools they do not. Reunions are so overwhelmingly social and emotional that many alumni are suspicious, distrust them, and will not participate. A traveler from outer space observing many a college reunion might think adolescents go to college (as one wag has facetiously suggested) to carouse until they are old enough to come out and behave themselves; certainly she would see little of the intellectual heart of the university that brought alumni together as students in the first place. Of course, we may want to distinguish between the celebration and the thing being celebrated; but there is something intellectually, aesthetically, almost morally and certainly spiritually inappropriate in the unrelieved raucous celebration of a serious intellectual enterprise. What would be wrong with an intellectual celebration of an intellectual enterprise?

Indeed, from now on all forms of alumni relations should be designed with the goal of nurturing alumni desires to keep in constant touch with the intellectual life of their institutions. There is enrichment of many kinds to be had, for the alumni themselves and for our institutions. The beneficial effect, not merely on fundraising projects (though certainly upon them, too) but also on current students and faculty and the curriculum can be enormous. We have always known that the real benefits of a university accrue not to adolescent undergraduates but to society at large through the efforts of educated adults. Through reunion (and many other kinds of alumni continuing education) programs that help to keep the spirit of intellectual pursuit and humane judgment alive in our alumni, we can help to ensure that our universities fulfill their richest roles in our world.

This discussion of alumni continuing education's contribution to alumni relations should close with a look at the alumni themselves. When all is said and done, perhaps the reunion tent—that symbol of pure human fellowship—stands proudly (if ironically, given its stereotypical baggage) at the very heart of the alumni experience, even today. Milton R. Stern reminds us that reunions inspire an important volume of serendipitous learning among old college classmates, quite apart from the contributions of the faculty at reunion seminars. No one has made this point more memorably than J. Michael McGean, who has been the driving force in alumni relations at Dartmouth College for nearly thirty years. He deserves the last word (originally written for his twenty-fifth reunion book in 1974):

> Reunions deserve a far greater understanding for what they mean to higher education than the all too stereotyped impression of a rollicking fun and games show that only alumni play. There is a simple but ap-

parently overlooked fact about . . . higher education . . . which is that,
by and large, those who build and preserve this remarkable system are
those [alumni] who arrange and attend reunions. Think about that for
a minute.

. . . higher education exists because there are those who believe in
it, . . . and it survives . . . because those same men and women in the
reunion tents do not come back just to see each other. Far more im-
portantly they return to check on an investment in what they consider
a significant national asset. It is they who will meet a cross-section of
the undergraduate body, evaluate the quality of the physical facilities,
and ask the important questions ranging from management performance
to the ultimate fulfillment of purpose. It is they who check out the college
and carry the word back. . . .

Perhaps a reunion tent is the wrong symbol for the most important
gathering of the college family each year. But the facts are clear, most
of those on whom the future rests are tent people. There will be no
pulling up stakes on them—unless to move their tents to heaven.

ADVANTAGES TO CONTINUING EDUCATION

Alumni continuing education is an effective recruiting tool
for more substantial noncredit and credit-granting continuing
education programs. It serves as a nonthreatening experiment
for tentative adults afraid that their academic skills are no longer
tuned for serious university study. It serves as an incubator for
new courses that will later be offered for credit. It generates
new interdisciplinary study and new courses by the faculty.
And it diversifies the audience with which the university can
interact and to which it can later turn for support of all kinds,
including political support in the state house where that is important.

Alumni continuing education, because in so many cases it
is partly or entirely operated from the alumni office, has access
to the larger travel budgets of alumni offices, which makes educational outreach on behalf of the university more affordable.
This in turn spreads the university's influence, its political support base, and its services to the community.

Alumni continuing education also has access to the "friendliest market" (to borrow James Pollicita's term) available to adult educators—the alumni of the university, who are already favorably disposed and therefore more likely than the general public to read mailed program announcements and to trust the product the continuing education office is selling. Furthermore, the mailing lists managed by alumni offices these days are sophisticated and computerized marketing tools, developed often for the purposes of the development or fundraising office but perfectly suited to the marketing goals of the continuing education dean. Finally, the promotional budgets of the alumni office can help the continuing education office. The alumni office is in business to keep in touch with thousands of adult members of the university's community, and so the potential to piggyback continuing education messages on alumni office promotional efforts is enormous. In fact, many alumni directors are delighted to offer educational programs to alumni that the alumni directors do not have to mount themselves.

THE NEW PROFESSIONALISM

Continuing education and alumni relations, with their long histories in American higher education, each can claim what CASE vice president for alumni administration John Hall refers to as elder statesmen, practicing professionals whose powerful leadership and vision for the field and for higher education have earned them wide respect. These exemplary men and women have advanced their professions and have served as mentors to successors. They were, and are, national treasures.

By striving for a new professionalism in our own time, we do not at all mean to denigrate the contributions of our grand old masters. We merely seek to make our professions as helpful to our institutions, as much an integral part of their missions, as they were in earlier times. This has always required diligence, hard work, and commitment. It also requires new vision and new programs to meet new institutional and national needs, sometimes replacing the old. That is the challenge of the new professionalism.

In continuing education, the new professionalism is the valiant struggle on behalf of all American adults to locate continuing education nearer the heart of our colleges and universities. Continuing education remains tangential to the mission of many institutions, and yet the future of higher education lies in providing lifelong education to our adults. The best leaders of continuing education will insist on making continuing education truly a continuing experience for their students.

In alumni relations, the issues are exactly the same. The most forward-thinking alumni relations leaders are determined to ally the power of the alumni body with the university's mission. They find that alumni continuing education helps to advance their cause.

As a result of the growth in alumni continuing education, alumni relations has begun to focus away from purely social, recreational, and athletic programs and more upon education itself. Specifically, alumni relations can provide two kinds of education for alumni: education about education, ensuring that the university's most important public (the alumni body) understands the mission and the kinds of support alma mater needs from them; and more substantive programs to keep alumni involved in the institution's intellectual life.

Like continuing education professionals today, many more alumni professionals in the future will earn doctorates before leading university offices,* and they will publish research into the needs and accomplishments of their fields. They have a start. Since 1980, the number of alumni officers with Ph.D.s, while still rather small, has increased. What could be more logical? Leaders whose vision links alumni to university intellectual life, either through programs or through financial support of the university's business, benefit from the academic training that makes them conversant with the mission of the academy and enables them to develop informed alumni support for it.

The new professionals in continuing education and in alumni relations will speak each other's language more and more

---

*In the mid-1980s, 85 percent of the deans and directors holding membership in the National University Continuing Education Association held earned doctorates.

fluently as time goes on. They will see that they are in the same business, the business of imagining, shaping, and servicing the richest possible lifelong relationship between our adults and our universities. What the one profession does not or cannot do, the other will. The continuing education professional will have become so interested in the whole person and the rounded relationship of that person to the university throughout a lifetime, and the alumni relations professional will have become so much less an entertainer and so much more an educator, that the two will become very nearly indistinguishable.

ADVANTAGES TO THE FACULTY

Faculty members primarily teach undergraduates. Currently, the majority of undergraduates are adolescents. The result is an educational generation gap, emphasized during the 1960s but always operating in a college classroom. This situation can present a serious disadvantage; at its worst, it can make teaching tiresome and burn out faculty members.

Consider the plight of the Shakespeare scholar who has published essays on *King Lear* that deal with the tensions of a family, not only between spouses but between parents and children—but always from the point of view of adults, and older adults at that. This scholar is going to have a frustrating time teaching *King Lear* to class after class of adolescents, who have never been adults, who have probably not yet been spouses (at least not in any traditional sense that will help them to understand Lear's problem), who have never been parents and may not even like parents (this will play havoc with our faculty member's attempts to elicit sympathy for Lear), and who may not have come to terms with the irrational and inhumane behavior to which some people subject others. The whole business will be utterly beyond redemption if the teacher faces a single-sex class. It is startling and important how much the classroom discussion is enriched by the participation of both sexes and older adults.

Continuing education classes have offered this advantage

all along. Now consider the benefit of alumni continuing education adding a final touch—alumni in the classroom who
studied *Lear* at this institution long ago when it meant something entirely different to them. These alumni are back for a
new experience with the play to compare with the earlier one
and to share that comparison in a classroom that includes undergraduates. We have here the makings of a marvelous educational experience for returning alumni, for the adolescent
students, and also for the teacher whose professional life is invested in that play and what it means to young and old through
a lifetime of readings.

At most colleges or universities that have gotten serious
about alumni continuing education, the faculty love teaching
these uninhibited, richly experienced alumni, even though this
teaching is often more demanding than the teaching of mostly
younger and more traditional students. If there is any disadvantage for the faculty, it is that going back to the regular undergraduate classroom may be disappointing.

For most faculty members, interdisciplinary teaching is still
a rarity. We are reminded of that marvelous formulation in
Marilyn Ferguson's *The Aquarian Conspiracy* (1980), bemoaning
among other things the arbitrary division of knowledge into
discrete disciplines:

> *If we are not learning and teaching we are not awake and alive. Learning
> is not only like health, it is health.*
>
> *As the greatest single social influence during the formative years,
> schools have been the instruments of our greatest denial, unconscious-
> ness, conformity, and broken connections. Just as allopathic medicine
> treats symptoms without concern for the whole system, schools break
> knowledge and experience into "subjects," relentlessly turning wholes
> into parts, flowers into petals, history into events, without ever restoring
> continuity.* Or, as Neil Postman and Charles Weingartner observed in
> Teaching as a Subversive Activity:
>
> *English is not History and History is not Science and Science is not
> Art and Art is not Music, and Art and Music are minor subjects and
> English, History and Science major subjects, and a subject is something
> you "take" and when you have taken it, you have "had" it, and if you
> have "had" it, you are immune and need not take it again. (The Vac-
> cination Theory of Education?) [pp. 282–83].*

Alumni continuing education offers an enthusiastic audience for interdisciplinary teaching, and therefore offers to the faculty a teaching environment quite often missing in their regular academic lives. Such programs are in concert with recent theories emphasizing that adults' educational needs and interests tend to be problem-oriented rather than subject-oriented, that adults would rather learn about international terrorism from a team of teachers representing political science, economics, Near Eastern or Asian studies, sociology, psychology, and religion than from the single teacher who offers an undergraduate course on the subject.

One important result of alumni continuing education programs is that members of the faculty may meet, strike up lasting and rewarding professional alliances with other teachers on these interdisciplinary teams, and in the end create new university courses. Continuing education and alumni offices looking for a route nearer the center of the university's life will be hard-pressed to find a better way.

Faculty members find alumni colleges abroad (foreign educational travel with alumni) not only a challenging test of their grasp on world affairs or the art of Florence, to cite two examples, but these programs can also provide teachers with opportunities to travel to those places in the world where their research is based. If a school has no Egyptologist (most do not), a faculty member from another discipline may be teaching the art, architecture, literature, and history of ancient Egypt as a sideline but based on little direct contact with the material: library reading has provided most of what the teacher knows about the subject. However, if, in 1979, during the height of the King Tutankhamun craze, this faculty member had taught an alumni college abroad based on a Red Sea cruise ship (as happened at Dartmouth College), the two-week program would have found that teacher in Cairo, at Giza and the pyramids, the Sphinx, and in the Valley of the Kings, Karnak, Thebes, and Luxor along the Upper Nile. Based on such an experience, which would include teaching adults on all these sites, this teacher could substantially improve the undergraduate course on ancient Egypt, complete with his or her own up-to-date slides.

Finally, there can be financial rewards in alumni continuing education for the best faculty. For their teaching in these programs the faculty should be paid honoraria that range somewhere between symbolic and significant amounts. Under the best of circumstances, where there is institutional support at all levels, including the tenure and faculty promotion policies, understanding among alumni, and the teachers' own interest in university relations, alumni continuing education can be part of the faculty reward system in which top teachers earn thousands of dollars a year for frequent overload teaching in these programs.

ADVANTAGES TO THE UNDERGRADUATES

Undergraduates benefit from adult participation in any class that normally lacks the adult perspective. In those few schools where some alumni continuing education programs allow direct undergraduate–alumni contact, the experience has been extraordinarily rewarding for the faculty, for the adults, and for the undergraduates.

Most alumni continuing education (and other adult education) programs do not operate directly in the undergraduate curriculum. Alumni colleges, even when they are on the campus, tend to be separate academic experiences, often held during the summer when the undergraduates are away or in the evenings or on weekends when working adults can attend but undergraduates do not. Some institutions, however, design the programs and promotion to encourage undergraduate participation and the undergraduates in fact do attend.

Even without direct participation, the undergraduates benefit in several ways from the presence of alumni continuing education on the campus. There is the beneficial effect on their curriculum when the faculty teach adults in short-term noncredit programs. Alumni continuing education, because it usually offers no credit, does not come under the usual scrutiny of the provost or dean of the faculty and therefore the result is sometimes more inventive teaching. Here, then, is an incubator

(to borrow Director of Cornell's Adult University Ralph Janis's
term) for new undergraduate lectures and courses. As we saw
above, the undergraduate curriculum also benefits from the interdisciplinary teaching of faculty members in alumni continuing education programs on and off the campus.

ADVANTAGES TO THE ADMISSIONS OFFICES

Those alumni continuing education programs that invite the
participation of children and teenagers, whether alongside or
separate from their parents, often serve as the very best introduction to a college or university. Instead of the overwhelming
rush of a weekend hit-and-run visit to a campus, these young-
sters become students in the everyday experience of the campus
for a week or more. It is not uncommon for these teenagers to
become enamored of a college during this kind of unpressured
visit and then to reappear a year or two later as undergraduates.

Nor is it difficult for alumni continuing education programs
to benefit the graduate admissions programs in at least two
ways. First, as Notre Dame's James Pollicita has noted, when
these adult programs take place near the time or place for, or
on the same subject as, credit programs, the possibility exists
that adults whose appetites have been whetted in the noncredit
programs will register for the more ambitious ones.

More important, short-term noncredit programs, like those
offered in alumni continuing education settings, grant adults
the perfect opportunity to dip their toes into the potentially
frightening waters of the university, where they can prove that
they have not forgotten how to swim before taking on more
substantial academic challenges. As Alan Knox (1977) has
pointed out:

> *Practitioners who work with adults sometimes want to help adults im-*
> *prove their own estimates of their learning ability. One way in which*
> *supervisors, teachers, counselors, and health professionals do so is to*
> *suggest that the adult engage in a relevant educative activity on a modest*
> *scale and see how it goes. For the adult with sufficient self-confidence*
> *to try, this approach has the great advantage of the direct correspondence*

between the modest educative activity from which the prediction is made
and the more major educative activity that the adult is considering.

At present there is no instrument or efficient procedure to establish
adult learning ability [pp. 412–13].

In other words, alumni continuing education is the ultimate
reentry vehicle. Any short-term noncredit continuing education
program has some of the same effect, but when the basic concept is offered to alumni who already know the university, we
are more likely to succeed in reintroducing those adults to our
intellectual communities.

Nothing brings home this important advantage of alumni
continuing education like a flesh-and-blood true story. It comes
from the wife of an alumnus who attended summer colleges at
her husband's alma mater:

> *[P]articipating in . . . Alumni College not only had a tiny bit to do*
> *with my decision to get my bachelor's degree but a great deal to do with*
> *it. When my husband first suggested that we go to Alumni College, I*
> *was not enthusiastic. But because he wanted to so much, I mustered*
> *my courage, I did the reading and found that when I attended the classes*
> *I was able to hold my own.*
>
> *That first summer gave me the inclination to seriously consider the*
> *idea of going back to school to get my BA degree. After the second*
> *summer . . . , that wonderful session concerning the Renaissance, I*
> *really felt the need, not just an interest, to complete my education. So*
> *in the summer of 1983 I enrolled at the National College of Education*
> *in Evanston, Illinois. It was a marvelous experience. I completed my*
> *junior and senior years in one year and graduated with honors. You*
> *may be interested to know that National College gave me five credits*
> *each for the two non-credit Alumni Colleges I attended.*
>
> *So as you can see . . . Alumni College made me realize how much*
> *education I had missed and how much I wanted to learn. Those programs*
> *got me started and the group discussion experience overrode my fear of*
> *returning to the classroom in a competitive atmosphere. The rest involves*
> *hard work with long hours of reading and writing, but it was all worth*
> *it. And, believe me, I felt three feet off the ground when that piece of*
> *paper finally arrived [letter from Barbara Horky to Steven L. Calvert,*
> *March 11, 1985].*

Robert Cooper of McGill University, an associate dean, Faculty
of Management, describes the advantages of alumni continuing

education for adult admissions programs, this time in classic marketing terms (1979). He first reminds us that "we are in the business of serving people's needs for learning and knowledge; for self-development; and for participating in the learning and development of others," and then suggests that we develop alumni programs as we would develop any other business product: by defining market segments and the needs of those market segments and then developing products for them. Remember how easy this will be for an institution that keeps alumni records coded by professional field, undergraduate or graduate major, geographical location, and age or college class. As James Pollicita also reminds us, the alumni office typically has big travel and promotional budgets, crucial tools for keeping in touch with far-flung alumni, and tremendous advantages to our admissions offices whenever the two offices cooperate.

ADVANTAGES TO THE FUNDRAISING OFFICE

Participation in continuing education programs seems to have greater influence on alumni donations than almost every other kind of alumni activity. When Stanford University studied over a decade ago the relationships between alumni participation and alumni giving, participation in continuing education programs ranked right behind service on the university's board or in the presidencies of its top alumni volunteer organizations. No other alumni programs had as powerful an ability to tune alumni to the academic quality of the university or to dispose alumni to support it financially.

Here are the comments of a first-time alumni college participant, which exemplify the almost instantaneous result these programs often have upon alumni:

> From the point of view of an uninvolved alumnus (this was my first time back after 43 years), I am proud of this college, realize what I've been missing, and must think about my future support for the College. I sense that such support will become important to me in a way it never has before [Dartmouth Alumni College evaluation form from Robert Ottman '40, August 8, 1983].

ADVANTAGES TO THE ALUMNI AND OTHER PARTICIPANTS

No matter how much the university (in so many of its offices) benefits from alumni continuing education, and regardless of the fact that it is in our own best interest to engage our closest adults in this way, the participants themselves may benefit more. We may rightly claim that we are providing a service to alumni, in some measure giving to them, which seems only fair, considering how much we ask in return.

Continuity of educational experience, an important goal of all education, and particularly of continuing education, derives most naturally from an educational perspective that begins with the moment a college or university accepts a freshman and continues until the death of the alumnus or alumna. This is the broadest definition of alumni continuing education and highlights the importance of taking this unique view of our lifelong relationship between our adults and our universities.

This continuity produces important developments in the individual, the more so for the individual alumnus. As William Jewett Tucker remarked, the important rejuvenation of alumni continuing education includes "returning there [to alma mater, and not to any other institution] from time to time [so] he can see with the eyes of a man what he may have missed seeing with the eyes of a boy." We are simply not who we were at that younger, formative age, and we cannot judge with as much assurance just how far we have come with our developing adult sensitivities unless we go back to their source and compare our reactions to the same issues, the same mentors, the same books. Joseph Epstein, in his August 1981 *Commentary* essay, "The Noblest Distraction," put it this way:

> Rereading can be a humility-inducing activity, when, on rereading, one learns that for the first time around with a book, one's politics or fantasies or personal anxieties were in fact doing most of the work. Rereading books first read when young, one is inclined to weep for the "naif one" you were at that time and, if you get to reread the same book some 20 years hence, you may weep again [p. 55].

Alumni need to keep learning, lest they lose intellectual powers requiring conscious application, like reasoning and analytical thinking, or the ability to read the best literature, hear the best music, and delve deeply into the best art. Here is a constant intellectual battle waged by alumni and alma mater against what John Mason Brown once described as the American myth by which "we expect the skin of a dead sheep to keep the mind alive forever" (quoted in Eklund, "The Alumni University . . . , " 1961).

Providing continuity to our alumni in their educational relationship to the university is normally aimed at the postbaccalaureate years. This seems to a very great degree a kind of marketing madness. As we mentioned above, no potential audience for our adult education programs is as favorably predisposed to participate with us as our own alumni. The odd fact, however, is that we fail to treat our matriculated undergraduate and graduate students as our best future market while they are right under our noses. The marketing is harder to do, and more expensive, after our students complete their degrees and leave town.

For all the advantages of this market, alumni are not so certain to return for continuing education that we can take them for granted or ignore basic marketing sense. After all, high school students do not beat down our doors without admissions offices, guidance counselors, and college-educated parents to push them, and we need to be smarter about creating those same kinds of encouragements to our students once they have had the initial experience of our undergraduate or graduate degree programs.

Relatively few parents have taken their own continuing education seriously; campus counseling offices concentrate on graduate degree program admissions or job searches; and continuing education admissions offices are generally not nearly so well staffed nor so well traveled as their undergraduate counterparts. This makes absolutely no sense. Undergraduate programs admit students for four years (whether or not continuous), whereas continuing education admission could be for a lifetime. In purely economic terms, why do we invest heavily in bringing students to the university for four years of tuition, but not spend a proportionate amount on continuing education recruitment that might result in a lifetime of tuition income?

One way of marketing our continuing education programs to our current students is to offer them two things before they ever graduate. One is a collection of short-term noncredit educational events, seminars, or programs for their spare time. The idea here is to create in undergraduates the habit of participating in continuing education activities beyond their vocational responsibilities though perhaps related to them. We must help our younger students to see that their undergraduate experience should take a shape they can easily adapt to the rest of their lives. We need to help them understand the pattern they are establishing, and even to help them practice making coherent sense out of all their otherwise disconnected educational experiences in and outside the curriculum. We might, for example, offer noncredit courses on continuing education, on educational skills-building, and other themes, to train undergraduates to think about their lifelong education and to make them competent continuing education consumers.

Currently we do little to make our younger students truly aware of the fact that they can be (but not necessarily are) learning how to learn while they are earning their first college degree. We will do them a great service, and serve ourselves in the bargain, if we begin graduating thousands of alumni who know how to recognize which life problems require a concerted educational experience; if we teach them how to define that problem in educational terms; if we make sure they can confidently build an educational package from the myriad educational resources available to them at alma mater, in their community, or through the media; if we model for them how to adjust their lives periodically so that education can take place; and if we ensure that they know how to evaluate their learning experience to see if it did the job.

Redefining the University Community

Of all the advantages of alumni continuing education, perhaps the most important lies in its potential to help redefine
the university community so that it includes active lifelong participation by alumni. Redefining the university community requires that we treat alumni like adults; and here, since we have
all the evidence we need that alumni want an enriched relationship, the responsibility lies primarily with the university
itself.

The fathers of alumni continuing education, those early college and university presidents at the turn of this century, took
responsibility for this new field of education because they saw
in it a way to respond to several pressing issues surrounding
alumni and alma mater: (1) alumni/ae are valuable resources
and no educational institution can afford to waste its resources;
(2) alumni relations must include direct participation by graduates in the institution's primary business of education; (3) fundraising among alumni should be a coincidental feature of a
more broadly defined alumni relationship; (4) failing to involve
alumni in the educational issues facing a college is dangerous,
the alternative being uninformed alumni meddling; (5) life is
speeding up, and alumni need both the perspective and the
refreshing intellectual change of pace that their college or university can provide; (6) an undergraduate education is not
enough education anymore; and (7) the problem is not to determine whether alumni should continue their education with
alma mater, but how.

In 1947, Cyril Houle, then a professor of education at the
University of Chicago, echoed this point of view:

> Sooner or later, some college or university will undertake in a systematic
> fashion, to plan a lifetime program of education. It will give to young
> people those basic and structural elements which best set the pattern for
> their later life. It will then offer a program of continued study for its
> alumni, giving them an opportunity to extend, broaden and modernize
> their education throughout life, as well as offering them a chance to
> learn the specific things which they need to know as they undertake new

responsibilities. Such an institution, when it appears, will have to survive a great deal of criticism, ridicule, and administrative problems, but we may hope that the force of circumstances will eventually make its practice the rule rather than the exception so that gradually American education will adopt a broader base of activity [Houle, 1948, p. 10].

"I am dreaming," said Amherst's President Alexander Meiklejohn in 1916, "of the college community as a body of thousands of men—teachers, graduates, undergraduates—all of whom are engaged in the same intellectual operation, in the same great enterprise of the mind." Meiklejohn is advocating that we expand our definition of the college community. As we work toward Meiklejohn's vision, we will be able to take advantage of mutual interests. On the one hand (as we saw earlier), alumni want a meaningful intellectual relationship with their alma mater (and increasingly with more than one alma mater). Why? In part because, geographical proximity notwithstanding, alumni know alma mater. On the other hand, alumni yearn for a lifelong, supportive relationship to alma mater because *it* knows *them.* Alumni offices symbolize this assurance that institutions know and want a relationship with their alumni. This combined sense of alumni belonging to alma mater, encouraged on both sides, goes a long way toward defining our lifelong "intellectual residence."

As demographics and funding sources change, more institutions will want to know their alumni. They will need alumni involved as students, and they will need financial and voluntary support. This means an exfoliation of alumni relations by many more institutions, including graduate and professional schools.

The question, then, is what *kind* of relationship to nurture on both sides. The new "community" about which Alexander Meiklejohn dreamed has been transformed over the last three-quarters of a century from a loose organization of alumni patrons emotionally motivated to a group asking for serious intellectual participation in the life of the university.

At the 1986 National University Continuing Education Association's annual convention, James Pollicita noted that the central question for professionals in both alumni relations and continuing education is: "Who are the members of this intellectual community?" (address in Portland, Oregon, April 26, 1986). His formulation resembles executive director of the Association of Yale Alumni Eustace Theodore's inaugural statement in the October 1981 issue of the *Yale Alumni Magazine:*

> *We are working here on one of the most critical questions in higher education today: What is the nature of the educational community? It's a question I have been working on for the last nine years [as faculty dean in one residential college].*
>
> *. . . People look to the church for spiritual strength, to the government for civic leadership, and to Yale primarily for a continuing educational relationship. You can see that in the requests of the clubs for faculty speakers, in the study trips for alumni, the alumni colleges, the educational underpinnings of the reunions, and the general desire to know about the state of education at Yale. The AYA mission is a very sound one [p. 18].*

On the continuing education side, Donald E. Collins, associate provost and dean of University College at Northwestern University, says,

> *It seems to me that the most satisfying alumni events would be those that in some way recreate the academic side of college life, as well as the social. . . . The programs serve also to bridge the gap between certain alumni and the university, providing intellectual stimulation for the participants and the faculty alike and increasing the sense of the university as a wider community [letter to Steven L. Calvert, May 16, 1986].*

Simply put, colleges and universities must take alumni seriously. Milton R. Stern, dean of University Extension at the University of California at Berkeley, suggests that we too commonly express our "disrespect" for alumni by "exploiting" them in our alumni relations programs. We expect much from these alumni but give little in return. He believes we must create an entirely new category of participation in academe. In his conception, there are faculty members, administrators, and students, all with well-defined relationships to the university. But what about those others who take their intellectual relationship to the university seriously but who fall outside the usual categories of participation? Stern views them as "members of the university." This group might include all alumni whose interest in alma mater goes beyond a gift to the annual fund, those who remain truly interested in education as an ongoing part of their lives. For Stern, who further believes that in the foreseeable future an individual's college will be as important as his or her politics or religion, such a category of membership could change the world of higher education for the better. Or, in the words of Professor Charles T. Wood, Dartmouth's most practiced teacher of alumni continuing education programs, "What I'm talking about, ultimately, is a revolution in the way a university should see its mission and function, and maybe the time isn't right. All I can say is that I see something like this coming at some future point. . . . The question really is when, not whether" [letter to Harvard's Chase Peterson, July 9, 1973].

An advantage of Stern's new category of membership in the university community is that it opens the doors to enriched interplay between this community and the greater community of which it is part—the town, city, county, state, nation, and even the world it serves. This is an important university responsibility, and according to Fred Harvey Harrington the time is right to take it up with vigor:

> Professors who are attacking problems of energy, environment, poverty, pollution, prejudice and population control have come to understand that research and campus teaching are not enough. To make an impact, they must also convince all sorts of opinion and policy makers. That is, they must become adult educators. Today is a good time to move in this direction, for the active public is worried about the future and is more prepared than before to listen to the message [Harrington, 1977, pp. 3–4].

These issues are as important for private liberal arts colleges, always struggling for the right balance between practical and theoretical knowledge, as they are for state or land-grant universities whose charters insist on community service. In serving the public, a college or university should turn its attention consciously toward its own alumni. At Cornell, an interesting combination of land-grant university and private college, the alumni university (summer liberal arts programs for alumni and other adults) was cited in 1974 as a valid part of the institution's land grant mission.

Universities have even begun taking seriously the influence they can have on world affairs acting through their alumni. The better informed those alumni are about the subtleties of personal, local, national, and global issues, the better. Ken Fredrick, alumni director at Canada's McMaster University, has put it this way:

> It is the "alumni response in society that effectively completes the educational process," observes Verne Stadtman, once director of alumni publications at the University of California, and a president of the American Alumni Council. And it is through the provision of continuing education, we would add, that a school helps its alumni to respond in fullest measure.
>
> Such learning—and we'll use Stadtman's phrasing—will "inspire the educated leadership in society our alumni can provide"; sharpen graduates' critical faculties and sustain "the adventurous spirit of the inquiring mind"; and "make more and more of the knowledge on the campus a part of the equipment of the alumnus in his everyday life."
>
> In short, it is through continuing education that our institutions can exert "continuing influence over their products," and, through them, make "discernible impact on the society" they serve [Fredrick, 1986, p. 8].

TREATING ALUMNI AS ADULTS

By and large, universities have not treated alumni as adults. They should. Ask yourself: If I had adults in my college, and adolescents in my college, and I could treat one to parties and sporting events, and the other to serious intellectual fare, which would I offer to whom?

We tend to waste our university resources on most of the adults who come into our orbit as alumni. Can anyone explain why, after concentrating on the intellectual lives of our adolescents in college, leaving them almost entirely on their own for their social lives, we suddenly on their graduation can think of nothing else for their reunions, homecomings, and the like? This may be the greatest travesty of American higher education.

Our colleges and universities are finite national resources. Ours is an age when more and more adults need education, when an aging population includes more adults than ever, when knowledge is exploding at such a rate that one's world changes every dozen years or so to the point where some retooling of the mind is necessary for mere survival, and when a new generation of college graduates expects to engage in lifelong learning. Our institutions of higher education must respond immediately to this self-evident challenge of alumni continuing education.

Universities are in the business of education. No university office can waste its university resources on social events. We need to establish serious, coherent, lifelong relationships with our adults, and the place to begin is with our own alumni. The reason is as much chronological as anything else. Our own alumni belong to us first. We make an educational compact with them very early in their lives, teach them our way of knowing, and show them how to use our resources, faculty, and support systems. We have, therefore, an absolute imperative to provide, in some measure and through whatever means within our grasp, for the lifelong intellectual residence of these, our own adults, our alumni.

If the moral imperative is not sufficient for us, then we can think in very practical terms. Americans spend over $100 billion every year on adult education, more than half of it going to providers outside the academy. How does the competition do it? They respond to the learners' needs, not merely to their own needs for students and for tuition income. And they adhere to simple market economics. They know that the easiest sales are repeat sales. Peters and Waterman (1982) say: "Stay close to the customer." Know what he or she needs. Sell to the same customer again and again. How short-sighted of us to graduate our best consumers and hardly ever seek them out when we sell our more advanced products. If we were in the business of video discs or luxury automobiles, we would not be so foolish. If we do not follow the simple rules of marketing, someone else will.

Conclusion

Having defined alumni continuing education and explored its importance and its advantages to the university, we can look in Part II at the varieties of alumni continuing education programs now in existence, and how to run them successfully.

Part Two

Developing Successful Programs in Alumni Continuing Education

CHAPTER 3

KNOW THYSELF:
Getting Started
in Alumni Continuing Education

Readers starting or expanding alumni continuing education programs will find it helpful not only to peruse appropriate chapters of this book but also to contact alumni relations and continuing education professionals who run successful alumni continuing education programs at colleges and universities similar to the readers'. Many helpful professionals are listed in the Appendix.

This part of the book will answer the most frequently asked questions about starting or expanding alumni continuing education programs. This chapter will tend to preliminary matters: ensuring that you know why you are starting or expanding such programs; that they will reflect your institution's mission and strengths; that you know your alumni, their interests and needs; that you have a professional and volunteer staff to do the job; that you can garner sufficient institutional support; and that you have a promotional and marketing plan.

Chapters 4, 5, 6, and 7 suggest dozens of successful program formats from colleges and universities with experience in alumni continuing education. This variety will allow any school the freedom to choose appropriate programs with a high likelihood of success. Examples will include summer alumni colleges, on- and off-campus seminars, alumni colleges abroad (alumni travel programs with the faculty), and many special program formats. Chapter 4 also suggests how to select the right program formats to begin with.

Chapter 8 looks at the faculty—its important administrative and teaching roles, how to earn faculty support, and what (or whether) to pay them—and suggests dozens of program topics especially appropriate to different kinds of alumni continuing education programs.

Chapter 9 presents sample budgets for each of the three major program types and explores funding sources other than program revenues. Closing Part II, this chapter also looks at mature alumni continuing education programs and provides long-range goals.

Analyzing Institutional Mission, Strengths, and Your Goals for Alumni Continuing Education

Begin with introspection. Ask questions like "What is this institution's mission?" "What are its goals?" "What is it good at?" Then, exploring the market, ask "Do we know our alumni (and the other adults we would like to serve)?" "What interests them?" "What do they want from this institution?"

When these questions have been answered by the right people, a college or university will be ready to ask the first question addressed in Chapter 4: "What kind of alumni continuing education program should we offer?" Of all the possibilities described in Chapters 4–7, an institution that knows itself well will choose the right place to begin.

Here is an example of an institution that carefully considered its strengths and weaknesses before opening its first alumni college. Johns Hopkins University knew it had a high-quality academic program and interested alumni whose support was very important, but its Baltimore campus did not seem particularly attractive for a summer alumni college. Their successful program now takes place on the campus of St. Mary's College on Chesapeake Bay.

Similarly, the University of Michigan uses its off-campus summer camps. Several institutions hold weekend alumni colleges in the West—at lodges in Montana, at the Aspen Institute or Vail in Colorado, and in Yosemite National Park. The University of Pennsylvania held several alumni colleges in the Catskill Mountains of southeastern New York State, and while these attracted too few participants, the alumni office yearns to restart them. There may be no point in some institutions running liberal arts alumni colleges if their real strengths are in engineering. And everyone needs an attractive location, even if it cannot be their own campus.

An institution also needs to be clear about its goals for an alumni college or other alumni continuing education program; and knowing the goals is crucial to soliciting the institutional commitment the program needs. One goal may be to provide adults with a nonthreatening, short-term continuing education experience. This goal should earn support from the continuing education unit because such programs can start adults toward more substantial programs. If one goal of your program is to produce extra revenue during quiet campus summers, you will be supported by the dining, housing, campus police, and other support service departments. Paying the faculty on an overload basis will help to interest the faculty dean and the provost. And the sum total of this backing will encourage institutional leaders to support alumni continuing education.

If your primary goal is to bring alumni and their families back to the campus so that their greater familiarity with the college or university today will lead to more productive fundraising, you will ask yourself different questions, especially, "Is this institution committed to the concept of alumni relations?" Most private colleges and an increasing number of public institutions across the country are committed to alumni relations and to its binary star, the annual fund. In this kind of atmosphere, it is reasonably easy to argue that an alumni continuing education program is worth doing because it is a logical and proven form of alumni relations. You may even, under these circumstances, convince campus leaders that these programs should not have to make money, any more than reunions or the alumni council make money. The reason is that the money eventually will come in through the door marked "fundraising."

State universities and other public institutions may have been less committed to alumni relations in the past. Such institutions valued more the general public relations value or the educational service offered by alumni continuing education programs. In 1978, Linda Carl found that many institutions (public and private) sponsored an alumni college in large measure to improve their public image (Carl, 1978, p. 20). Today, with public funds drying up, public institutions are increasingly interested in good alumni relations and therefore in alumni continuing education.

Still, to be realistic, few on-campus summer alumni colleges pay all their bills for the first three to five years, and so, with funds always in short supply at colleges and universities of all kinds, an institution may want to consider where back-up funds would come from if it started that kind of program. In this sense, one strength a sponsoring institution might look for is a commitment to new alumni programs, supported by real dollars.

Other strengths to look for are the campus itself and its facilities. Is the campus an attractive place for adults? Is there a conference center, or are the dormitories adequate for adult occupancy? Are support services (food, transportation, audio-visual equipment) adequate? Are the staff and the faculty prepared to run the new programs? Alumni continuing education puts new, and relatively high, pressures on the professionalism and energy of everyone involved.

Some professional schools (business, law, engineering, and medical schools) began getting into alumni continuing education in the 1980s. In many respects the reasons, and the questions these schools must ask themselves, are identical to those for parent colleges or universities. There may be some differences, too. For example, a rapidly increasing number of professions now require recertification based on continuing education credit or certificate programs. Where geography is not a serious deterrent, professional schools may find that offering continuing professional education to their own alumni makes perfect sense. Most profession-mandated continuing education makes money, so this kind of alumni continuing education should not need to ask tough fiscal questions. Nor will new programs be hard to invent: it cannot be far from medical seminars abroad to alumni colleges abroad for medical school alumni. Indeed, an improved educational image and less risk with the IRS could result. From the participants' point of view, some such programs can still be written off as business expenses.

Organizationally, some early programs of this type have taken advantage of cooperation between an alumni officer's expertise and a professionally oriented academic program. William L. Hathorne, director of alumni relations at Bentley College in Waltham, Massachusetts, reports that "we offer continuing education credits for one of our Saturday morning seminars. A great draw for a business college with many CPAs!" And James R. Hopson, assistant for services at the University of Connecticut Alumni Association, reports that the alumni office cosponsored with the School of Business Administration an outreach educational program in the state.

The University of Pennsylvania's Wharton School (of business administration), on the other hand, has drawn up plans for a "cradle-to-grave" alumni continuing professional education program. Still in its very early stages, this program would give expression to Wharton's feeling of responsibility toward its students and its graduates throughout their professional lives. Once Wharton has the program up and running, and business school applicants learn about it, other schools may be expected to follow suit.

"Nothing can come of nothing," wrote Sir Joshua Reynolds in 1774. No successful alumni continuing education program ever appeared out of the blue, nor would it succeed if it did. The faculty would not understand it. The alumni would be so surprised by it that they would not participate. And the institution might not know how to organize or support it. The secret for any college or university is to build alumni continuing education upon strengths already in place. Then, because alumni continuing education is the most logical way for alumni to relate to alma mater, it almost cannot fail.

Look at existing programs of the alumni office and of the continuing education office, for example. Few alumni offices entirely exclude faculty from their programs. If reunions include faculty presentations, build on them: make seminars out of them by choosing academic subjects, allowing sufficient time for audience participation, and suggesting advance or follow-up reading. If your faculty members occasionally speak to the annual dinner meeting of your largest alumni chapter or club, spin off a half-day academic seminar for the same alumni group with that teacher. If your alumni office sponsors alumni travel, add faculty and a teaching program. The continuing education office or even the undergraduate deans may be able to help, especially if they already send undergraduates abroad with the faculty.

Which Alumni Will Participate?

It is important to recognize that some alumni participate actively in the intellectual life of the institution whether they are expressly invited or not, and others never will, no matter what the enticements or admonishments. As Cyril Houle suggested in *The Inquiring Mind* (1961):

> The desire to learn, like every other human characteristic, is not shared equally by everyone. To judge from casual observation, most people possess it only fitfully and in modest measure. But in a world which sometimes seems to stress the pleasures of ignorance, some men and women seek the rewards of knowledge—and do so to a marked degree. They read. They create or join groups in order to share their studies. They take courses. They belong to organizations whose aims are wholly or partly educational. They visit museums and exhibits, they listen to radio and watch television with discrimination, and they travel to enlarge their horizons. The desire to learn seems, in fact, to pervade their existence. They approach life with an air of openness and an inquiring mind [p. 3].

In other words, alumni are not different from the students they were, and it helps to remind the faculty of this before they teach in an alumni continuing education program. Some students come to the university to learn. Of those, some love learning for its own sake; others love the advantages of learning. One respected and senior faculty member of a major state university believes that three-quarters of the undergraduates do not belong there; they simply are not ready to take advantage of the academic experience. This may mean that alumni need to be encouraged to come back to the university later in life, when they are ready.

Among the participants in an alumni continuing education program, some come having read every word in every book sent them in advance, having read further in local libraries, and having discussed the subject with their spouses for months. Others read a little during the program, a little more afterward. Some read nothing, take no notes during lectures, but still take away something of value to them. On the whole, the proportion of enthusiastic learners is much higher in these programs than among undergraduates, which helps to explain the faculty's enthusiasm for teaching alumni continuing education programs.

Who comes to alumni continuing education programs? Every institution that has looked closely reports that these programs attract, among others, alumni who do not participate in any other kind of alumni program. In some summer alumni colleges and off-campus alumni weekend seminars, between 60 and 95 percent of the alumni participants had never been involved with the university since graduation. It is not uncommon for alumni college participants to be back on the campus for the first time in forty or fifty years.

This is an astonishing and significant fact. Not that previously uninvolved alumni are the only participants of these programs. Far from it. Many are club officers, class officers, annual fund volunteers, parents of undergraduates, season football ticket holders—all looking for a little balance in their ties to the university. But we must remember that alumni relations offices at many institutions have concentrated on social programming, which means that alumni whose interests in the university are primarily intellectual have been left out. If we mean to have them back, we must give them what they want. If we do not, we will never know what human resources lie out there waiting to share in the life of the institution, taking and giving. The goal is not to supplant social programming but to round out a complete alumni program in which each graduate can find programs they value in which to participate. This means that from now on our alumni programs need to be sometimes social, or cultural, or recreational, and sometimes intellectual.

Many colleges and universities have done alumni surveys that show the discrepancy between programs the alumni association offers and what alumni want. These surveys at all kinds of institutions (public and private, large and small, university and college) show far more interest in alumni continuing education than the institution or its alumni association satisfies. It does not matter whether the alumni office, the continuing education unit, or an individual faculty member puts on the educational program many alumni are waiting for. What matters is offering that program.

In 1977, Linda Carl, then at the University of Illinois (Urbana-Champaign), conducted the only national study of alumni college participants—who came and why. It is worth reiterating her findings, but keep two caveats in mind.

First, she studied only alumni colleges: thirty-seven five- to seven-day, primarily on-campus, summer alumni colleges as they existed in the middle 1970s. She would have found some differences in the participants of off-campus, weekend, alumni club or chapter seminars, or alumni colleges abroad (academic alumni travel), even in those days.

The second factor to bear in mind is that America's population has changed in ten years in ways that affect who comes to an alumni college. Many of Carl's findings are still valid (for example, what kinds of professional backgrounds are typical in alumni college participants), but the age profile has changed at many alumni colleges in the 1980s. That group is aging. Fewer young families are returning to the summer alumni college on the campus, partly because two-profession couples are finding it difficult to coordinate traditional family vacations. Their own work schedules are hard to manipulate and children today can choose their own vacations from a bewildering variety of specialty summer camps.

In short, times have changed since Carl figured out who came to alumni colleges in the 1970s. Still, many of her findings apply today. First of all, she discovered that participants were by no means all alumni. In many cases most were spouses, parents or other relatives of students or alumni, and members of the general public that most colleges and universities judiciously refer to as friends. There is no point excluding non-alumni from an alumni continuing education program. Not a single institution surveyed for this book excluded others, and indeed nonalumni may help to support an alumni college financially while enriching the participant group. Faculties are wary of intellectual in-breeding; alumni colleges might recruit nonalumni for this reason, but this group seems to show up without the extra effort.

At some alumni colleges, as many as one-quarter of the participants were parents of the sponsoring institution's undergraduates. This trend has become stronger in the last ten years, perhaps because parents are checking up on their educational investment, or are experiencing rekindled intellectual excitement from talking with their children. Either way, an alumni college provides an ideal focus for a parent relations program.

Most participants are college graduates. Continuing education research suggests that the more education one has, the more one wants. This fact should encourage us to focus more attention on continuing education for alumni.

Participants come heavily from four professions: medicine, law, business, and education. Some primary and secondary school teachers take participation certificates back to their school districts and receive continuing education credit toward advancement and salary increases. It makes sense that all these serious-minded, highly intelligent professionals would find an alumni college an efficient way to accomplish two things at once—escape from the office and intellectual stimulation. Also, as undergraduates these were the students who concentrated on preprofessional courses and may still harbor unfulfilled loves for the liberal arts, especially art and art history, philosophy, religion, world affairs, and literature. These are, in fact, the most successful subjects for alumni colleges.

Participants are typically over 50 percent repeaters, and over 50 percent women. The women of couples make most of the original decisions to attend. Carl found a healthy distribution of ages, starting with alumni seven years out of school (in other words, old enough to be out of graduate school altogether); but again, many alumni colleges see fewer young participants every year. Many alumni colleges are convenient to a large geographic concentration of alumni and others, and a high percentage of participants commute, rather than live in student dormitories. As advancing communications technology makes convenience more important to continuing education delivery, we would expect that commuter participation in alumni colleges will increase.

Why Do They Come to Alumni College?

George H. Ebert studied the participants of Iowa State University's alumni continuing education seminars in 1972. The seminars were Friday-Saturday programs of lectures and discussion on liberal arts themes held once or twice a year. Ebert found that the three most important factors stimulating participants were a desire to be intellectually curious, a desire to share intellectually with a spouse, and a desire to serve others through intellectual pursuits. Over 50 percent of the participants followed up by discussing the seminar topic with others, reading additional material or sharing seminar readings with others, discussing a theme-related issue at some other meeting after the seminar, or a combination of these activities.

Carl asked alumni college directors why they thought participants came. There is no reason to think participants' reasons for attending alumni colleges have changed in ten years. Carl reported that two motivations were particularly important. One was intellectual stimulation; the other was the combination of intellectual and physical activities. Few seemed to come primarily out of emotional attachment to alma mater, and whether or not this makes intuitive sense, it is nice to know. After all, we run alumni colleges partly on the theory that they attract a different group of alumni than those who return for the mostly social and emotional reunions.

Anecdotal evidence supports the surveys. Earlier we quoted Barbara Horky, a Dartmouth Alumni College participant who had been motivated by her experience to finish one degree and start another back home. It seems fair to quote her husband (in this case, the alumnus), Rudy, who described his reasons for attending as both intellectual and emotional:

> All in all, it is the atmosphere you create that lures us into the great annual game called Dartmouth Alumni College. For it is a wonderful game, and we all love to play it. We play at being students again, meeting old and making new friends in much the same way that we did many years ago. And as it was many years ago, we learn something that stays with us. In March or April, sometimes, the reading looks like a big hill to climb, but at the end of August, we feel we have climbed an intellectual Mt. Moosilauke [a mountain and lodge near the campus where deans and presidents have traditionally initiated most Dartmouth undergraduates into the College experience]. It is a joyful, relaxing, yet stimulating time. I can say for my part that it is a two-week period during which I am completely separated from the other fifty weeks of the year. All else is out of mind for that two weeks among convivial people in one of the most beautiful spots in the world.

Adult learning theory helps to explain who comes to alumni college and why, although few alumni college directors come from continuing education backgrounds and know the research. Therefore, there has been very little application of theories popularized over the last fifteen years by Alan Knox, Pat Cross, Carol Aslanian and Henry Brickell, among others. Neither have directors consciously applied landmark adult development theories from Erik Erikson (or the more derivative Gail Sheehy), Daniel Levinson, or George Vaillant; or the so-called stage theories (that adult development occurs in discrete stages) of ego development by Jane Loevinger, moral development by Lawrence Kohlberg, or intellectual development by William Perry. However, interested professionals and other readers are urged to review these development theories, beginning with the helpful listing on pages 153 and 176 in K. Patricia Cross's *Adults as Learners* (1983). An alternative is simply to involve more continuing education professionals when developing these programs.

With these adult development theories at hand, one can design age-specific educational program themes. The perfect time and place is the alumni reunion seminar. Here the audience is going to be age-specific no matter what you do, and you may as well take advantage of it. Chapter 5 will suggest subjects that work well during reunions. Here, it is worth distinguishing between those reunion occasions when age-specific programs based on adult development theory make sense and the kind of audience that is preferable for other alumni continuing education programs that result when location, topic, and other variables succeed in bringing together a range and balance of participant ages.

With adult development and learning theory in our heads, we are in a better position to develop alumni continuing education programs. It helps to know that we are trying to respond to what Cyril Houle calls "margins of energy and attention" (1961, p. 61), that is, those times in adults' lives when they reach plateaus of development and are ready for change—because that is often when they are also ready for more education.

Or, if we are wondering who will come to a certain kind of program, we will be glad to know that

> there are basically two kinds of learning associated with the learning society: self-directed learning, for which the base of knowledge is the work of Allen Tough and others . . . ; and participation in organized instruction (including learning for credit and certification), for which the base of research is primarily surveys and census data. In general, educators who want to increase participation in self-directed learning concentrate mainly on individual motivations. . . . In contrast those who wish to encourage participation in organized instruction start [by] opening up new opportunities and removing existing barriers [Cross, 1983, p. 132].

That is, some alumni who will not attend our educational seminars may nevertheless accept our educational counseling, reading programs, videotapes, and other educational materials for self-directed learners. Eventually, all of these services will become part of the alumni continuing education service package. In fact, the long-term future of alumni continuing education depends upon training competent, self-directed learners in the undergraduate program, and then supporting their lifelong education through both advice and materials. No institution can put even a substantial fraction of its alumni through residential programs. Our goal must be to support in any way we can what Harvard's brochure, "Institute for the Management of Lifelong Education" (1986), refers to as the "inner curriculum" in each graduate.

Smith, Aker, and Kidd (1970, p. 399) cite John W. C. Johnstone's *Volunteers for Learning* as showing why adults learn. Second on the list is leisure learning, that is, learning entirely for pleasure, precisely what alumni continuing education does best.

Two final points about adult learning theory. First, an understanding of adult development helps to explain why few young alumni participate in alumni continuing education. At this stage they are busy with new marriages, young families, and budding careers. Later in life, many of these young adults will be ready to return to alma mater and the informal classroom offered by alumni continuing education. At the 1985 Minary Conference on Alumni Continuing Education (held each fall at Dartmouth College's Minary Conference Center on Squam Lake in central New Hampshire), Eustace Theodore suggested that the life cycle of alumni programming must allow for graduates to be out of school from seven to as many as fifteen years before we should expect them back for serious intellectual activity. University of Vermont Alumni Director Suzanne A. Villanti agrees, finding that young alumni attend mostly social events, whereas older alumni value reunions and homecoming seminars, lecture series, and alumni travel programs with the faculty.

The second point is that educators from Plato to Alan Knox have remarked upon the appropriateness and predictability of adults' interest in certain subjects, depending upon the adults' ages. Plato's *Republic* assumes that young men seek physical challenges, so military service precedes demanding intellectual activity. This Platonic perspective offers a nice corrective to errant modern notions that older adults cannot learn. Alan Knox notes that "almost all adults can learn almost anything they want to" (1977, p. 424). He then characterizes some general differences between childhood, young adulthood, and maturity, in terms of the ideas and modes of thought most natural to these ages:

> *Young adults tend to be goal oriented. Older adults are more likely to emphasize reasons related to content and activity. Another type of expectation concerns the learning process. Many adults have a preference for some learning procedures, such as reading, observation, or group discussion.*

And

> *The innocence of childhood yields a natural curiosity and growth. For many people adolescence and young adulthood brings a false maturity in which surety is more important than wonder and answers are more important than questions. For those who achieve a mature capacity for growth, the wisdom of age born of experience is not innocence but simplicity.*

Finally,

> *Adult development is affected by the outlook of the individual adults, including the sense of current self and ideal self. The ideal self includes attention to competencies and priorities for responsible action, openness to feelings and creative efforts, and concern for others. The humanities have much to contribute to adults who seek a fuller and more enduring sense of their ideal self, along with enriched aspirations. The self is in turn authenticated through involvement. . . .*
>
> *Adults who are more open but have a sense of direction are able to reconcile contradictions between the old and the new and achieve growth through action and contemplation [Knox, 1977, pp. 427, 17, 13].*

The payoff for all adult educators, including those interested in alumni continuing education, is that the human mind is best prepared for the most fascinating subjects of study later in life. J. Roby Kidd has put his finger on the reason in Smith, Aker, and Kidd's *Handbook of Adult Education* (1970); he draws strength from thinkers of Plato's time:

One of the problems of the schools has always been how to teach certain ideas or achieve certain kinds of growth in an individual when a lengthy time span is necessary for maturation. How do you teach honour, or justice, or courage? How do you help students to welcome the innovator, to learn to be innovators themselves and at the same time cherish the "eternal verities"? How do you arm people against propaganda and against crushing pressures to conform? How long does it take to assist a man to become healthily critical of society, of ideas, and of himself, without becoming a sceptic, one who has faith in nothing? Or how, in a curriculum, do you find time to get a hearing for ideas that are merely important against the clamour of those that are urgent? It is much too simple an answer to these baffling questions to say that the time span for education must be extended. But, as the Greeks knew, "time is a kindly God," and, only where education is available when and as needed, will some of life's most important problems be solved [p. 404].

Here we are very close to answering the question, "Why do adults come to alumni college?" They come to continue asking those timeless questions about human existence that we taught them to ask when they were adolescents—back when they were too young to develop sophisticated answers.

We are also close to the theory about the lifelong relationship between adults and universities offered in Part III of this book. In that theory, the goal is a rationalized sequence of adult ties to higher education.

Marketing and Promotion

Once an institution has reviewed its mission and knows what it expects of alumni continuing education, it is time to entice alumni to these new programs. That is where marketing and promotion come in. Promotion here means the ways those in a target market are encouraged to purchase a product. By this time the promoter has already done the marketing, using expert advice or surveying potential participants to find out who is interested in a particular program; designing a program for a particular market; and designing program evaluation aimed at improving the product for further promotional campaigns.

MARKETING

The term marketing turns many people off. Doing a market survey, and calling it a market survey, seems potentially risky with the sensitive and intelligent people we want to participate in alumni continuing education. Do it tastefully.

There are two other reasons to be careful about market surveys. One regards Jerold Apps's fear that continuing education has not decided whether to base curriculum on surveys showing what adults already buy (assuming they know what they want) or on a theory about what adults need (assuming they do not know).

On the first, whether market surveys provide good guides to adult curricula, K. Patricia Cross is adamant:

> We should be cautious . . . about using the data directly to develop learning components into programs for adults—a procedure becoming alarmingly popular among educators conducting "needs assessments" and among legislators requiring evidence of "demand." Educators responding to "demand" as revealed in surveys may find themselves selling the ice box that the learner remembered rather than the refrigerator that the learner wants. . . .
>
> While some teachers insist that nothing will ever replace the standard classroom lecture as sound and efficient pedagogical technique, that is a little like saying that nothing will ever replace sneakers as the standard American sport shoe, or meat and potatoes as the universal American diet. Tastes do develop and change, and as people are exposed to alternatives, whether in physical fitness, cooking, or in education, large numbers are likely to find something that suits their particular needs better than the standard fare. The role of educators in the learning society is to develop gourmet learners and to be responsive to their interests by providing a wide range of high-quality educational options [1981, pp. 219, 251].

She was even firmer in her earlier formulation in *The Missing Link: Connecting Adult Learners to Learning Resources* (1978):

> The point is that planning for the learning society cannot be done safely on the basis of marketing surveys and consumer demand. The average adult can only respond on the basis of relatively limited knowledge and experience. Progress in uncharted domains is not generally made by responding to requests for the things people have already experienced;

it is more likely to come about through the imagination of people who see a need and can propose a better way of doing things. This is not to recommend doing away with needs assessments and certainly not to suggest remaining aloof and out of touch with the learning needs of the average adult. It is to suggest that planning for the learning society will be inadequate and always somewhat behind the times if planning and funding are based on a pedestrian implementation of the "demand" figures from the admittedly valuable background information provided by the needs assessments [p. 24].

To repeat: use market surveys carefully. We want to understand potential students, but in the end education should lead, not follow. Even some proprietary providers, including commercial television, would do well to remember that few consumers have experienced high-quality, innovative programs and delivery systems. Certainly our colleges and universities need to remember their leadership role in higher education, even in times of fiscal hardship.

Of course, survey marketing can contribute to successful promotion. Not only can surveys find existing markets, but they can also help develop new ones. In this sense marketing can become a kind of promotion (normally, we think of promotion as one phase of marketing). For example, when a college or university surveys its alumni to find out how many own video-cassette recorders (VCRs), the hint is communicated to owners that video programming might be forthcoming and to be alert for it; and it tells nonowners that they may soon wish they had a VCR.

Since marketing means understanding potential consumers, tailoring programs for them, and aiming promotion at them, we can measure alumni interest in alumni continuing education through methods other than market surveys. Jon Keates, in his article, "The Alumni Auditor Cometh" (1980), suggests one way:

For the Alumni Relations Office, the course audit program serves both as a barometer of alumni interests and as a market survey for the design of on-campus alumni programs. With this information, we can work to make the supply meet the demand. For example, more than 125 alumni registered for an introductory course in accounting two years ago. The following semester, we put together a special series of lectures on business accounting for alumni [p. 21].

James Pollicita suggests ways to link participation in one educational program to registration in another. We can hold registration for one set of programs near the entrance to another program's classroom, or we can follow up one subject with a related one. Duke University faculty members give campus-reunion previews of upcoming off-campus alumni seminars.

Ernest McMahon believes that marketing to repeat customers is more than good business practice; it carries out a university responsibility for alumni continuing education:

> *Observation leads only to the conclusion that most persons omit the graduates . . . from their concept of the college community. . . . [I]t is hypothecated that presidents, trustees, and faculty seldom consider the alumnus as related intellectually to the institution. The day of Commencement is the day of departure on which he passes beyond the Sheepskin Curtain. The alumnus has rolled off the academic assembly line, but the producers feel no obligation for service and maintenance. The automobile manufacturers feel a stronger obligation to their product [1960, p. 19].*

Four final comments on marketing. First, there is a huge market out there for adult education. Cross believes that something like one in three adults participate each year in some form of "organized learning activity, ten percent for credit or certificates" (1981, p. 52). That may mean 50 million adults engaged in continuing education, many of them college and university alumni.

Second, McMahon, Cross, and others suggest that we recruit learners through "membership and reference groups." Alumni comprise such a group to whom we can market very effectively.

Third, test-marketing tells us who will come to which programs. Young alumni may attend weekend seminars on personal finance, while retired alumni flock to longer alumni colleges on world affairs, literature, and the arts. Keeping in mind that our alumni offices keep address lists of potential participants that can be segmented by geography, by age, by professional background, and other useful categories, we should turn right around and market future programs to the right subgroups of our alumni.

Finally, alumni continuing education marketing and promotion serve two educational purposes at once. These activities attract participants. But they also enhance the relationship between alumni and alma mater, even for those alumni who never attend a program. It is hard to overestimate the effect of such mail in alumni mailboxes after a century of promoting social events. Remember Milton Stern's point that alumni must be tired of not being taken seriously as members of the university community. Mailing them promotional invitations to programs with the university's best teachers goes a long way toward solving that problem. It may be the biggest problem colleges and universities must solve, as we will say in Part III of this book. Therefore, in great measure, the medium is the message.

For more on marketing, readers can consult such other helpful resources as *Marketing Higher Education: A Practical Guide*, which Cornell's Robert Topor published through CASE in 1983.

PROMOTION

We know a lot (by intuition, instruction, experience, or as recipients) about promotion, but still a professional can be a big help. Use volunteer alumni with professional promotion backgrounds to write and design the brochures, and even to develop the marketing strategies, for alumni continuing education.

Whoever prepares the promotion should keep in mind that, because these programs are new to many alumni, early promotion should both explain the concept of alumni continuing education and sell the idea of participation in specific programs.

Especially in the early promotion, alumni need to be convinced that alumni continuing education programs are fun. They are education-vacations, with the intellectual challenge left in and the hazards (grades) removed. Once in the programs, the more serious-minded alumni continuing education participants have asked to write papers for faculty evaluation, and the faculty have cooperated. The best papers can be shared with the whole class, presented as valedictory addresses at closing banquets, or printed in alumni magazines or bulletins. The point is that any pressure is self-imposed by the participants themselves. Program directors should reduce barriers to participation by making sure alumni know how little pressure and how much intellectual excitement is available to them. In addition, it is important to spell out the other campus attractions available to participants. Remind them about the libraries, museums, recreational facilities, and interaction with undergraduates. It may even help to let participants register with credit cards.

Each sponsoring institution will develop its own list of special attractions for its alumni colleges and other programs: special faculty stars, alumni stars as guest speakers, extraordinary campus events running in conjunction with or alongside your program and accessible to alumni participants, and more. Perhaps the hardest thing to express in a printed brochure is the effect on the human mind of a stunning campus, but we should try. School songs, lore, and presidential quotations do this. Draw on them. Use all the arms in the arsenal. It is also hard to describe verbally in a brochure, or in its photographs, the excitement that goes on in a participant's mind when reacting to a faculty member's or other participants' ideas. Try to capture that stimulating moment. Take pictures that show faces lit up from within. Use past participants as ambassadors to alumni clubs, class reunions, and mini-reunions; as alumni magazine authors; and in word-of-mouth promotional campaigns. Past participants are the best salespersons.

Further, point out that alumni continuing education is a bargain. There are few cheaper ways to spend a week or two away from home. We have to be honest. Student dormitories may be offered at low rates, but participants only get what they pay for (except where some schools, like Notre Dame, subsidize the summer dormitory occupancy of alumni). But alumni almost can't afford to stay home for these prices.

The promotional brochures should use sophisticated direct-mail techniques. Only past alumni continuing education participants await the arrival of this year's brochures with bated breath. Most alumni find those brochures in their mailboxes with a lot of other attractive mail, and so our promotional pieces need to compete for attention. Color helps. So does photography and interesting writing. Brochures, designed to draw readers from the attractive outside to the detailed message inside, must make it easy for alumni to respond: tear-off registration forms help; postage-paid envelopes are even better (but expensive). If these techniques can sell soap, they can certainly help to sell education, especially if we take advantage of this audience's past happy association with alma mater's educational product.

The trick is to make that first sale, to get an alumnus or alumna to try his or her first alumni continuing education program. *Be seductive.* Many alumni continuing education programs have gotten started by sneaking faculty into existing alumni events that had not previously included an educational component. The annual alumni club or chapter dinner suddenly has not merely a faculty member's report on the campus year but a little taste of insight into the most exciting and accessible idea that the teacher can bring to an alumni audience. The seduction works. Alumni have been starved for intellectual contact with their university for so long that many of them have forgotten what a joy it is, and how important it is to them. Once seduced, or otherwise invited back into this stimulating role in the university community, many never go away again. That is why the repeat rate among alumni college participants can be as high as 50 or 70 percent.

Good promotion for a brandnew alumni continuing education effort may take two years before the first program, and thereafter it may take five years before extra effort is no longer needed. Again, we are reeducating alumni about our hopes for their relationship with alma mater. That takes effort, and it takes time.

It also takes money. A mature alumni college (more than five years old) may still spend 5 to 25 percent of its gross budget on promotion and postage. A good response is 1 to 3 percent of those receiving invitations, so mail to as many as the budget will allow. Those who cannot attend still get the message, including a little education on the seminar's subject from your promotional description. Direct mail is usually necessary; alumni magazine advertising, although helpful, proves less effective. One alternative is to piggy-back on other alumni mailings, like those sent to alumni club members or alumni classes. Announcements at club meetings avoid postage and printing costs altogether, but again serve best to support rather than to replace direct-mail promotion.

The Council for Advancement and Support of Education (CASE) maintains a large library of award-winning promotional brochures for alumni programs, some of them in alumni continuing education. In addition, the experts listed in the Appendix will usually share samples of their work.

Organization and Staffing

Who will run alumni continuing education? Almost anyone who thinks of it.

ORGANIZATION

Organizational and staff strengths or weaknesses must be part of the "know thyself" phase when planning alumni continuing education. "What do we do best?" is directly related to "Who does what we do best?" If the right people do not work for the university, they can be hired to help alumni continuing education succeed. Most institutions find the talent already on board, somewhere. If the existing organization of alumni relations or of continuing education is decentralized, that talent may be harder to find. On the other hand, experience has shown that the talent often identifies itself: a champion for the programs volunteers to direct them. This fact helps to explain the great variety of successful organizational structures that supports alumni continuing education at institutions around the country.

Linda Carl found that 89 percent of alumni colleges were

sponsored or co-sponsored by an alumni office or alumni association. The alumni office (at Ohio Wesleyan, for example) or the alumni association (at Notre Dame) may run the alumni college entirely alone. Continuing education (at Northwestern University, for example) may go it alone. The original sponsor may not keep the program: the extension office ran the University of Michigan's earliest Alumni University, while more recent programs came entirely from the alumni association (see Carl, 1978, p. 13). Occasionally different programs land in different offices: the College of General Studies (continuing education) at the University of Pennsylvania runs weekend off-campus seminars and tours, while the alumni office planned the early summer alumni colleges.

Alumni continuing education could encroach upon the continuing education unit's market for liberal arts programs. Ideally, where a continuing education unit exists and wants to serve the alumni market, it will find cooperation with the alumni office an attractive arrangement. With cooperation, each office gains a program and an increase in staff, without having to pay for all of either. Carl found one-quarter of the alumni colleges before 1978 run cooperatively. At Indiana and Penn State Universities, for example, continuing education creates the academic content and the alumni office promotes it. At Harvard the alumni college has become a subdepartment of the faculty of arts and sciences, even though the alumni association's full-time professional continuing education officer takes overall program responsibility. Cornell's Alumni University began under the Office of Public Affairs and Educational Programming, then changed its name to Cornell's Adult University before moving under the academic dean for the summer session. At the University of North Carolina at Chapel Hill, the alumni association co-sponsored with the Program in the Humanities (itself a cooperative program of the Division of Continuing Education and the College of Arts and Sciences) a successful series of weekend seminars. At Duke University, the alumni director pays part of the continuing education dean's salary in return for her planning several academic programs for alumni each year (she also teaches in some of them). Carl predicts that as a result of such close cooperation some continuing education offices will hire Ph.D.s for alumni continuing education assignments.

Continuing education and alumni office cooperation may also result in splitting up the alumni market. For example, continuing education may be better prepared to serve local alumni with on-campus programs, while the alumni office, already organized for outreach programming, can serve the alumni who live farther away. Experience shows that continuing education offices are less likely to engage in off-campus programming at alumni clubs and in alumni colleges abroad.

Sometimes an individual takes on the project virtually alone as a special love. Later, the continuing education and alumni offices get involved. At Colgate University, the summer alumni college ran through the late 1970s out of the hip pocket of foresighted biology professor William Oostenink. Professor Grace Graham started and ran the University of Oregon's alumni college, among the first in the country back in the early 1960s; in her memory the program is now called the "Grace Graham Vacation College." A volunteer ran Tufts University's Special Events Courses for alumni for almost fifteen years before 1964, but this alumna eventually ran out of steam working alone. She was succeeded by a continuing education committee of volunteer alumni/ae, which selected topics and faculty for ensuing programs while the alumni office promoted them.

Several colleges and universities use volunteer alumni committees either for moral support or for administrative help (including promotional and marketing advice) in running alumni colleges. Some of these institutions and their professionals associated with alumni continuing education swear by this use of volunteers, others would swear it off if they could. It is the classic dilemma about the role of volunteers, with which all alumni directors are familiar. Volunteers do not always follow through on assignments or step down when no longer effective. Professionals control most sophisticated alumni continuing education programs, and direct the volunteers.

Joint sponsorship by two or more colleges and universities can produce an alumni college. The five-college system in central New England (Smith, Mount Holyoke, Amherst, and

Hampshire Colleges, plus the University of Massachusetts at Amherst) threw in together for a summer alumni college, rotating the management responsibility from year to year. This arrangement broke down. For a program as complicated, time-consuming, and potentially campus-specific as a summer alumni college, rotating management almost always falters. On the other hand, off-campus seminars of shorter duration (up to a full weekend) have worked beautifully when co-sponsored by as many as half a dozen similar (emphasis on similar) institutions. The same can be true of alumni colleges abroad for which a travel agent does much of the logistical planning.

Where a general alumni association and the alumni offices of component schools or graduate programs within a university all offer alumni continuing education, the potential for conflict exists. But the smaller units can offer alumni continuing professional education and not compete with liberal arts programs sponsored by the general alumni association. Cooperative promotional forethought might lead alumni participating in one such program to try the programs of other alumni offices at the university. At the University of Tennessee, the National Alumni Association cooperates with the Knoxville Campus assistant vice-chancellor for alumni affairs to produce the summer alumni college.

The Organizational Role of the Faculty: The Academic Director of Alumni College. Ernest McMahon believes that serious faculty commitment is crucial to alumni continuing education:

> *Regardless of the position of the governing board and of alumni leaders, it is not likely that any institution can maintain a really good and continuing program of alumni education without strong faculty interest in the program. Perhaps "dedication" is too strong a word, but at least there must be some leading faculty members who believe in alumni education enough to give time and energy to it.*
>
> *The participation of the faculty depends upon the support of the central administration, because full institutional recognition must be given to participation of faculty members in the alumni program. Such participation cannot be regarded as a casual activity done for a few dollars or for sentiment. Unless the central administration looks with full favor*

upon the enterprise, the faculty member will hesitate to take from research and writing—the touchstones of promotion and recognition—the necessary time to prepare for the alumni college.

For the same reason, the support of recognized leaders among the faculty is necessary, because they are the faculty members who determine departmental personnel policies and select from among the junior members those who will achieve promotion and retention [1960, p. 40].

What does faculty support mean? First, it means that teachers will teach enthusiastically in the programs. We want to be in the position where, when asked to do an alumni college, alumni college abroad, or alumni club seminar, a teacher accepts with pleasure. In mature programs, this happens because so many faculty members have already enjoyed the advantages of adult teaching. Getting faculty members involved in a new alumni continuing education program is harder: the idea is new, strange (given the history of alumni programs at most schools), and looks at first blush like a new burden.

A successful strategy begins with the support of the central administration and the faculty deans. They must give value to this kind of faculty service in decisions about promotion, tenure, and salary raises. Almost without exception faculty leaders do support such teaching, because it fits all three of the criteria normally used to evaluate faculty performance: scholarship, classroom teaching, and service to the university community.

Any participation in alumni activities is viewed as community service. That is the easy part.

But high-quality alumni continuing education programs also demand the best classroom teaching of any academic setting. The adult students who attend are among the smartest, most highly motivated, and therefore most demanding in the university community. They bring the experience of age to their evaluation of the faculty's lectures; they are usually paying full freight for their participation, and typically they are alumni, or parents of current university students, who think of themselves as stockholders checking up on the quality of their investments in the institution. Finally, they are not in the program for grades and their criticism flows freely. Teachers who stand up under these conditions prove themselves master teachers, and their deans should acknowledge it. Alumni continuing education directors can help by promising letters of thanks, sent to the academic deans for deposit in the faculty members' files.

Finally, new scholarship is often required in preparation for such tough teaching for an entirely new audience in a program developed just for the occasion. One reason for the new scholarship is that teachers from different disciplines often work together in alumni continuing education programs. As for publication, teachers make more of their original thinking truly public in alumni college and alumni club seminar lectures than in publishing in many little-read academic journals. Publication through alumni continuing education lectures can even help a faculty member to receive promotion. Ideally, the institutional service represented by teaching in alumni continuing education programs (whether or not pay is involved) will be formally recognized in the tenure and promotion policy of sponsoring colleges and universities.

Having a full-time faculty member serve as academic director of alumni college is highly recommended, especially early in the life of the program. By naming a dean or academic director, we can increase the faculty's investment in these programs. When a full-time faculty member plays a key part in the alumni continuing education organization, the value in credibility among every university constituency (not just the faculty, but the administration, the alumni, and the students who are observing and will soon become alumni) is enormous. This arrangement puts a teacher, not an administrator, in the role of hiring other faculty members (this way, teachers respond more favorably and more often) and gives the faculty a sense of responsibility for alumni continuing education.

At some colleges and universities the academic director leads all programs; at others different faculty coordinators run individual programs. A few institutions, wishing to keep more control in the sponsoring administrative office, omit this strategy altogether.

Some kind of academic director seems important, politically as well as pedagogically. The idea has the credibility of history on its side. As early as 1924, Vassar had an educational secretary in the Alumnae Association. Ohio University calls the faculty director the dean of Alumni College; the administrator in charge is the director of Alumni College. At Duke, the dean of continuing education acts as academic director, and also teaches in some alumni seminars she designs. Each college or university will devise its own best policy, depending in part upon the strength (and especially the credibility among the faculty) of the administrators who are available to direct alumni continuing education.

The responsibility is usually an overload for faculty members, and should be compensated accordingly. This puts both money and control over some exciting new educational programs into the hands of faculty members used to unwieldy approval procedures for their teaching ideas.

STAFFING

What about nonfaculty staffing? As with organization, any staffing arrangement that works will be the right one for each institution. The key is talent. It matters less in the end where we place the line officer in the university structure than who sits in the chair. As Jerold Apps advises,

> it is not a thorough understanding of procedures in continuing education that brings success to an educator of adults but a basic understanding of human beings, of how learning occurs, of viewpoints regarding knowledge and the purposes of continuing education, and of the characteristics of adults as learners. These form the rationale for how one teaches—for the procedures one uses in working with adults [1979, p. 145].

Temporarily, an oversupply of Ph.D.s can help fill the need for well-qualified directors of alumni continuing education. They know the university, their classroom experience gives them a feel for the academic environments they will create for the alumni and the faculty, and they bring credibility and collegial relationships with teachers who need to be hired for the programs. However, nearly all institutions still assign alumni continuing education to existing staff members. This may work for a time. But alumni continuing education is quickly becoming a profession in its own right, and needs professionals to run it.

Professionalism in alumni continuing education already means that an administrator of these programs should have an intimate working knowledge of both alumni relations (or institutional advancement from some angle) and continuing education. Extraordinary speaking (even teaching) and writing skills are crucial, and these new directors must bring or develop credibility with the faculty and with administrative colleagues, alumni, and students. Budgetary, marketing, and promotional skills are needed. This administrator directs both long-term planning cycles and short-term infinite program detail. We are talking about a combination of innovative program manager and university ambassador.

This is not the job description of a part-time, junior administrator. It is to be highly recommend that, before any alumni continuing education program gets very far off the ground, it deserves most of the attention of a highly qualified and talented academic administrator, of an educator in administrative clothing. Several institutions with long and successful records of alumni continuing education have a director of alumni continuing education or the equivalent person with a similar title. McMahon envisioned a future in which the "Dean of Alumni College" essentially ran the alumni operation, which in turn focused mainly on the intellectual relationship of alumni to alma mater. During the 1960s and 1970s, Lowell Eklund served as Oakland University's dean of continuing education with alumni relations and continuing education under him. This is our future, but only if we begin now hiring and developing professionals in alumni continuing education.

Because of alumni continuing education's high potential to improve alumni relations, continuing education, and many other aspects of the relationship between adults and universities, the program requires volunteers, but their use is a delicate business. Volunteer advisers should represent the alumni on committees that establish or expand alumni continuing education. Some institutions use volunteer committees to set policy, to choose faculty and themes for individual programs, to raise funds that back up budgets, and to develop institutional or alumni support for alumni continuing education. Some professional directors like these arrangements; others find them unwieldy or confining.

Once alumni continuing education is up and running, volunteers can be most helpful in planning and operating programs on the road. Most colleges and universities have too many alumni and too few professionals on the staff to serve them, especially after the alumni get a taste of these educational programs and want more. The secret is to find, train, and use volunteers to run off-campus seminars. They are used to setting up off-campus meetings for the institution. Alumni seminars are merely a special kind of meeting. Hiring faculty and defining the academic programs is staff work, but volunteers should be consulted even on those matters, because part of their motivation comes from their investment in the seminar topics and faculty. This involvement begins to give alumni a sense of themselves as self-directed learners. Once they have worked with the director of alumni continuing education to set up major alumni seminars, alumni volunteers can often run smaller academic programs for themselves with little or no staff help. This is to be encouraged. But we want to remember to provide the training, handbooks, and other support these volunteers need.

Some experienced directors would never turn over this much responsibility to volunteers, especially as they worry about the faculty having a good experience on the road. But given the pressures of supplying more alumni continuing education than the staff can possibly produce, volunteerism offers a proven and logical staffing solution.

Gathering Support

No book could adequately prepare proponents for the intricacies of gathering support for alumni continuing education. At each institution, the real expert on this subject is the person reading this book, whether he or she is a volunteer or a university employee. It is crucial to remember, however, to gather support from every university constituency *before* launching a program of alumni continuing education. As with any new venture, this may be either frustrating or easy; it may take months or years.

Support for alumni continuing education must begin at the top. At public institutions, this may include the legislature and the governor, especially if any of them are graduates. Ideally, the board of trustees or regents and the president will become vocal advocates.

Internally, you need (to borrow the concept from Peters and Waterman's *In Search of Excellence*) a champion for alumni continuing education. This will probably be the administrator or faculty member who brought up the subject in the first place. It may be the reader of this book. The champion needs to get appointed to key campus committees. If there is a committee on continuing education, that one is crucial.

Alumni reading this book may become champions for alumni continuing education. Indeed, that is where the idea began at some institutions. As volunteers, however, alumni will want to sell the idea to one of the university's well-placed administrators or faculty members before going much further.

Support from alumni and the faculty is indispensable. Use the alumni council or alumni association executive committee. Work with the faculty dean initially, then follow his or her advice to gain faculty support. Involving these groups not only puts the right heads to work planning a successful program; it also alerts them to programs in which they can become involved.

When the alumni and faculty begin working together on these programs, long-standing stereotypes and certain kinds of distrust tend to disappear. The result is very beneficial to the university even without the resulting seminars and alumni colleges.

Gathering alumni support may also turn up the discrepancies between what alumni want from their university and what we currently provide. If we take complete notes during these planning sessions, we may be able to improve alumni relations in more ways than one.

In general, remember that nearly everyone benefits from
alumni continuing education—the alumni, the faculty, the
administration, and the institution's current students. Therefore
everyone should play a role in planning and running alumni
continuing education, and that early support will guarantee
success in the long run.

CHAPTER 4

"WHAT KIND OF ALUMNI CONTINUING EDUCATION PROGRAM SHOULD WE OFFER?"
Planning Alumni Colleges

Whether one is proposing the first program in alumni continuing education at one's institution, expanding or otherwise altering an existing program, or adding new program types so that the variety will attract more alumni, it helps to know what kinds of programs have already worked for other institutions. Therefore Chapters 4, 5, 6, and 7 will describe the many kinds of programs that exist today.

A variety of program types has existed at least since the 1920s. Ernest McMahon, surveying the field for his 1960 monograph, found residential programs (on-campus but disconnected lectures), short courses (integrated lectures, sometimes residential), lectures (perhaps on a broad theme, but not integrated), extension courses (including evening classes), and discussion groups (McMahon found two, both started spontaneously by alumni).

By 1978, when Linda Carl studied alumni colleges (closest, perhaps, to McMahon's short courses), she also found credit programs for alumni, intermittent seminars, weekend seminars, regional and international alumni colleges, national and international study tours, a vacation college for nonalumni (and future plans by surveyed institutions for lengthening a current alumni college), audiotape and videotape self-study programs, a single evening alumni college, a one-day alumni college, off-campus seminars, weekend off-campus seminars, an alumni college at a winter vacation site, a better-packaged two-week summer session, foreign travel colleges, one-day cultural events in the performing arts, some early interest in the Elderhostel, and exploration of a year-round adult vacation college.

McMahon and Carl found definitions sticky. Where could McMahon draw the line between residential programs and short courses? What differences did Carl find between international alumni colleges, international study tours, and foreign travel colleges?

Definitions are still sticky, but today the increased variety of program types gives us an advantage. The more kinds of alumni continuing education activity exist, the more we fill in the picture and notice the important differences between one kind and another.

We will categorize alumni continuing education programs this way:

1. *alumni colleges,* usually on-campus, residential programs normally extending beyond a third day;

2. *alumni seminars,* some on-campus, some off, with club seminars especially popular off-campus and reunion seminars very successful on-campus;

3. *alumni colleges abroad,* academic alumni travel or travel study programs, occasionally within the United States; and

4. *special programs,* a catch-all category for the myriad innovative, sometimes unique programs not fitting other categories, including offerings through the media (news-

papers or alumni magazines, radio or television, and computers).

Related programs are not quite alumni continuing education, but they are so close either in format or in audience that they are worth mentioning; especially since some related programs make a good place to start an alumni continuing education program. A few related programs will be described alongside the alumni continuing education programs they resemble. The others will appear at the ends of the chapters.

Two caveats. First, we will be illustrative, not exhaustive, in describing this diverse and expanding field. And second, while some categorizing will help make sense of the field, our definitions are not meant to be rigid. Some institutions call their longest alumni continuing education program their alumni college, even though it is not quite one day long. At others, such a program would be called an on-campus alumni seminar. Not many institutions agree on the term "alumni college abroad" for their alumni travel or alumni study tours. There is no uniform use of the term "alumni continuing education" or of the title "director of alumni continuing education." These irregularities make for imperfect definitions, but, more important, they offer hard evidence of programmatic ingenuity by institutions that know themselves and invent programs to fit their own needs.

WHAT PROGRAMS WORK BEST IN THE 1980s?

Many schools believe they should begin their alumni continuing education programs with a summer alumni college. In fact, most of them probably should start with another kind of program.

In the 1960s and early 1970s, when many new alumni colleges were born, they offered attractive summer vacations for families with young children. The baby boom generation seems to have changed all that. Families with children are not coming as much, which means that alumni college participants are getting older. As a result, several of the larger and more mature alumni colleges have shrunk.

Experienced directors posit several factors that may be caus-
ing the decline of summer alumni colleges. One is that the baby
boomers' two-profession families cannot as easily coordinate
long vacations, and therefore do not find residential alumni
colleges as attractive as did their predecessors. The homemakers
who accounted for one-sixth of Cornell's Alumni University in
1978 are a vanishing breed in the late 1980s. Those adults
(mostly women) used to welcome a vacation featuring mental
as well as physical exercise. Many of today's women, like men,
enjoy plenty of mental stimulation in the workplace, and may
need to rest the mind at vacation time. Alumni college offers
a refreshing kind of mental exercise, for many adults an attractive combination of relief from mental work pressure and
healthy mental exercise. For an increasing number of adults,
however, nothing will do but a visit to the lake.

For these young parents, American life has changed in other
ways that hurt alumni college attendance. The pace of family
life seldom allows vacations longer than one week, and the most
popular alumni colleges therefore last between three and six
days. When the University of Vermont surveyed alumni who
were already participating in the one-week alumni college, they
overwhelmingly favored two- to three-day or weekend programs for the future. Also, a phenomenon called market seg-
mentation means that each family member has different recreational and athletic interests, many of them offered at specialty
summer camps or resorts. These therefore compete with alumni
colleges.

Modern life offers so many accessible fascinations that one
is hard-pressed to give even one whole week to any one vacation
spot, including one's alumni college. The long weekend is fast
becoming the standard family vacation package. Inexpensive
air travel makes world-hopping a vacation possibility for more
and more couples and families; facing a choice between a week
at Club Med and a week at alma mater, only a few special people
will choose the dormitory. Nor does the competition come only
from outsiders in the vacation industries: many schools offer
alumni colleges abroad in direct competition with their own on-
campus alumni college. Directors see some of their old regulars

in the alumni college now traveling abroad with the faculty in the summer.

Continuing education professionals see the effect of these factors in adults' increasing interest in nonresidential educational opportunities. For many institutions, this trend translates into less alumni interest in the summer alumni college and more interest in the convenient alumni seminars near their homes.

Also, costs have escalated since the 1960s, with the result that alumni college is no longer the bargain vacation it once was, by comparison with other vacation possibilities. In many cases, these cost escalations result from institutions, in budget crises, leaning on every department (including food and housing services) to maximize profits. Every alumni director knows how myopic this is, considering the long-term fundraising results of effective alumni relations programs like the alumni college; but presidents still have to pay today's bills with today's revenues, and an occasional alumni college suffers.

Given these demographic and cultural shifts, for most colleges and universities alumni colleges are not where the action is; shorter on- and off-campus seminars (including reunion seminars) and the alumni colleges abroad will work much better.

Ernest McMahon put it this way in 1960:

> The present trends are encouraging. There is something heartwarming about the spontaneous action of the Swarthmore faculty in launching evening classes for alumni and about the equally spontaneous reaction of the group of Boston University alumni in creating a discussion group. The summer month at Wisconsin, the thousand Yale alumni, the long history of the Alumni University at Michigan indicate that alumni will return for intensive programs. It is probable that they will find the time if the program is sufficiently stimulating.
>
> But there are time considerations which must not be overlooked. The development of educational programs for adults can seldom be reduced to a set of rigid procedures, and one of the practical problems to be faced in programming for alumni is the variety of demands which their own personal and professional commitments make upon their time. It may well be that the most faithful members of the Allentown discussion group could not arrange annually to spend a week on the campus in a residential seminar. Conversely, some of the alumni who returned for a month to

the campus at Madison, Wisconsin, might not be able to commit a night
a week for twenty weeks of the year.

An initial caution, then, is that the institution truly interested in
the continuing education of its alumni may have to consider a variety
of programs rather than a single format, although the beginning might
have to be limited to one type of program [p. 46].

This is worth noting because most alumni volunteers and
university officers who are considering alumni continuing education ask experienced directors for advice on starting alumni
colleges, by which they mean three- to five-day residential programs on the campus. Most of them would be well advised to
consider reunion seminars, alumni club seminars, and alumni
travel programs instead. Many institutions may wear out themselves, their budgets, and their alumni advocates by pushing
for an alumni college instead of thinking freely about other program formats that make more sense.

At the same time, institutions that consider all the varieties
of alumni continuing education and still believe the summer
alumni college is right for them should go ahead with confidence. Several colleges and universities have done so since the
late 1970s. For example, Washington and Lee University in
Lexington, Virginia, and the College of Wooster in Ohio boast
relatively new alumni colleges which, in their fifth and seventh
year, respectively, were still experiencing steady growth and
good participation by younger alumni.

The summer alumni college is important to these and other
sponsoring institutions. It offers alumni the chance to participate
in substantial intellectual interaction with alma mater, and
alumni college becomes the flagship for other programs.

The Life Cycle of an Alumni College

An alumni college's effectiveness should be monitored con-
stantly. It may not be the right format from the beginning. Or
it may lose its effectiveness if alumni, faculty, and directors turn
their attention to alumni club and reunion seminars and to
alumni colleges abroad. These variations suggest that an alumni

college has a natural life cycle at each institution, which differs from place to place and which operates to some degree independently of the effects of shifting demography and American lifestyles.

For some institutions, the alumni college waxes and wanes; it always provides inspiration and therefore partly accounts for the success of other program types, but may need some adjustments or even a rest from time to time. At other institutions, the alumni college format never works very well, but symbolically the birth of the alumni college sends a clear signal to alumni that their participation in the intellectual life at alma mater is welcomed; once alumni interest has been aroused, it can be shifted to other forms of alumni continuing education.

Stanford University began a ten-day alumni college in 1966. In the early 1980s attendance dropped radically, but by cutting the program to eight days (one work week plus the surrounding weekends) and offering an attractive program on the Soviet Union, Stanford saved the program in 1984. The national economy also recovered in that period, which probably helped. Stanford was committed to its alumni college, and reacted rationally and flexibly to solve specific problems with it.

Yale University, disappointed with attendance at its multiple one-week summer alumni colleges, reorganized the program for 1986. Quite probably competition from their many summer alumni colleges abroad affected participation in the one-week, on-campus, summer alumni colleges. By operating four quite different themes in one long-weekend format and by promoting to parents and through alumni club communications in addition to direct-mail brochures, Yale doubled attendance and attracted a new group of younger alumni as well.

The University of Michigan has a long history of leadership in alumni continuing education. Its extension service started an Alumni University in 1930. This prototype of the modern alumni college disappeared in the early 1960s because the Alumni Association, under the direction of Robert G. Forman, developed a four-location family camp archipelago called Camp Michigania. It began at Walloon Lake in the upper part of Michigan's Lower Peninsula, and proved so popular that Forman added three more in New York's Adirondack Mountains, California's Sequoia National Forest, and Switzerland. By 1986, more than 4,000 alumni families representing a total (not correcting for family repeaters) of 50,000 campers had attended. Alumni voted with their feet for the new format, and the Alumni University was let go in the early 1960s.

Pomona College in California ran twelve alumni colleges beginning in the early 1970s. Director of Alumni Relations Lee Harlan suspended operations, but he intends to reestablish the program, perhaps on a biennial basis.

Nancy Levitt, assistant director for special events at the University of Colorado at Boulder, reports that the Alumni Association sponsored an alumni college for two years in the early 1980s with some success. The relatively low participation, lack of profit, and heavy time commitment by the staff caused cancellation, even though the 90 to 100 participants were extremely pleased by the experience. Under Executive Director Richard Emerson, formerly vice president for alumni administration at CASE and a proponent of alumni continuing education, the Alumni Association now runs other educational programs and plans to expand them. Tradition and experience are on their side: the University of Colorado helped start the modern alumni college movement in 1958.

Duke University offered alumni colleges in 1974-1976. Alumni director Laney Funderburk, wishing to take advantage of the 400th anniversary of British-American relations scheduled for that region of North Carolina, tried to bring it back in 1984. The theme may have been too esoteric, and the program never took place. But the interest in alumni continuing education at Duke, awakened by the alumni colleges and enlivened by a new cooperation between the alumni and continuing education offices, has blossomed into successful shorter alumni seminars on and off the campus.

Notre Dame ran one-week theme-oriented alumni colleges in 1977-1979, then canceled the last one due to low registration in 1980. Yet Notre Dame actually does more now, offering three weeks of Elderhostel and three alumni mini-college weekends instead.

The University of Pennsylvania started its alumni college in 1971, the same year as Pomona and Harvard. Penn has wrestled with its Philadelphia campus location ever since. For a few years the alumni staff tried a summer camp site in the Catskill Mountains of southern New York State not far from Philadelphia. Like Pomona and Stanford, Penn is committed to the concept of alumni continuing education, both in its alumni office and more recently in the School of Continuing Studies. When there is not an alumni college, there will be off-campus alumni college weekends and other educational opportunities for Penn alumni.

At Northwestern University, the alumni office started an alumni college, could not sustain participation, and let it die. The program has been reborn, thanks to a new champion, Associate Provost and Dean of University College Donald Collins. At the University of Oregon, the Vacation College begun in 1964 by Professor Grace Graham may get a new lease on life, thanks to a new interest by alumni director Philip Super.

Brown University has shown great flexibility with its alumni college. Started as the third modern alumni college in the nation in 1961, it ran several years, then rested several more, having inspired most of the other Ivy League institutions to start up their own alumni colleges. Brown brought back its alumni college in 1972, canceled the program in 1985 due to staff needs in other areas, but returned with a summer alumni college in 1986.

To summarize: a canceled alumni college does not mean the end of alumni continuing education at a sponsoring institution. The institutions named above have used their alumni colleges with patience, intelligence, and flexibility. As a result these colleges and universities have much more to share with their alumni today than one summer alumni college. The summer program may need a rest; it may be in a quiescent period in its life cycle. But the minute we consider it dead, it will find a way to be reborn.

Two final points, before looking at a variety of alumni college formats in this chapter, and then at alumni seminars, alumni colleges abroad, and related programs in the next three chapters.

DESCRIBING A PROGRAM'S CHARACTERISTICS

In addition to describing individual programs, we will also analyze the characteristics that distinguish one program type from another—an on-campus alumni college from an alumni college abroad, and so on. The way an alumni college is planned differs from the way a half-day on-campus alumni seminar is planned. We will recommend an appropriate planning schedule or (where a program repeats predictably and periodically) planning cycle before describing each program type. Other preliminary matters will include joint or cooperative programming with other institutions or their alumni, financing, staffing needs, and participant differences from program to program.

COOPERATIVE PROGRAMS

Alumni continuing education programs can be sponsored jointly by two units of the same institution, often the alumni and the continuing education offices; they can be co-sponsored by on- and off-campus entities, such as an alumni club or chapter and the home alumni office; or they can be mounted by the joint effort of two or more colleges and universities.

Ernest McMahon hoped in 1960 for extensive cooperation between institutions, although he did not find much in existence then:

> Joint action not only has merit for correspondence instruction but also for discussion groups, extension courses, and off-campus lecture series. Except for a few activities, such as the regional plans which are gradually developing for professional or specialized instruction, there are not too many examples of educational cooperation among the colleges of the United States. The continuing education of alumni may be one area in which such cooperation can be extended.
>
> Why should an eastern university fly a professor to the West Coast to give a short course to the alumni? Why not utilize the faculty talent of one of the western institutions? Might not one of the colleges in Los Angeles provide courses in international affairs for all college alumni in the city—except possibly those of other local colleges—and another college provide all the courses in human relations? Similarly, the in-

stitutions in New York City could provide a joint service for the thou-
sands of college graduates living or working in New York [p. 48].

Many institutions now jointly sponsor alumni seminars or
alumni colleges abroad in which they share not only alumni
but also faculty.

It does seem, however, that sharing faculty in the way
McMahon suggests requires a leap from the kind of alumni
continuing education we can see in the 1980s to a continuing
education of some future time less oriented to alumni relations.
That is, as long as alumni relations offices have much to do
with planning alumni continuing education, there seems likely
to be at least enough parochialism to insist on alumni colleges
bringing together a school's own alumni with its own faculty.
This parochialism does not preclude several schools from sharing alumni and faculty in the same cooperative gathering,
whether on one of their campuses, in the hinterlands, or abroad.
In these cooperative ventures, it can help to give most of the
planning responsibility to one sponsor, or even better, to one
person. Next year the partner can take a turn.

Alumni Colleges

Bearing in mind that sponsors should consider all program
types before deciding what to offer, let us begin our description
of program types with a variety of alumni colleges.

An alumni college is a summer, residential, usually on-campus, primarily academic program for alumni, between 3½ and
12 days in length. Because nearly all alumni colleges are university-wide offerings (not provided to the alumni of one school
within the overall institution), nearly all of them take liberal
arts themes, frequently from the humanities.

THE PURPOSES OF AN ALUMNI COLLEGE

Perhaps most alumni colleges focus on the humanities because universities believe that, no matter what one's profession,

one still needs to keep in touch with the arts and humanities throughout one's life—for perspective and for their humanizing, liberating influence. Some institutions say so in alumni college brochures. At Georgetown University, School for Summer and Continuing Education, Dean Michael J. Collins writes a letter to alumni before the theme is even picked, expressing the philosophy of the alumni college:

> *Alumni College at Georgetown is an opportunity to re-visit a place where lifelong memories were made, to share with spouses and children some part of the past or to come to know better the place where one's children learn and grow, to enjoy the beauty of Washington and its unrivaled cultural and political resources, to take part in lectures, short courses, seminars, and field trips. But above all, it is an opportunity to put by, for a time, the tempests of a world "too much with us," and, like Prospero on his island, reach a "still point," a place for reflection and discussion, with teachers and other participants, on the meaning and value of things [January 1985 letter to alumni, parents, and friends of the University].*

The longer time frame for an alumni college allows institutions that organize their alumni college academic programs this way to show off many members of the faculty from all over the campus. Alternatively, it allows other institutions to explore a single broader interdisciplinary theme in some depth over the entire alumni college period. These alumni colleges often suggest advance and follow-up reading to extend the experience well beyond the on-campus program itself. Some alumni colleges offer two or more separate single-theme weeks in a row, and participants can stay as many weeks as they choose. Others offer two or more theme choices in each of several one-week segments. In at least one alumni college, participants take one course in the morning, another in the afternoon. Usually, though, afternoons are a time for more esoteric optional workshops on subjects from hands-on arts activities and writing or video workshops to cooking.

Most alumni colleges include some touring of campus centers and other attractions, plus campus or local theater, concerts, museums, and other educational resources, often related to the alumni college theme. Large alumni colleges actually have the power on campus to influence the choice of plays, concerts, museum exhibitions, and the summer focus for other resources.

THE PLANNING CYCLE

Because it is the longest alumni continuing education program a college or university offers (except for some travel programs), the alumni college also requires the most sophisticated planning. It is not unusual for the most experienced schools to plan more than one year in advance for each annual alumni college, which means starting the production of next summer's alumni college before this summer's arrives.

There are several advantages to this long planning cycle—and predictable disadvantages to planning an alumni college with less time ahead. It is much easier to get faculty teaching commitments a year or more in advance. The faculty deans and department heads plan slightly under a year in advance, in order to submit course offerings for the undergraduate and graduate school course guides. It is worth beating these deans to the faculty, in case teachers wish to plan their lives with alumni college in mind.

It can take a year to pull together the most complicated alumni colleges, integrating an interdisciplinary study by several teachers from different departments. The resulting faculty team may grow so close that they go on to initiate a university seminar or to design and teach a new course in the regular curriculum. Much of the faculty's motivation in teaching an alumni college lies in this collegial opportunity.

A good alumni college promotional campaign also takes a year. Shorter weekend programs operate nicely on shorter planning and promotional schedules. Alumni participants need less warning to clear their calendars for a Saturday or weekend seminar. But asking an alumni family to plan its summer vacation around the alumni college dictates a first mailing notice at least nine months ahead. This is both a courtesy and a practical necessity.

Schools planning a first summer alumni college will ideally plan and promote the program for two years. This cannot be emphasized strongly enough. The entire university community needs time to get used to this new idea. The first year is really for internal promotion—gathering support, staff, and faculty; making preliminary reservations for teaching space; and placing orders with housing, dining, and other campus centers. Early announcements should appear in the alumni magazine and other alumni communications. The academic and administrative directors can spend time on the road talking about the upcoming alumni college at alumni club meetings. If many alumni live near the university, media promotion (using newspapers, radio, and television) may be in order. Budgets can be adjusted over a two-year period. This is especially important if old money currently in other program budgets needs to be reallocated to back up or subsidize the alumni college. Institutions that start with academic modifications to existing programs like reunions and offer the longer alumni college after success in shorter formats can reduce the planning cycle for a first summer alumni college.

COOPERATIVE ALUMNI COLLEGES

Jointly sponsored short alumni seminars often do very well, especially off-campus, because they solve the problem of how to serve small numbers of alumni in far-flung locations. This has never been true of on-campus summer alumni colleges.

The problem with sharing an alumni college is that, if one institution plans the alumni college for several others one year, and the management responsibility then rotates, much accumulated experience goes to waste. Also, there is a potential public relations loss in sending your alumni to someone else's beautiful campus for more summers than you invite them to yours. Or, will your alumni go to a strange campus for your alumni college at all?

Generally, a summer alumni college needs to be sponsored by one college or university on its own campus. Linda Carl (1978) believed that Johns Hopkins was the only institution that succeeded on another's campus, but in that case the program was Johns Hopkins's only, not a joint production.

BUDGETING THE ALUMNI COLLEGE

Chapter 9 details an alumni college budget, but a few notes should be mentioned here as well.

Alumni colleges can break even. A very few earn considerable revenue. More commonly, alumni colleges pay their direct costs and cover some indirect costs like staff salaries. There are also sponsoring institutions that subsidize the alumni college every year to keep costs down and attract more alumni.

As a rule of thumb, summer alumni colleges need three to five years to achieve peak fiscal health. Normally the institution will recoup the investment many times over in increased alumni giving, not to mention the extra revenues that will end up on the housing and dining balance sheets and in faculty pocketbooks.

The promotional budget for an alumni college can be 5 to 25 percent of the gross budget, and that money is spent up front. Therefore an alumni college budget of $50,000 implies that the institution could be out $2,500–12,500 for about half a year between the promotional mailing and the program. Other parts of the budget will be spent long before tuition income arrives, too—for books sent to registrants for advance reading, for printing participants' notebooks, for deposits on theater or concert tickets, and more. Most institutions are used to spending before billing; and where the fiscal year closes near the program date, the summer alumni college budget may end one fiscal year in the red, and turn black early the next year. This may mean putting the alumni college on a rotating or two-year budget, as Harvard has done.

THE ALUMNI COLLEGE STAFF

Hiring a faculty academic director can be a big help with the summer alumni college. Most administrative directors can handle the hiring of two teachers for a short seminar or one for an alumni college abroad, but orchestrating large numbers of faculty members for the summer alumni college is another matter.

For off-campus alumni colleges, the staffing challenge increases and the number of participants that can be handled decreases. Most off-campus alumni colleges serve fewer than fifty participants. More help is required to care for large numbers of summer alumni college participants for one or two weeks than is required to operate a Saturday seminar on or off the campus. Therefore, administrative directors of the alumni college usually add professional staff, volunteers, and student workers before and during the program.

ALUMNI COLLEGE PARTICIPANTS

Cared for day and night for a week at a typical alumni college, participants should enjoy the privileges of other students in terms of housing, dining, parking, transportation, tours, recreation, evening events, and the use of facilities, including the library. But remember that they will be older than most other students, so the schedule should allow them time to move between events, and adequate time for rest and sleep at appropriate hours. Housing near the local fraternity may not work well. Directors must communicate this need to nearby fraternities and dormitories, which operate on other-worldly diurnal, not to say nocturnal, schedules.

JUNIOR PROGRAMS

Participants in successful alumni colleges range in age from fifteen to ninety. Teenage participants can sample the institution's academic fare prior to applying for admission, so it is a good idea to reserve a few interview times with the admissions office during alumni college.

Participants younger than fifteen years of age may be uncomfortable (and make others uncomfortable) in the adult program, so some institutions provide junior programs for the children of adult alumni college participants. Junior programs have ranged in character from residential summer camps to children's alumni colleges with an academic flavor. The camping atmosphere seems to have been the most successful. However, most junior programs have died out as demography, the complications of two-profession families, and the proliferation of specialty summer camps for children have changed the clientele for the alumni college from the family to older couples and individuals. Many institutions never considered a junior program in the first place. Linda Carl discovered four reasons why sponsors eschewed junior programs: lack of space; alumni did not want to bring their children; the staff was too small; and child safety was a problem. Others decided not to compete with specialty camps for children.

Cornell probably has the largest, most successful junior program in operation today. Indiana, Georgetown, and Washington and Lee Universities, and Whitman College in Walla Walla, Washington, have junior programs. In conjunction with its nine-year-old Alumni College, Ohio University runs a Junior Alumni College for children aged six through twelve, and a Teen Alumni College for thirteen- to fifteen-year-olds. The University of Tennessee offered a youth program with its first Alumni Summer College in 1986. Penn State operates Youth Programs for preschoolers and up. This program also introduces high school juniors and seniors to Penn State during the Alumni Vacation College. More and more colleges and universities are developing similar applicant recruitment programs; in this case the coincidence with the alumni college multiplies the benefits to all family members and to the university.

Carl's 1978 study found that Stanford University, the University of California at Berkeley, the University of Illinois, and the University of Michigan had family camps, some of which included a little teaching for the adults. Notre Dame offers an Alumni Family Hall, inexpensive dormitory accommodations for families with little or no programming. Neither the camps nor the Family Halls are alumni colleges, but they do offer an attractive way to involve whole families in university life, and could be turned into alumni colleges by the addition of academic programming.

SAMPLE ALUMNI COLLEGE FORMATS AND SCHEDULES

What do successful alumni colleges look and feel like? From the following examples, the reader will understand why some alumni colleges are successful, and also will know whom to contact for advice. Let us begin with the shortest and simplest and end with the longest alumni colleges in the country.

Remember that the natural life cycle of alumni colleges may have altered some of the particular programs described below. Some may even have been shelved. This seldom happens with shorter alumni seminars or alumni colleges abroad; a particular weekend seminar on Cape Cod or Puget Sound may only run for a year or two, but the outreach seminar concept goes on in different locations with new themes and faculty.

The Weekend Alumni College. Notre Dame runs a typical weekend alumni college. Actually, the university runs three on consecutive weekends from mid-July to the first weekend in August. Each weekend has a different theme. The price is right, thanks to subsidized dormitory housing.

There are variations on the weekend alumni college worth noting. Connecticut College runs a program called A Weekend in the Country. It is actually a weekend alumni college on the road, for it never sees the campus. Instead, the program takes participants to the Williamstown Theater Festival one night, the New York City Ballet at Saratoga Performing Arts Center the next, and to Tanglewood for a Boston Pops concert the third night, staying at first-class inns along the way. Transportation is included in the fee.

In 1985, Yale ran a summer series of alumni colleges. The first, held shortly after commencement and reunions, used a variation of the weekend alumni college format by starting Thursday and ending Saturday. This was followed by an alumni college in Pebble Beach, California; a third program went to

Vail, Colorado, for one week. By 1986 Yale had honed its on-campus weekend alumni college further, changing the program's name to the AYA (Association of Yale Alumni) University Seminars and offering one topic in each of the academic areas—humanities, the arts, science, and social science. Despite the name change and the short format, it still seems right to characterize this Yale program as an alumni college (and not a seminar), since it is still the longest on-campus alumni continuing education experience planned entirely by the alumni association.

With Eustace Theodore, a faculty member, serving as executive director of the alumni association, and alumni who demand an intellectual relationship with their university, Yale has become a leader in alumni continuing education. Therefore, we should pay attention when Yale makes a significant change in its overall alumni continuing education strategy. Through the 1970s and early 1980s Yale offered several consecutive weeks of summer alumni colleges in which alumni had a choice of themes each week. But during this period Yale also began offering several off-campus alumni colleges in the long weekend (Thursday-Sunday) format, a few shorter alumni seminars for the alumni clubs, and by 1980 the alumni college abroad program was expanded to some eighteen programs a year, many of them in the summer. By 1985, Yale realized that it had created competing programs and therefore reduced its on-campus summer alumni college to the shorter, multiple-theme format. Theodore takes a practical view of attracting participants: he enters "multiple race horses," knowing that only some will be winners. This is true both within the shortened summer program on the campus, and in the overall summer menu that now offers Yale alumni a choice of on- and off-campus domestic and abroad programs.

The Midweek Alumni College. Smith College's Alumnae College runs for three days in mid-week. The program takes advantage of and immediately follows the commencement and reunion period.

The Long Weekend Alumni College. This format brings in participants late Thursday afternoon for registration and a social evening. Friday and Saturday are packed with events, and on Sunday the program ends, allowing most participants to get home for the next work week.

Middlebury College offers an alumni college in this format. Its Labor Day Alumni College was eleven years old in 1986. Middlebury, like Smith College, also runs an alumni college each year immediately following reunion, but Middlebury's is a week-long program, Monday through Friday. For this captive audience, the topics are lighter or more practical: in 1985 participants chose between personal computing for the home or office, and watercolor painting.

Rutgers, The State University of New Jersey, started its alumni college in the weekend format about 1980, but expanded to the long weekend in 1982. Ohio University held its ninth annual alumni college in 1986, also in this format.

The University of Illinois at Urbana also offers its Alumni College-Illini Union in the long weekend format with a variety of informal lectures, discussions, tours, and dinner theater.

The University of Tennessee's Wednesday–Sunday program provides a transition from the long weekend format to the one-week alumni college. It has more in common with the long weekend programs, since only two days (Thursday and Friday) focus on classroom fare, while Saturday is used for field trips.

Before we discuss the most popular alumni college format by far, the one-week alumni college, notice that, even in the shorter alumni college formats, the entire summer, from the day reunions end to the very end of August, is available for the summer alumni college. These programs cater to the vacation college crowd, even if they closely follow reunions. It is far less common for schools to use the term, alumni college, for programs that take place outside the summer months. There, the more common term is alumni seminar.

The One-Week Alumni College Format. By far the most popular format for the on-campus summer alumni college is the five-day to one-week program. It may seem a fine distinction between the long weekend format (up to four days) and week-long alumni colleges. It is a real distinction, however, for it takes institutional strength in staffing and budget—and a strong pull on alumni, parents, and friends—to get participants for a full week of their vacation. The long-weekend format does not ask that commitment; it sneaks participants out of work or retirement routines for one or two week days, plus most of a weekend. This is an important difference, and most one-week alumni colleges are sponsored by strong colleges and universities of all types—public and private, small and large.

The one-week alumni college allows plenty of programmatic flexibility. There is time to study a single theme in depth or to showcase a wide variety of the university's best departments and teachers. No need to choose between a campus tour and enough time in the classroom; both will fit. There is even time for recreation or social events—a formal dance, a night at the theater, a day for hiking or other outdoor activities, or family time—without short-changing the academic program.

Examples of the One-Week Alumni College. These programs vary according to how tightly they organize academic materials around a single theme. Some feature just a few, others more than a hundred, faculty presentations. Some focus presentations upon a single theme; others offer participants a choice of themes. Some programs with integrated themes nevertheless add lectures and week-long workshops in the afternoons and evenings not tied to the central academic theme.

Here are the existing types of one-week alumni colleges:

the alumni college as faculty collage

the theme collage

the teacher-a-day collage

two transitional formats leading to single-theme programs:
   the course collage, and
   the teacher-a-day loose theme alumni college

the tight single-theme alumni college

the tight single-theme alumni college with afternoon workshops, and

the choice-of-themes one-week alumni college.

The Alumni College as Faculty Collage. Indiana University's Mini University, fifteen years old in 1986, brings 350–400 participants for a choice of over a hundred one- to two-hour faculty presentations. Each participant selects up to three a day, fifteen during the week. The Mini University is aptly named. Participants must feel a lot like undergraduates thumbing through the entire university course catalog, and indeed they probably see faculty members teaching subjects they ordinarily teach.

This is not always true of other alumni college formats. In the single-theme programs, interdisciplinary teaching can offer participants a chance to interact with faculty members who are stretching beyond their specialties, experimenting with material not yet included in the university curriculum.

The determined, perspicacious, self-directed learners among participants in faculty collage programs can piece together groups of individual faculty presentations to create their own mini-courses around a theme that occurs to them, like an undergraduate selecting a dozen departmental courses to form a major. Of course there is no major adviser here; that is a role played by the academic director (faculty director) in single-theme alumni colleges.

Slippery Rock University in Pennsylvania offers over thirty different academic, skills-oriented, and recreational subjects in this format. The University of Texas at Austin's nine-year-old Alumni College thinks of its program as an update of university expertise and activities, so this collage includes presentations on current events and new campus strengths. This kind of alumni college is related to "the university today" programs to which many schools invite top fundraising prospects.

The Theme Collage. The University of Alabama offered its first annual Alabama Chautauqua Sunday-Friday, June 9-14, 1985. The difference between Alabama's and Indiana's programs was the superimposition of several loose categories upon the thirty-nine otherwise free-standing faculty presentations. For example, "Business in Your Life" included individual lectures on "Interesting Comparisons of the Educational and Business Systems in China and the United States" by a teacher from the School of Accounting; "So You Want to Buy a Computer?" by the director of the Center for Business and Economic Research; "How to Finance Your Child's College Education" by a faculty member from the department of economics, finance, and legal studies; and eight other subjects. "Your Alabama" allowed a little local architecture into the curriculum. Wednesday included time for special events, when participants could take tours, rest, and enjoy the campus informally.

The New York State University College of Arts and Sciences' Alumni College runs from Wednesday to Sunday (it was July 9-13, 1986), offering a loosely thematic collage of activities.

The College of Wooster in Ohio uses the theme collage organization for its program, which began in 1976 and brings 70–80 participants to the campus in mid-June. Three morning classes take place daily, for which the faculty always includes one alumnus or alumna; and evening cultural activities balance the program. The loose theme for 1986 was "Lessons from the Past: The Worlds of 1886 and 1986."

The Teacher-A-Day Collage. At the University of the South in Sewanee, Tennessee, the Sewanee Summer Seminar offers a collage; the activities of the Sunday–Saturday week focus on five precisely defined themes, like "The U.S. in the Middle East" and "Southern Literature." The important difference here is that an administrative director or academic director is helping participants organize their intellectual experience. This is far different from turning adults loose in the unstructured environment of the faculty collage format, which from the point of view of participants is really an "alumni collage."

No attempt is being made here to judge the relative merits of organizing experiences for alumni during alumni college, or of turning them loose to organize the experience themselves. Continuing education theories (whether we refer to them as pedagogy, or "andragogy" after Malcolm Knowles) support both approaches. Ivan Illich might decry the single-theme alumni college as paternalistic, manipulative, Orwellian. But for anyone looking at the whole field of alumni continuing education, or trying to decide what format to use in an alumni college, it is clear that almost every conceivable format has been used successfully somewhere. The secret is to know thyself and thine alumni and to choose the right format for both.

Here are two transitional formats leading to single-theme programs:

The Course Collage. Georgetown University offers a course collage of eighteen discrete courses, from which each participant chooses up to six. Not only does the Georgetown Alumni College lead us toward other alumni colleges that carefully orchestrate alumni participation around one theme, but it offers an example of a program that has the right shape for its alumni and its own staffing strengths.

The Georgetown University Alumni College is directed by Michael J. Collins, dean of the School for Summer and Continuing Education. Collins teaches English at Georgetown; he also teaches English in the alumni college and in some of the spinoff alumni seminars on and off the Washington, D.C., campus. As a dean and faculty member, he is used to thinking about the regular weekly schedule of matriculated students in the university. Therefore, his alumni college schedule looks more like an undergraduate's course schedule for a week than does any other alumni college in the country. Participants choose offerings like "*A Distant Mirror:* Barbara Tuchman's Fourteenth Century," "Graham Greene: A Look at Two Novels," or "Critical Issues of Contemporary Middle Eastern History." Each day, participants have three choices in most time slots; they attend two course meetings each morning and a longer one in the middle of the afternoon. There is no rest mid-week, but Collins knows his students will be tired by Friday, so on that day he features a choice of field trips: "A Day on Capitol Hill," or a day-long program on Shakespeare conducted at the Folger Library and its Shakespeare Theater.

The Teacher-A-Day Loose Theme Alumni College. At the University of Virginia every faculty lecture or discussion contributes to a single theme. In the Sunday–Thursday program, June 9-13, 1985, the theme was "Pluralism in the Americas." This is a broad theme to attack in one week with one teacher a day, but the program offers a lot, and alumni can scan, if not thoroughly cover, the waterfront.

The theme is loose only compared with longer alumni colleges that focus on a single, sometimes narrower theme. This alumni college format coordinates faculty input so carefully that it makes sense to alert registrants to advance reading in preparation for alumni college. Each teacher suggests a book or two for the University of Virginia's Summer on the Lawn, and some general further readings are added. These are the beginnings of real continuing education in an alumni college.

Ohio Wesleyan's Summerweek extends from Sunday to Saturday in early June, giving a little more room for teaching, campus touring, and rest (Wednesday afternoon is entirely free). Faculty members generally spend part of a morning giving a lecture and answering participants' questions, although the program is flexible enough to allow an entire morning with a teacher who is especially important to the theme. The president also meets with the participants. We sense the hand of an academic coordinator here, and in fact a faculty member serves as moderator for Summerweek.

These alumni colleges are directly related to those at Harvard University and elsewhere that bring in teachers for single appearances within the overall framework of a single theme. The difference is that Harvard offers more than one tightly organized theme in each of two or three consecutive weeks. Cornell offers five consecutive weeks, and adds many separate afternoon workshops to the tight morning themes. Before discussing these programs, let us have a look at true single-theme programs at Wellesley College, Duke and Northwestern universities, and the University of Alaska-Fairbanks; and at Brown University's single-theme mornings with smaller afternoon workshops.

The Tight Single-Theme Alumni College. Wellesley College's Summer Symposium is an alumnae college. It offers a classic single-theme program with virtually no distractions (in other words, the academic structure is very tight). When a Wellesley alumna receives the Summer Symposium brochure in March, she knows exactly what she will study from the day she registers until after the Sunday–Thursday mid-June program is over. The faculty director's introductory (it is much better than a promotional) letter immediately inside the brochure is enough to transport the reader to distant times and places all by itself. Here is an example of a promotional brochure as a teaching device. But the brochure is not all that is good about this program. For participants in Wellesley's program, not a moment is wasted: the evening films, presentations, and concerts relate to the theme. Literally, one cannot eat without thinking thematically: a medieval banquet was included in the 1980 program, called "The Spirit and the Flesh: Exploring the Middle Ages."

Anne Mitchell Morgan, executive director of the Wellesley College Alumnae Association, offers a Summer Symposium that has inspired a Freshman Cluster Program, an interdisciplinary course option for first-year Wellesley students living in one dormitory cluster. Because the Summer Symposium benefits from planning input by the Alumnae Committee for the Annual Symposium (a committee of five or six members including the Alumnae Association's chair of academic programs), Wellesley benefits from graduates' influence upon the undergraduate curriculum. This intellectual tie between adults and undergraduates makes Wellesley a leader in developing new relations between adults and universities.

Northwestern University used to offer two consecutive one-week programs in its alumni college. The Office of Special Programs began Northwestern's alumni college in 1983 as a single one-week session with one central theme, then expanded upon initial success by going to the longer format. In 1984 their two one-week programs were reasonably separate thematically. In 1985 the faculty directors of the two one-week programs consciously worked out

> related topics. In the first ["The Making of the Self"], we will explore the awareness of individuality that emerged in personal expression and in science from the Renaissance to the 20th century. In the second ["The Modernist Revolution: Breakdown or Breakthrough?"], we will examine modernism, the cultural upheaval of our century, which often seems to be individual self-expression run amok [from the opening lines of Northwestern's 1985 Alumni College brochure].

Although this innovation at Northwestern did not last, it is worth remembering because the program recognizes that most participants want a one-week alumni college, while taking advantage of thematic continuity to make a two-week experience possible, not only for those participants who stay on, but also for the faculty, the dean, and the university. Northwestern went back to its original one-week single-theme format for Alumni College 1986 on "The Persistence of Myth."

The University of Alaska–Fairbanks featured its setting in a comprehensive introduction to Alaska (the land, natural wonders, wildlife, people, and problems) in a Workshop on Alaska for its week-long, mid-summer program.

The Tight Single-Theme Alumni College with Afternoon Workshops. Brown University's late June Sunday-to-Saturday Summer College concentrates on one or two themes for all participants, but adds workshops in the afternoons. These are week-long mini-courses, hands-on by comparison with lecture-and-discussion morning themes; afternoon topics range from art, historical architecture, theater, dance, creative writing, and geology through bookbinding, computers, jazz, journalism, and videotaping. As at Georgetown, the work at Brown comes fast and without break, but evenings are for rest and recreation, and the Summer College always ends with a clambake on Narragansett Bay. An alumnus in advertising often writes and designs the Summer College brochure for the alumni relations office.

The Choice-of-Themes One-Week Alumni College. Whitman College in Walla Walla, Washington, started its one-week alumni college in 1976 with a choice of two morning themes, afternoons for recreation, and theme-related evening events. Just once, the sponsoring alumni office canceled this summer program.

Off-campus One-Week Alumni Colleges. Before we get to the multiple-week on-campus alumni colleges, let us note that a few alumni colleges take place off the campus. We saw earlier that not every campus is an attractive place for a summer alumni college, and that Johns Hopkins University uses the campus of St. Mary's College on the Chesapeake Bay. Hopkins's Alumni College began on the campus in 1975, but soon moved off-campus and never went back. The university ran the program for two successive weeks with different integrated themes in the late 1970s, but now offers a single-theme, one-week (Sunday–Saturday) program.

In most alumni colleges to this point, teachers seldom participate for more than a day. The Johns Hopkins Alumni College's off-campus location encourages teachers to take part in the whole program, including less formal interaction on academic questions over coffee and at mealtimes. Especially at institutions that pride themselves on a close relationship between faculty and students, the best way to replicate this experience in the alumni college is to engage faculty for the week, not by the hour.

Brown University's 1982 week-long summer college off-campus took place just once, which may be instructive. Southern Methodist University in Dallas ran an alumni college off-campus. Princeton University, Amherst College, and Franklin and Marshall College have each run summer alumni colleges at Red Lodge in the Beartooth Mountains of Montana. Princeton's has been a perennial favorite. These are fairly tight single-theme programs that take advantage of the cultural and natural history of their rugged setting. Indeed, taking advantage of where one is teaching can be a good idea in many kinds of alumni continuing education programs, as we shall see with some off-campus alumni seminars and with most alumni colleges abroad.

Princeton's summer offerings in 1984 included a Monday-Friday on-campus alumni college in June, plus the one-week Red Lodge alumni college, August 13-20 (Monday-Monday, oddly enough), and early in the fall at the peak of color season for the turning leaves a Martha's Vineyard alumni college in a Thursday-to-Sunday long-weekend format.

Many schools have used this long-weekend off-campus format successfully for several years. In effect these are shortened off-campus alumni colleges. The sponsors call them alumni colleges, and not alumni seminars, which is why our definitions consider anything longer than three days an alumni college, while alumni seminars last three days or less. There are few substantial differences between a two-and-one-half-day alumni club seminar at Mount Hood's Timberline Lodge and a Red Lodge alumni college. The difference is primarily administrative. Most alumni colleges are conceived from the start as big summer vacation programs; some take place on the campus, others are transported elsewhere. In both cases the audience for promotion is the entire alumni body, or everyone west of the Mississippi for a California alumni college. When the same director creates shorter programs for alumni of one region only, the concept has become an alumni seminar.

The Longest Alumni Colleges. There are three on-campus alumni colleges longer than one week, at Stanford University, Penn State University, and Dartmouth College.

Penn State's Alumni Vacation College closely resembles the University of Alabama's Chautauqua theme collage format. It is slightly longer, letting participants settle in on Saturday for the Sunday–Friday program in mid-July. Most participants leave the second Saturday. Programmatically, there were nine sub-themes under the overall theme, "A Star-Studded Spectacular."

The Stanford Summer College, in its twenty-first year in 1986, focuses on a single theme. When alumni studied "The Soviet Union: Rut, Reform, or Revolt?," they heard from four Stanford faculty lecturers, two of them joint deans of the Summer College, plus five non-Stanford teachers from campuses of the California state university system. Stanford gives little time to activities not related to the theme.

For years Stanford used a ten-day, Sunday-to-Sunday format in mid-August. For a variety of reasons in the early 1980s, the program dropped from over 200 participants, to under 200 the next year, then to under 100, at which point the Alumni Association took stock and remounted their program in a trimmer eight-day format requiring only one week away from work for working participants. This adjustment seems to be working.

Dartmouth's twelve-day Alumni College began in 1964. The format has never changed: four lecturers from different departments in an interdisciplinary study of a single theme. Two lecturers speak each morning, followed by seventy-five minutes of small-group (about fifteen to a group) discussions led by faculty members, all of whom spend the entire twelve days in the program. Discussion leaders read in advance the same books as the participants and attend all lectures, evening films, concerts, and plays during the mid-August program. Follow-up reading is distributed on the last day, so that repeat participants can study alumni college material around the year.

Multiple One-Week Alumni Colleges. Cornell, Harvard, Washington and Lee, and the University of North Carolina at

Chapel Hill offer two or more consecutive one-week alumni college programs each summer, each week focused upon an integrated theme plus some academic extras. Only Williams does more for alumni in the summer.

Cornell's is the most intricate program. The Cornell Alumni University began in 1968 as a single-theme, two-week program based on Dartmouth's model. In 1969 Cornell expanded to four weeks, offering two sets of faculty who alternated their teaching: two worked the first and third weeks, the others the second and fourth weeks. In 1972 single topic workshops were added in the afternoons to allow participants to study a special topic intensely, sometimes sixty hours in a week.

Today, it takes most of a small office's year to prepare and operate Cornell's Adult University (CAU) for more than 1,000 participants. Ralph Janis, the current director, holds a Ph.D. He started his 1986 summer with the third annual Reunion Week CAU, Sunday–Thursday in early June, just before the long weekend reunions began, with a choice of four themes led by one faculty member apiece.

The four weeks of Family CAU began the week of June 29–July 5 with two main themes and four smaller ones to choose from. Until recently Cornell offered a choice of two morning themes and several afternoon workshops; this new configuration, which concentrates on six courses meeting morning and afternoon, gives the faculty more room to work with, but Wednesday afternoon is kept free for a mid-week break and time to explore the campus. The old CAU repeated some courses in alternate weeks; the new CAU offers different courses every week. The Youth College at Cornell serves hundreds of children, dividing them by age.

In August, after the last week of CAU on the campus, Janis is off on four CAU programs out of town. One is a geology and natural ecology week in the foothills of Colorado's San Juan Mountains; the other three are field seminars in marine and mainland ecology at Appledore Island, Maine (Cornell joins the University of New Hampshire in directing the Isle of Shoals Marine Laboratory off the Maine-New Hampshire coast).

Harvard University's Alumni College, begun in 1971, has run as many as three consecutive one-week on-campus programs during the early summer. There has usually been a choice of themes each week. Two features of Harvard's attitude toward these on-campus summer alumni colleges are worth noting. First, Harvard is flexible. It cut back in 1986 from three one-week programs to two, freeing director James Quitslund for a substantial amount of work on academic seminars for the university's 350th anniversary celebration. Harvard did this (here is the second feature worth noting) despite the fact that it makes money on alumni colleges. It is nice to have an example of an alumni college that makes money, although Harvard's setting is unusually conducive to a successful alumni college. Cambridge is full of the kinds of adults who participate in alumni colleges, and indeed an unusual number of Harvard's participants are local area commuters.

Similarly, the University of North Carolina at Chapel Hill benefits from a tri-city area with the highest percentage of doctorates in the nation. Not surprisingly, UNC-Chapel Hill's Vacation College looks a lot like Harvard's two one-week programs, with a choice of two central themes in each week. Participants can earn continuing education units (CEUs).

Few schools describe their alumni colleges as helpfully in their promotional brochures as does UNC. Here is the lead paragraph from the 1985 mailing piece, an example of succinct, effective brochure writing:

> *Vacation College seminars explore interesting and important cultural, moral and social topics from the perspective of the humanities. Each seminar draws on at least seven faculty members from a variety of disciplines, and with the varied backgrounds participants bring to the seminars, new insights are all but guaranteed. While a lecture forms the basis for each session, lively discussion follows. The faculty coordinator is present at all sessions to provide continuity and to guide discussion. And the discussions continue informally during coffee breaks, over lunches, and at social events. The seminars are held in comfortable rooms conducive to good conversation. . . . Sessions usually begin at 9:30 in the morning; afternoon sessions end at 3:00. Most evenings feature films or social events. Enrollment is usually limited to fifty participants.*

After discussing social events, meals, lodging, and tuition, the brochure describes in careful detail, well thought out months ahead, the rationale for all four seminars, complete with the faculty names and the title of each of the dozen lecture/discussions in each course.

Washington and Lee University in Lexington, Virginia, opened its Alumni College doors in 1981 with a single week, including junior programs for the children of participants. By 1984 the sponsoring Office of Summer Programs had expanded to three one-week programs on the basis of earlier successes. Total attendance reached 179, with 28 children that year. In 1985 three more one-week programs in July offered "Great Writers, Etc." (which offered participants a choice among Mark Twain, Russian novelists, or Marquez's Latin American novels; art topics covering great late-Renaissance painters and Greek art history; and baroque music masters Bach and Handel), "Society and Health," and "Classical Athens." An Alumni College Abroad to England followed in August. It was not linked to any of the on-campus Alumni Colleges, but a small number of schools have made this linkage. For 1986 Washington and Lee cut back to two one-week programs in its Alumni College.

Chadron State College in Nebraska offered two one-week programs under the rubric Western Heritage Experience in July 1986. Four topics contributed to the overall theme, and a children's program was available.

ALUMNI COLLEGE RELATIVES

The programs we have been discussing are alumni colleges, not because everyone who comes is a graduate and not because alumni offices run them, but because, when asked whether they offer an alumni college, the institutions named the programs above. The variety in length and in program content is healthy, and gives credence to the theory that alumni colleges that survive take on a shape unique and appropriate to the sponsoring institution.

Some close relatives of these alumni colleges are worth mentioning here. They take place mostly in the summer on a campus, they offer noncredit access to the faculty, and alumni are only one clientele. Indeed, some institutions pay no attention to the fact that some participants are alumni. Some programs have sprung up without any involvement by the alumni office (even where another campus office runs an alumni college, it is with the knowledge, involvement, or support of the alumni office). Some offer topics that would not be appropriate for more than a subset of alumni and so could not be thought of as "the" alumni college for the institution. Some invite alumni and their families but offer little or no teaching. Or they meet most of the criteria for an alumni college, but another, more clearly defined alumni college already exists at the sponsoring institution.

Elderhostel. Elderhostel at some colleges and universities seems to take the place of an alumni college, or it may warm the institution up to one. Elderhostel started in New England more than a decade ago, quickly spread across the country, and then came Interhostel abroad. President William Berkeley directs the national headquarters in Boston. James Pollicita, director of Alumni Continuing Education at the University of Notre Dame, became a fan of Elderhostel while a graduate student in Boston, and took the idea to Notre Dame. To quote his advertising:

> *During our second season of Elderhostel, outstanding Notre Dame faculty and staff will offer courses on a wide variety of subjects including Mark Twain, The Art Museum, King Lear in Our Time, Biosocial Genetics, and a Fiction Writing Workshop.*
>
> *Elderhostel is a network of over 700 educational institutions in the U.S., Canada, and abroad which offers low-cost, short-term residential educational experiences for people 60 years of age and over, or those whose participating spouse or companion qualifies. Three separate weeks of Elderhostel programming will be offered by the Notre Dame Alumni Association from June 9 to June 29, 1985. Three different courses will be offered each week. The $195 fee per week per person covers double room accommodations in Alumni Family Hall, meals, instruction, course materials, social and recreational activities. To register, or to obtain further information, please contact* ELDERHOSTEL. . . .

This is almost an alumni college. It combines the course collage format from Georgetown University, where a single teacher stays with a class for the week, with the multiple-week alumni college concept. Notre Dame also offered three Alumni Mini-College Weekends (Friday–Sunday) in late July and early August 1986. At the University of Maine at Presque Isle, the Office of Conferences and Special Programs combines Elderhostel with its own program, offering a one-week Body Recall program for people of all ages, but linking its evening activities to Elderhostel's.

With his own mini-colleges, why does Pollicita offer Elderhostel, too? He knew that promotion for a new alumni college would be expensive and that Elderhostel offers access to a nation-wide promotional campaign. And he had subsidized housing, an important point, because a disadvantage to Elderhostel is the tight budget control from the Boston office, which sets tuition fees so low that sponsoring institutions may lose money. Also, Elderhostel is limited to adults aged sixty and over, which excludes many alumni.

Still, Elderhostel is popular. At the very least, this tells us that the alumni college concept aims at a large potential alumni market, assuming that older alumni would prefer alma mater to a strange campus.

Chautauqua Institution. This institution in Upstate New York, begun in 1874 and which Linda Carl says helped inspire the first alumni colleges, continues to offer many intellectual summer programs on the original site. The current facilities in Chautauqua, New York, include a Center for the Arts, programs in education, religion, and recreation, plus access to symphony, opera, drama, and dance.

The Aspen Institute. Begun in 1949 in Aspen, Colorado, the Aspen Institute spread to the East Coast in the mid-1980s. A kind of nondenominational Chautauqua, Aspen has provided some inspiration for a number of alumni colleges.

Alumni Family Hall. A Notre Dame alumnus does not have to pay the Elderhostel fee and take courses to spend a week's vacation in South Bend. Alumni Family Hall offers university-subsidized housing and access to much of the campus.

Family Camps. Several institutions offer their alumni non-academic family experiences during the summer. Some, like Notre Dame's, are on the campus. Others, usually called family camps, are off the campus. Carl found family camps sponsored by Stanford and Indiana universities, and by the universities of California-Berkeley, Illinois, and Michigan. The last put Michigan's thirty-year-old Alumni University out of business.

Writing Workshops. No stand-alone writing programs for alumni exist to our knowledge, but there is no reason why a program like that at Breadloaf in Middlebury, Vermont, could not be adapted for alumni. Bennington College, also in Vermont, offers early summer writing workshops on its campus in two-week and four-week formats. Portland State University in Oregon offered seminars and workshops in writing, the visual arts, and music under the name Haystack '86.

Computer Alumni Colleges, Alumni Language Programs, and Other Specialty Alumni Colleges. Programs offered to alumni in special subject areas often act like alumni colleges. Participants take special skills courses with immediate goals. Since the most successful of these programs deal with languages (computing, foreign languages, music, or arts and crafts), they allow whole families to learn together.

The personal computer has spawned computer alumni colleges, some of them at colleges and universities that feel responsible for upgrading the diplomas of alumni who missed the computer revolution. A computer alumni college has immediate value to participants, so it can charge higher tuition than a liberal arts program, and it can involve participants twelve hours a day, including hours of hands-on time at the personal computer. A few sponsoring institutions, anticipating computer communications with alumni, believe that the computer alumni college will also benefit the institution over the long run.

Lehigh University offered a weekend program, "Personal Computers for the Home," for the third time in April 1983. The next summer, Dartmouth started its one-week Computer Alumni College. And in 1985 Stanford offered "The Power of Personal Computing," a series of personal computer programs, including (1) "Personal Computing Lab I: Introduction to Spreadsheets," a two-session program; on a Saturday morning and the following Tuesday evening in February; (2) "Personal

Computing Lab II: Business Applications," in the same format the following week; and (3) "Personal Computing Camp," in the Thursday–Sunday format, May 30-June 2 at the Stanford Sierra Camp near South Lake Tahoe. Ohio State University offered its own computer camp for three years in the early 1980s.

Institutions that have superb foreign language departments can offer alumni language programs. Like computer alumni colleges, they offer immediate value, and can charge more. Students willingly submit to very rigorous language and culture experiences.

Institute, Professional, and Technical School Summer Programs. The programs described above represent technical or skills programs for generalists: they teach nontechnical adults basic computing, languages, and more. But professional and technical schools also offer on-campus summer programs in the fields of their expertise. If their own alumni come back, these can amount to professional alumni continuing education. The Black Hills Natural Sciences Field Station of the South Dakota School of Mines & Technology in Rapid City offered three summer programs in 1986 with credit available for two semester credit hours.

The Rensselaerville Institute in New York State offered a one-week program in July 1986 called "The Last Humans?," featuring "social evenings" with Isaac Asimov. Given Asimov's range from science to science fiction, such a program might stretch participants from technical to humanist spheres.

The Massachusetts Institute of Technology combines the institute's science focus with liberal arts undergraduate strength in some of their alumni programs. For example, it sponsors Enterprise Forums (a copyrighted term), where the heads of technically oriented businesses volunteer for technical and management analysis by an expert group of M.I.T. faculty, alumni, and others, with the public invited to observe.

Executive Programs in the Humanities. These programs can feel like alumni colleges, except that the primary market is not the alumni. The Stanford Alumni Association offers a number of executive programs, including a Tuesday–Thursday Financial Seminar for Executives in April, an Engineering Executive Program for two weeks in late June and early July, the Thursday–Saturday Conference on Design, and a one-week Advanced Management College in the fall. The flagship is the summer Executive Program in the Humanities, identical in length to the twelve-day Dartmouth Alumni College. Dartmouth started its month-long executive program, the Dartmouth Institute for Continuing Education, in 1972, using its Alumni College and the Aspen Institute as models. Administratively it differs from the Stanford program in operating entirely apart from the alumni office. At Washington and Lee University, a two-week summer Institute for Executives in late June uses the same daily format as many alumni colleges: morning lectures, afternoon small-group discussions, late afternoon recreation, and evening films and other events.

Yale's and Dartmouth's business schools turn the tables on these executive programs, inviting corporate officers to teach and offering them the chance to submit "their lifetime experience to exhaustive student inquiry and analysis."

Religious Schools' Summer Programs. Chautauqua started this way. Brigham Young University's summer programs for alumni and others often fall in this category. Notre Dame makes religious and family issues one staple in its alumni continuing education diet. For variety, consider the Academy for Jewish Studies, which has headquarters in New York City but which moves around during the summers: two of its 1986 programs were at Skidmore College in Upstate New York and at Williams College in Massachusetts.

SUMMER EDUCATIONAL OPPORTUNITIES, WILLIAMS STYLE

Let us close our discussion of alumni colleges with a look at Williams's busy alumni summers. R. Cragin Lewis, director of alumni relations, offers the Williams College Society of Alumni five one-week alumni continuing education programs, two on the road (on Cape Cod and in the Rockies), and three on the campus. A twelve-day maritime history program at

Mystic Seaport museum and at sea comes first during most summers, expanding the menu to nearly seven weeks. The 1984 summer line-up looked like this:

OFF-CAMPUS:

June 23–30	A Naturalist's View of Cape Cod
July 1–7	Alumni College in the Rockies

ON-CAMPUS AFTER A ONE-WEEK BREAK:

July 15–21	Alumni Seminar Week (in the course collage format)
July 22–27	Computer Literacy
July 28–August 4	Alumni Theater Week (a play a day at the Berkshire Theatre Festival in Stockbridge [MA], the Dorset Playhouse in Vermont, Shakespeare and Company in Lenox [MA], and the Oldcastle Players at Bennington College, featuring Professor Fred Stocking '36 who "has stimulated and delighted four decades of Williams students")

A few schools come close to this, but the variety, balance, and length of Williams's alumni continuing education summer set it apart. This is achieved both by offering access to Williams's strengths and by sending the faculty out with participants into the rich cultural environment that surrounds Williamstown in the summer.

This comes close to an entire alumni semester. One might imagine that a summer alumni semester will one day appear somewhere, in which each week would offer access to faculty and a different aspect of the intellectual life of the college. The opening and closing weeks could be reserved for something like Notre Dame's Alumni Family Hall, where alumni could reside in campus dormitories at low rates in order to fulfill personal sabbatical goals, which only a superb academic campus environment can satisfy, in the company of other adults doing the same thing.

A FINAL WORD ABOUT ALUMNI COLLEGES

The flagships of many alumni continuing education programs, alumni colleges require special care by those professionals and volunteers who plan them, but they also reap special rewards for participants and institutional sponsors. A good alumni college's daily schedule looks like a bus schedule. Participants need help getting around; alumni college "bibles" become a necessity at such universities as Indiana, which prints a 100-page handbook, covering everything from where the banks are located and how to get laundry done overnight, to the busy schedule of events. Morning newsletters handle unexpected changes. These touches ensure participants that someone is paying attention to them during their visit.

For all its demands upon participants and sponsors, nothing in the world of alumni continuing education matches the effect of an alumni college's intellectual reflection with superb faculty in the old, familiar haunts. Few university programs produce more enthusiasm than those described in alumni college brochures. One participant, a graduate of the 1920s, had attended all of one institution's thirteen alumni colleges; another participant wrote a Shakespearean sonnet in response to advance reading before she even reached the campus. Cyril Houle calls such participants "learning-oriented," and they are, to be sure, possessed of inquiring minds. They are also the unmistakable products of an alumni college.

CHAPTER 5

PLANNING ALUMNI SEMINARS

Alumni seminars are even more difficult to describe than alumni colleges. A few institutions can recall some early seminars. Dartmouth's *Alumni Magazine* reports alumni seminars through the winter of 1918–1919 in Manchester, New Hampshire. In 1929, the University of Michigan established "courses of lectures in Detroit and elsewhere held for a number of years under the auspices of the University of Michigan clubs" (*Encyclopedia*, p. 338). Cornell held reunion seminars (reported as alumni colleges) in 1935 and 1936, although college reunions go back to 1800 and some must have included academic content. In the more recent past, Reed College has records of "The Reed Alumni College, Seattle Session" on Saturday, March 28, 1953, a program featuring a presidential address at lunch, two lecture sessions, and a closing reception. Total tuition: $2.75.

Another reason alumni seminars are hard to get a handle on is that anything from a ten-minute after-dinner alumni talk to a four-day weekend program falls into this category, making description, categorization, analysis, and understanding a challenge.

After we discuss the purposes, planning, and other characteristics of alumni seminars, we will look at successful seminar formats in this order: those most like alumni colleges (some are called alumni colleges, although they are too short for our definition); seminars that use alumni to teach alumni, or where alumni teach the faculty; the true seminar formats themselves; and finally a few close relatives. We will then draw some conclusions and look at the future of alumni seminars.

A Definition of Alumni Seminars

By alumni seminar we mean any brief academic opportunity for the faculty and the alumni to interact. Most seminars stand alone, and last from one hour up to a weekend. Beyond that, the purposes, planning, sponsors, financing, staffing, participants, and topics may all differ.

The Purposes of Alumni Seminars

Seminars are the simplest programs that bring faculty and alumni into academic contact. A few seminars study the academic life of the university, but most investigate specific academic themes.

Many alumni gathered for other purposes welcome a little academic exercise for variety. Seminars can leaven such multiple-purpose alumni events as a reunion or football weekend. Seminars can also enrich cultural and other educational events. A television series on a specific academic subject can benefit from an introduction and conclusion by university faculty. A play, concert, or art exhibition means more to alumni viewers after an alumni seminar. But be prepared that, no matter how varied the program, some alumni will show up only for the seminar.

Planning Schedules and Cycles for Alumni Seminars

Generally, the shorter the program, the shorter the required planning cycle, because alumni participants need little time to plan for a one-day or evening seminar. The exceptions occur when a major event like a traveling world-famous opera, concert or theater tour, or art exhibition (remember "The Treasures of Tuthankhamun," "The Search for Alexander," and "The Vatican Treasures") will sell out six to twelve months in advance.

With these exceptions, alumni seminars need three to twelve months' planning. Promotion is the key. At a minimum, if you allow two weeks to develop faculty and theme, two weeks to write and design the promotion, two weeks to print and mail, and three weeks for brochures to reach alumni mailboxes third class, you want over two months just to get the program from your head into alumni heads; and they need a month or two before the program to clear their calendars.

Alumni Seminar Finances

Seminar finances are just as volatile as those of alumni colleges. You can be surprised by great successes and by dismal failures. Fortunately, the stakes are much lower with seminars, so you can take more chances. This means that the general advantage of alumni continuing education—the ability to run experimental curricula—is even greater for alumni seminars. If you guess wrong about "Death and Dying," the moribund event is over before the pain becomes unbearable. If "What Is 'The Good Life' " sells out and no one wants to leave at the end of the day, you can always bring it back as a full weekend event later in the year.

Chapter 9 gives a detailed seminar budget, but here are some of the issues to consider. Do you pay the faculty? The answer should be yes, if you expect good teaching. How many faculty members can you afford in the program? One or more: one to four in integrated single-theme seminars; dozens in on-campus reunions. Because seminars are small programs, they produce little revenue. This reduces the number of faculty you can pay. Sometimes faculty members will contribute very short set pieces requiring little new preparation for a reunion program, but in general you should pay teachers to teach, and the financial facts of life may reduce the number of faculty members in shorter seminars.

The farther the seminar travels from the campus, the fewer

teachers you can afford. Once air travel is required, the squeeze is really on the budget. Some colleges and universities use faculty from local or sister institutions, or alumni in the field, when they hold seminars far from the campus. This reduces cost but also quality control over the event.

Topics are related to costs, too: seminars on financial planning attract higher participation than seminars on the romantic poets. Dorothy DiIorio at the Chicago campus of the University of Illinois offers this and other important hints about alumni seminars:

> Our Chicago area program events are of a general nature such as financial planning and retirement planning and are put together by our staff and marketed to alumni members in geographic areas where the event is being held. We sometimes do break down by class years depending on the topic. These events are self-supporting although we do have some developmental funds from the Alumni Association [12 May 1986 letter to Steven L. Calvert].

Who Comes to Alumni Seminars?

The same kinds of people come to alumni seminars as come to alumni colleges. And a few more. If alumni fall along a continuum, from those Cyril Houle considers inveterate learners to those who never darken a classroom door after commencement, seminars pick up a group closer to the center than do alumni colleges. Seminars require less commitment of time and money by participants. More young alumni can attend, because travel and child care add less cost. And alumni colleges almost never teach retirement preparation or financial planning, which means that new groups of very practical-minded alumni will attend shorter seminars that offer help in these important subjects.

Some institutions find to their surprise that the percentage of alumni attending seminars is higher than that for the alumni college. Fewer than a quarter of the participants in some alumni colleges are alumni, with two-thirds having some family connection to the sponsoring institution; but in alumni seminars nearly everyone is a graduate, spouse, parent, or child. Therefore the benefits to alma mater are probably greater from seminars.

Sallie Riggs reminds us of an important relationship between participants and seminar location:

> *Even the distance of alumni within cities can make a difference. Saturday day-time offerings in some sections of town will be better attended than those in the evenings in the same sections, either because of the quality of the neighborhood or of the time necessary to get there for the largest number of alumni [material provided to Steven L. Calvert].*

Breaking down the alumni audience by age can be important if the topic is retirement, investments, family life, or some other age-specific topic. At Northwestern University, a long-running program for alumnae offers a weekday seminar series throughout the year which most men and working women cannot attend because of the scheduling. It should be interesting to watch this program adjust to the increasing number of women in the workplace.

Organization and Staffing for Alumni Seminars

A summer alumni college ought to showcase your best faculty, but seminars offer more freedom to use someone else's faculty, or alumni, or other experts, especially when the program goes off-campus. The risks from bad teaching go down in short programs: if someone teaches badly, the event is over at four o'clock. But it is also easier to involve your own busy faculty in shorter programs than in longer ones, and so alumni seminars may be the only place you can show off your prolific faculty authors or researchers, for example. They do not mind helping with a short program that fits their schedule, but cannot bear the thought of a week or more away from their grant or work-in-progress.

Volunteers can play more important roles in alumni seminars

than in alumni colleges. More and more institutions see the future of alumni club and reunion seminars in the hands of volunteer alumni leaders, because the professional alumni office staff back home has its hands full. Sometimes, the alumni office will find out about a top-notch alumni club seminar after the fact. It is better to know in advance, but the point is that this cannot happen with an alumni college.

Colleges and universities that use volunteer alumni seminar directors in the field not only discover that local judgment about successful seminar topics and locations creates better seminars, but that volunteers who run seminars become very devoted alumni. And, while other alumni club offices turn over as rapidly as the club charter allows, club seminar directors like to keep the job. The key is to train these volunteers through personal contact and handbooks from the sponsoring campus office.

At some institutions the continuing education office runs alumni seminars and may include some alumni relations (in addition to academic) programming. Duke's Judith Ruderman does: in the May-June *Duke* (alumni magazine) she describes her Martha's Vineyard alumni seminar weekend as consisting of "absorption in political science, in geology, and in Duke." The program on "Our Resourceful Earth" included an evening showing of videotaped "life at Duke" (Bliwise, 1986, p. 37).

At the University of Pennsylvania, the College of General Studies under dean David G. Burnett offers several alumni continuing education services. Philadelphia area alumni aged 35 to 60 receive the quarterly noncredit course catalog and many alumni participate, especially in career development programs. A special College Alumni Series of fall and spring weekend seminars often takes advantage of alumni connections, as well as faculty teaching. In 1986 an alumnus in charge of the Jazz Festival helped to arrange an alumni seminar in New Orleans, and a Chicago alumnus-architect contributed expertise and a cocktail party to a faculty-taught alumni seminar on art and architecture. The College of General Studies also works with travel agents to produce alumni colleges abroad.

Cooperative Alumni Seminars

Different schools within a university may cooperate, as in the case of the business school or medical school putting on workshops for the general alumni association. The alumni office may cooperate with a strong alumni chapter in a distant city. But the most interesting cooperative seminars result from two or more colleges and universities working together in the field.

Institutions with far-flung alumni cannot afford to take high-quality seminars to smaller club areas. But when two or more institutions pool their alumni mailing lists in those distant areas and each contributes a faculty member, the result can be a high-quality seminar attended by dozens or even hundreds. Participants in these cooperative seminars like them nearly as well as programs for fellow alumni only, if they have ever experienced the difference. For many of them, this is the only way they will ever see an alumni seminar. When the best scholars from each institution get together on a good topic, the result can actually be better than either institution could have done alone—for the faculty members as well as for the alumni. The key is adequate advance faculty preparation by telephone and letter.

Themes for Alumni Seminars

Some topics are appropriate for alumni seminars and others are not. It is hard enough to get something of value from a week on "The Middle Ages." It is nearly impossible in half a day. On the other hand, these shorter formats can be perfect for subjects that could not sustain a week-long discussion.

Not all themes determine program length, however. At the University of North Carolina at Chapel Hill, Linda Carl once used nearly the same China seminar in a one-week, two-session format; a weekend, off-campus seminar; and a weekend on the campus. She also sent a three-week alumni college abroad to China.

It makes good business and educational sense to follow Carl's example and repeat seminars. Whether we redesign the alumni college theme for an alumni seminar on the road, or plan several seminars in different cities to take advantage of the development time and money we have invested, there is no inherent reason for providing a new theme and faculty team for every seminar. At its most efficient, the repeating seminar might take the same faculty team of two to four teachers to several clubs during one week, then return to those clubs for as many weeks as the course lasted. No such program turned up in the research (one teacher expressed fright at the thought of teaching the same alumni seminar in five cities in the same week), but it could work, especially during term breaks when faculty members have fewer conflicts.

Examples of Alumni Seminar Formats

Beginning with one kind of alumni program that is related to alumni colleges and alumni seminars but not clearly in their camp, we will turn to true on-campus alumni seminars, including reunion seminars. Next will come off-campus formats, including club or chapter seminars, before we take a look at the future of alumni seminars.

ON-CAMPUS ALUMNI SEMINARS

On-campus Programs Related to Alumni Seminars. Some institutions invite alumni back to the campus for a "romp" not specifically linked to fundraising or other campus programs. There is nothing wrong with this. In addition to its alumni continuing education programs, Williams College has invited alumni back to an annual Alumni Winter Weekend in February since 1983. Co-sponsored by the Society of Alumni (the alumni office), the Athletic Department, and the Williams Outing Club (a college club that involves undergraduates in the out-of-doors), this program invites alumni and their families to "Come join Williams Students" for a weekend of participating in or watching athletics. Alumni have access to the libraries and museums, but without specific programs to entice them to those facilities.

On the face of it, this has little to do with alumni continuing education. The faculty is never mentioned. No one from the college or among the alumni themselves plans to say a word about academics; no one plans to say anything at all. But athletics are a part of university life because they teach skills and values to students. Further, some alumni associations promote ski trips to Switzerland as alumni travel programs, and think of all alumni travel programs as educational even if faculty members do not go along. The winter festival weekend format fits right here. It offers all the potential for an educational experience but with nothing educational made explicit.

On-Campus Seminars Within Other Events. Add one short seminar to the winter festival weekend and we are back in the world of alumni continuing education. Williams offers Saturday morning seminars on the campus before all home football games. Ohio Wesleyan University offers half-day alumni seminars before football games, too, and the university president ends the morning with a talk about life on the campus today.

Attaching an alumni seminar to a cultural event like a play, concert, or museum exhibition makes a popular alumni evening or matinee richer for the faculty's participation than these events might be for alumni otherwise. Rutgers University gives theater parties with a preplay discussion led by the director. Such programs also work well off-campus.

In programs where alumni seminars are organized in conjunction with programs featuring campus life, we have yet another mixed format, which Linda Carl calls conference programs. The University of Wisconsin at Madison calls these events Fall Day on Campus and Spring Day on Campus, where returning alumni choose among morning seminars and then attend luncheon, an early afternoon talk with the president, a short musical performance, and any of several mid-afternoon tours to interesting university centers. Northwestern University has run NU-DAY for more than two decades.

Seminar Days on the Campus. Northwestern also offers a full day of alumni seminars, called NU Seminar Day, where alumni choose four out of eighteen faculty presentations. At the University of Illinois at Urbana-Champaign this event is called University Day; even the luncheon features an academic talk.

Penn State and Stanford offer one-day, on-campus seminars on a single theme. At Penn State, Alumnae Day 1983 (a Saturday) studied "Investing in yourself—at home, at work, in your community." At Stanford, a winter Saturday was devoted to "Managing Your Money."

Mount Holyoke College alumnae, studying "A Play in Progress," spent a winter Saturday learning "how a script is transformed into the performance we enjoy as an audience." Participating with alumnae were the director, designer, production team, and cast of Stephen Sondheim's *A Little Night Music.* The resulting performances appeared later on the campus.

Loyola Marymount College in Los Angeles invites alumni to President's Day, including the celebration of Mass, a coffee break, twenty-four short academic courses, a lecture at lunch, and an afternoon convocation, all of which has proven attractive to younger alumni. Loyola admits that its president carried the idea west from Fordham, where he had been dean when he introduced a similar program, called Dean's Day.

Turn About: Alumni Teach the Faculty. At the University of San Diego, alumni put on a seminar for the faculty on grantsmanship. They discussed "How to find a home for a proposal" and "Mechanics and the cost of proposal writing" (Cummings, 1976, p. 12). Most institutions could make more frequent use of this alumni (and other adult) expertise to assist the faculty.

Evening Seminars on the Campus. The University of Illinois Alumni Association has offered "Time Management for the Two Career Family" on a fall evening. To keep costs down, the program managers did not include dinner, but the brochure pointed out a nearby cafeteria. This format is also used for alumni seminars based on museum exhibitions.

Swarthmore College brought back six star alumni/ae for an

evening liberal arts symposium, and promoted the event in a monthly alumni newsletter. The stars were 1975 physiology and medicine Nobel Prize-winner David Baltimore '60, Harvard psychologist and author Carol Gilligan '58, former University of California president and Carnegie Commission on the Future of Education chair Clark Kerr '32, Swarthmore board chair Eugene Lang '38, Harvard sociologist and author Sara L. Lightfoot '66, and former Stanford University president and Rockefeller Foundation president Richard Lyman '47. Swarthmore College president David W. Fraser moderated. Here again, we see alumni/ae as teachers. Events of this magnitude can often be opened to the public, and do the university much good with many constituencies.

The On-Campus Mealtime Seminar Series. A good on-campus mealtime seminar series can be habit-forming. Reed College in Oregon and Southern Methodist University in Dallas invite alumni to breakfast discussions on topics of current and often local interest. Reed's Commons Club breakfast series takes place in the college's dining facility from 7:00–8:30 A.M. One year's series featured important politicians including gubernatorial candidates; other years have featured a symphony conductor, newspaper editor, and business speakers, among many others. SMU's Alumni Breakfast Lecture Series, in its third year in 1986, attracted 240 participants per event, up from thirty-five the first year. Alumni director Gary Ransdell plans to expand the series.

The Massachusetts Institute of Technology (M.I.T.) offered a 1985–86 dinner-seminar series. M.I.T.'s Boston Seminar Series featured a unified theme, "Alchemy for the 21st Century: Water, Air, Earth and Fire," to explore "global resources, population management from control to space colonies, and a concluding look at the overall quality of life in our biosphere in the next century." In its second decade, the "Series is designed to offer alumni, their spouses and guests an opportunity to explore critical issues facing society." Held in the M.I.T. Faculty Club Main Dining Room with cocktails at 5:30 and dinner at 6:15, the six sessions cost $90 per person including dinner, and ran the first Monday of every month except January—easy to remember and work into busy schedules. While Illinois had a perfectly good idea in avoiding the evening meal cost, M.I.T. shows that dinner can sometimes be included with a seminar at a reasonable price.

The University of Illinois Alumni Association has offered short evening-without-dinner series, in addition to the one-night seminar format noted above. "Personal Financial Planning" took place on two consecutive Tuesday evenings in April 1983, while "How to Start Your Own Business" ran the same two weeks on Thursday evenings. All programs were from 6–8 P.M., without dinner but with Illinois's usual advice about a convenient and inexpensive cafeteria.

Stanford used four Wednesdays in April and May (every other week) for an on-campus evening series called "Shakespeare on Stage." Between the first two programs, also on Wednesday night, they showed Zeffirelli's *Romeo and Juliet*, and discussed the play the following week.

Brown University ran two weekday evening seminar series in 1982, "George Washington: A Hero for All Seasons" was scheduled on two consecutive Tuesday evenings in March in the campus library ($14 for the two sessions), and "Following in the Footsteps of Alexander the Great," off-campus but nearby, on two Mondays two weeks apart in April.

Alumnae and Women's On-Campus Seminars, Series, and Weekends. Northwestern University has a Women's Board, and women are members of the John Evans Club. These women, plus wives of the Young Presidents' Organization, were invited in September 1985 to their second annual Wednesday morning seminar series, in this case about the field of medicine. Coffee at 9:00 A.M. preceded each of the ten programs, with optional box lunches afterward, all for a $350 suggested donation to the University. In addition, Continuing Education Daytime Courses, organized by volunteers of the Alumnae of Northwestern University, run on weekend mornings and generate scholarships, gifts, and grants to the university.

The University of Illinois Alumni Association provides an on-campus Women's Day on a central theme one Saturday in March; the 1986 program featured nine speakers. Pomona College aimed a weekend of discussions about women in society at alumnae and women students. The Women's Council of the University of Tennessee's National Alumni Association sponsors six to eight seminars a year at different UT campuses. The University of Iowa's "Eminent Alumni Series" began as a program for women and now admits everyone including current undergraduates.

Academic programs for women make sense. Some program directors surveyed believe that women make the decisions for many couples who attend alumni continuing education events. As the working and family patterns of women change, however, weekday programs will serve fewer women. Programs will shift to evenings, weekends, holidays, and summers.

On-Campus Weekend Seminars. The format of on-campus weekend seminars resembles that of many alumni colleges, and for good reason. As family life becomes more complicated, adults' weekends are becoming the most convenient time for education.

There is little difference, other than a fraction of a day's time, between a weekend alumni college and Colby College's Wednesday–Thursday Alumni College before June reunions. Colby offers graduates a choice of four courses by six faculty members in two days. Colby correctly calls this its Alumni College, because the program stands alone, despite its proximity to reunions; because the promotion goes to all alumni; and because it is Colby's longest alumni continuing education program.

Participants would be hard-pressed to distinguish between Colby's Alumni College and the University of North Carolina's Weekend Seminars, offered sixteen times a year. These seminars on "cultural, moral and social topics of interest and importance," were in their eighth season in 1986, began late on a Friday afternoon and ended on Saturday at 1:00 P.M. Four or five faculty members lectured and tuition was $50 per course, for which one Continuing Education Unit (CEU) was available.

North Carolina's weekends focus on single themes. So did the University of Notre Dame's on-campus winter weekend on "Ethical Issues in Medical Practice" in 1986. Faculty and guest lecturers spoke during the weekend. Participants earned 10.5 American Medical Association continuing education credits, and paid a fee of $295 without housing.

When the Stanford Alumni Association adopted the weekend format for its summer "Stanford Conference on Design" in 1985, it brought in fourteen outside experts from all over the state of California to join one faculty member.

Mount Holyoke College's winter symposium on recombinant DNA began with a Friday evening after-dinner reception and hands-on tour of a new campus laboratory facility. Most of the seminar took place Saturday, ending before dinner. By including only Saturday lunch, the price was kept to $35.

Dartmouth College featured its Robert Frost collection and participation by the poet's daughter, Leslie Frost Ballantine, and amanuensis, Kathleen Johnston Morrison, for a winter weekend seminar at the campus inn. Eight English department faculty members lectured, and they and three undergraduate English majors led small-group discussions of the poetry.

Reunion Seminars. Reunions are probably the oldest form of alumni relations, and have often (but by no means always) included a little academic programming as a reminder of what is being celebrated. Some of the most fascinating stories alumni directors have to tell about their own or their institution's histories feature reunion characters and settings.

No story, however, is nearly as interesting as the events themselves. Daniel N. White, in a 1978 article in the *Princeton Alumni Weekly* called "The Festival and Fantasy of Princeton Reunions," argues persuasively for a balance of the cultural and the social at reunions. Alumni directors who agree make certain that alumni have access to the faculty in addition to time with each other and the freedom to explore the campus of today.

While the thought is not often expressed, effective reunion programs reunite the four aspects of an undergraduate experience: the intellectual, cultural, recreational (including athletic), and social. The days of purely social reunions are numbered. Adults these days expect more. Perhaps they always did. Working together, alumni relations and continuing education professionals can provide a reunion experience that alumni

want, need, and deserve if sponsoring institutions expect anything in return (and they do).

The formats for alumni reunion seminars show great variation and ingenuity, and often display precise self-knowledge
by the sponsoring institution. Notre Dame packs forty-two
seminars and workshops into two and one-half days of reunions; the university encourages additional mini-seminars sponsored by the reunion classes themselves; religious events also
play a prominent role.

Not all reunions take place near commencement in the
spring. Stanford's fall reunion format, Rediscovering Stanford,
features six lectures by prominent faculty in addition to more
traditional, less academic reunion fare.

Reed College also sets aside a day for a symposium as part
of its late May reunion weekend. Now ten years old, this tradition focuses upon a single theme, such as the 1986 "The Human Spirit and the Computer Age," which must feel a little like
a one-day alumni college. Most of Friday at Vanderbilt's Friday–
Saturday reunion period features lectures and campus tours to
academic centers. At Simmons College, six seminars dominate
the day on Saturday at reunions. Williams devotes all of Thursday afternoon and Friday before reunions to seminars and campus academic center tours. At Brown University, where reunions began in 1823 to raise money for medals to be won at
declamation and other academic contests, the ubiquitous Commencement Forums dominate the landscape for an entire day
of the reunion weekend.

At Southern Methodist University, the fifty-year class members enjoy an hour's seminar on the morning of the second day
of their two-day "golden mustangs reunion." M.I.T. used to
invite only the fifty-year class to a campus reunion, but now
insists that all five-year classes return for such events as M.I.T.
Night at the [Boston] Pops and a symposium, memorial service,
luncheon, and induction event called Technology Day.

At the University of Illinois the individual professional
schools hold their own field-specific reunions and the seminar
topics are particularly suited to those fields. The Medical, Den-
tal, and Pharmacy Alumni Weekends provide their graduates

with professional reunions: the dentists spend a full Wednesday in October; doctors attend an educational convocation and awards dinner in early June.

The Unique Educational Opportunity of the Alumni Class Reunion. Too often ignored as an education setting, reunions can be powerful opportunities for colleges and universities to provide educational programs for age-specific groups of adults.

In the first place, reunions gather educated adults. In addition, the identical age of adults in a reunion class offers the advantage of predicting successful subjects for reunion seminars. Adult development theory can help us choose those subjects. So can Ralph Waldo Emerson:

> *Historically, there is thought to be a difference in the ideas which predominate over successive epochs, and there are data for marking the genius of the Classic, of the Romantic, and now of the Reflective or Philosophical age. With the views I have intimated of the oneness or the identity of the mind through all individuals, I do not much dwell on these differences. In fact, I believe each individual passes through all three. The boy is a Greek; the young, romantic; the adult, reflective. I deny not however, that a revolution in the leading idea may be distinctly enough traced [Emerson, 1969, p. 52].*

Emerson wanted us all to be scholars, and to be independent in that enterprise from our European cousins. He also subscribed to the Platonic notion that different times of life suit us for different modes of thought and subjects of study.

The Dean of Reunions. If reunions are going to include substantial study of age-appropriate topics, someone should serve as the dean of reunions. It can be the alumni director. It might be the dean of continuing education, a faculty member, or a qualified member of each reunion class.

This dean of reunions can organize some seminars appropriate to alumni of all ages, others aimed at individual reunion classes. Younger alumni want to know about career choices, the politics of modern marriages, child-rearing, and money management; or they can return to liberal arts seminars about specific novels or poetry. Midlife alumni have different concerns: career change, family changes including divorce and remarriage or the empty-nest adjustment, financial planning, and the constellation of midlife crises studied by the faculty in psychology, sociology, psychiatry, medicine, and other fields. This midlife group also thinks hard about world affairs, local and national government, and issues of political and interpersonal power. Older alumni want to discuss the transition to retirement or retirement itself, and they tend to favor philosophical themes from the liberal arts, as opposed to the topics popular with more practical-minded young alumni.

The dean of reunions can encourage two other kinds of intellectual activity besides seminars. Alumni should be urged back into the university library. Some will need an introduction to the electronic library. But it is also important to send them back into the stacks for half an hour to sniff around (literally), and to browse among the collections.

The dean of reunions should also foster reentry into a special part of the undergraduate's residential relationships, something we might call the adult late-night bull session. Since much of what one learns in college comes from conversation with peers outside the classroom, a reunion should provoke these serious but informal conversations between classmates about issues facing adults of the same age.

An alumni director can take advantage of reunion seminars to increase his or her visibility as an educator in the eyes of colleagues and alumni alike. Alumni relations will move closer to the heart of the institution if the director is seen as an educator. Alumni relations will achieve its purposes more effectively if the director is seen by the faculty and by continuing education officers as a colleague, and if he or she is also respected by alumni as their link to the educational purposes for which the institution needs alumni support. Therefore, alumni directors should organize and moderate faculty panels during reunions. The symbolic educational leadership alone will go a long way toward increasing the credibility of alumni relations as a serious part of the institution's educational enterprise.

Reunion Seminars by Academic Department. Nearly all alumni continuing education programs invite alumni of the sponsoring institution without regard to their major or special field of interest. However, at colleges and universities with sophisticated alumni programs it is not uncommon for departments to keep directly in touch with their former majors. Occasionally departments will hold receptions or afternoon teas during the formal reunion period.

In one or two cases, alumni have been invited back to the campus for departmental reunions. At Reed College, the Alumni Association cooperated with the psychology department for a one-day symposium with two alumni prominent in their field and two faculty members as speakers. A two-day professional conference followed. As of mid-1986 Reed was working with other departments on the academic reunion concept. Dartmouth's earth sciences (geology) alumni ran two departmental reunions, one in 1974 to celebrate a move to new campus quarters; the other in 1984 in honor of two retiring professors. Relatives of continuing professional education seminars, these events provide a nice balance to alumni club seminars based on geography or reunion seminars based on the age of participants.

OFF-CAMPUS ALUMNI SEMINARS

A few extra challenges come with off-campus seminar planning, but just as the Alumnae of Northwestern University use volunteers to organize their on-campus continuing education program, colleges and universities can take advantage of alumni expertise when mounting off-campus seminars. When these are club seminars, the club organization can pitch in. Some alumni offices prefer arranging the seminars themselves, and save volunteers for help on seminar day. The question is whether directors or deans risk a false economy when they keep the staff at home, since the faculty could have a bad experience on the road in a setting over which the home office has little direct control. Other alumni offices find that alumni do a creditable job of organizing seminars when they know their role is crucial.

Institutions sponsoring off-campus seminars taught by someone other than their own faculty can build on these events when they start off-campus seminars featuring their own faculty. Reed College uses alumni to speak at annual meetings of alumni groups around the country. Their programs may not qualify as seminars, but they are close enough to provide a foundation for later off-campus seminar development.

To get one step closer to a true seminar, instead of holding the alumni club's annual dinner meeting with a nonacademic after-dinner speech about the football season or local politics, the sponsoring institution can send a faculty speaker. It helps to hold such events in a nearby museum or in an academic setting, rather than the local hotel.

The Off-Campus Football Saturday Seminar. The simplest off-campus seminars serve an alumni audience already gathering for another purpose. The University of Northern Iowa's "Knowledge Network" sends four faculty members to speak to out-of-town alumni the morning before away football games.

The Off-Campus Evening Seminar. Ohio Wesleyan used an alumnus with expertise in Japanese manufacturing technology and organization for an off-campus Wednesday evening alumni seminar in New York City. The University of Connecticut Alumni Association sent a Business School Faculty on Tour program to three cities in the state, one teacher per evening, with cocktails at 6:30 P.M. and then the talk and discussion. A local graduate handled the registration in each city. Some schools find that including dinner with evening seminars raises the total program price too high.

The Off-Campus Seminar with Cultural Event. A very popular alumni seminar format adds a lecture/discussion to an attractive cultural event. A special museum exhibition, play, or concert has several advantages. Some alumni are going anyway and value the extra appreciation of the event that a faculty member or other lecturer can provide before or after the event. Further, such events provide their own promotion, usually more than a local alumni group could afford, and the alumni seminar team can piggy-back on that visibility when announcing its related seminar. The museum may be willing to provide its logo, or the exhibition logo, to help alumni recognize the program in seminar brochures. Sometimes special access to the cultural event can be included—backstage privileges, a talk with the director afterward, a private viewing of an art exhibition—

something the alumni may not be able to get without the university's help.

These kinds of events can work nicely on the campus or in the university's own city or town. When done off campus, it is especially helpful to engage volunteer alumni to make local arrangements and to handle registration.

Sculptor Henry Moore's reclining figures became the center of attention at the evening seminar with wine and hors d'oeuvres that Ohio Wesleyan sponsored at the Columbus Museum of Art on a Tuesday evening in October 1984. Talks at 7:00 P.M. were followed by docent-guided tours of the galleries and a 9:00 P.M. reception. Notice again the judicious avoidance of full dinner expenses.

Ohio Wesleyan's is one example of the most popular museum seminar format used today. An exhibition making local or national news becomes the focus. The seminar takes place on a weekday evening (less frequently a weekend day or evening). The program begins with wine or cocktails after dinner or substitutes hors d'oeuvres for dinner, and adds a faculty talk and discussion before or after the cultural event. Prices can be as low as $10 per person if the museum cooperates and food comes reasonably priced. On the other hand, the alumni association that buys a block of scarce tickets for a nationally promoted exhibition can charge up to $50 per person for the evening and may still attract hundreds of alumni, spouses, parents, and friends of the institution.

Ohio Wesleyan added its own faculty member to a visit to "The Vatican Treasures" at the Chicago Art Institute on a fall Saturday morning. Participants heard a museum staffer's introduction, took a taped guided tour through the exhibition, then joined their teacher for discussion over lunch.

Brown University makes a habit of spotting touring art exhibitions and creating alumni seminars around them. On a Sunday evening it sent two teachers to Washington, D.C.'s National Gallery of Art for the Dégas exhibition; 6:00 P.M. lectures and discussion were followed by a narrated tour through the exhibition by one of the teachers, which ended at 9:00 P.M. Brown has also made alumni seminars out of a Renoir retrospective at Boston's Museum of Fine Arts, and the Vatican Treasures on display at the M. H. de Young Museum in Golden Gate Park, San Francisco.

Lehigh University made three of New York City's great art museums available to alumni in one weekend seminar package. In October of 1981 a Lehigh professor of art took participants through parts of the Metropolitan Museum of Art, the Museum of Modern Art, and the Guggenheim Museum. Wisely, program directors focused on "the origins of 20th century art in the original works of Cézanne, Gauguin, Munch, Picasso, Braque," and a few others, especially works created during thirty years of revolutionary change in art between 1880 and 1910.

Seminars in art museums work best when they put the faculty on first with slides of exhibition pieces, so that alumni enjoy the exhibition itself with an enriched sense of the objects. Sending less prepared adults through an exhibition and telling them afterward what they should have noticed gets things backwards.

But museums are not the only focus for alumni seminars. Brown took a program on "The Business of Show Business" to two different sites. On a Saturday in March participants visited the Arena Stage in Washington, D.C., with a faculty member and two alumni—one a Tony Award winner, the other a manufacturer of products for theater, television, and film. The presentations were separated by an arena tour, lunch, and group discussion. At their option, participants could move directly from the seminar to a matinee performance and cast reception on the site. Two members of the same teaching team put on a similar program at Chicago's Goodman Theater, where the afternoon seminar ended in time for participants to have dinner on their own and then attend a performance and postproduction reception. For both these events, a volunteer from the local Brown Club handled registration.

Holy Names College for Women offers family science excursions in which anything from seaside tidepool life to an organic farm might be the setting.

Of course, institutions can feature their own art museum exhibitions, musical performances, and dramatic productions in alumni seminars.

The Off-Campus Seminar Series. Off-campus seminar series can be expensive, because faculty travel costs weigh in heavily. As a result, most off-campus alumni seminar series stay close to home. The University of Illinois Alumni Association's Executive Director Lou Liay took faculty off-campus to the Oak Brook Marriott Hotel in the Chicago suburbs for a seminar on four winter Tuesday evenings on "Planning Your Retirement" for $55 per participant. The same association co-sponsored with the Office of Continuing Education and Public Service a Faculty Star Series on two Tuesday evenings in June 1983: teachers from the Urbana-Champaign campus were thus made available to alumni in two Chicago suburbs. This is mostly a series from the sponsors' point of view, although truly devoted Chicago alumni could have attended both seminars. Brown University held a Wednesday series called "Lunch at City Hall" in Providence, Rhode Island, where the university is located. One speaker at each lunch discussed a different problem of local or national concern.

We did not find any distant off-campus alumni series like those Peter Shultz imagined while at Harvard in the 1970s. Shultz's plan would have sent the same faculty team to several distant clubs, hitting one each night for a week, and then would have returned this same team to the same clubs one or more times to continue the series seminar. Shultz's model is intriguing. It offers real educational continuity to alumni at considerable distance from the campus, in a format that provides alumni with greater access to the regular university faculty than is normally possible. However, his plan would require extensive planning and promotion, continuous administrative monitoring over weeks or months while the program took place, and devoted faculty members.

Dartmouth ran a program sharing some of the Shultz model's characteristics over the winter of 1978–79 in Denver. Faculty flying to the annual Pacific Northwest Dartmouth Alumni Seminar stopped off in Denver and gave a seminar on the topic, "Where Have All the Heroes Gone?," to open this six-month experiment. They left study materials, including syllabi, discussion questions, and one videotaped academic lecture by the president of the college. Alumni from the Denver club organized the ensuing monthly discussion groups and local guest speakers for the next six months on the same topic. In March, when the alumni club normally held its weekend alumni seminar, the faculty returned for a weekend wrap-up.

The experiment worked, but still has not been repeated—a statement about the administrative difficulty of managing it. Advanced electronic technologies may make new models for long-distance alumni continuing education seminars more feasible.

The Off-Campus Saturday Seminar. On-campus half or whole-day seminars attract alumni on Saturdays. The same is true off the campus. In fact, next to the single evening lecture, the one-day Saturday seminar is probably the most common format for off-campus alumni seminars. The programs reach distant alumni; the faculty and the alumni can find the time; younger alumni/ae keep child care costs to a minimum; and interesting sites are available.

Ohio Wesleyan sent a Saturday seminar about American education, featuring two faculty members, to Chicago's Newberry Library for independent research. This might have been described as an off-campus university conference program (see below), except that the new Ohio Wesleyan president addressed the central seminar theme in his afternoon discussion, rather than talking about the university, as would normally be the president's role in a conference program.

Ohio University did not use a unified seminar theme when four teachers offered an "Alumni College in Cincinnati." This Alumni College on the Road is an annual event, drawing strength and program name recognition from the four-day, eight-year-old summer Alumni College on the campus: brochures reminded alumni that the "dean of Alumni College" was Dr. Samuel Crowl, professor of English and dean of University College, who had helped start the first Alumni College in 1978, even though Dr. Crowl did not teach in the Cincinnati Saturday seminar. The brochure also identified the executive director of the Ohio University Alumni Association as the "director of Alumni College," gaining him and the association credibility as educators. The tuition of $21 including lunch is typical of many institutions' Saturday seminars for alumni.

Georgetown calls each of its Saturday seminars an Alumni College Day and takes the programs to several major cities each year. In October 1985 Georgetown was in New York City, where each participant chose six of nine teachers' presentations (all on different themes), to go with coffee, lunch, and a closing reception. On May 3, 1986, the university was in Los Angeles with a similar program using eight teachers, of whom participants chose four.

While in New York, Georgetown borrowed Fordham's campus for a seminar setting, just as Ohio Wesleyan has borrowed Yale's Alumni House. Experience recommends this practice. An academic setting is important to an academic seminar, and it is worth finding a campus instead of calling the local Holiday Inn. Museum or theater seminars can be an exception, but if they cannot provide teaching space even these programs may benefit from a campus setting for the seminar before the group moves to the exhibition, play, or concert.

The Off-Campus Alumni Conference. Many (especially public) institutions, most of whose alumni live nearby, hold alumni conferences on campus. That is ideal. The conference's overall purpose is to give alumni a university update. For many institutions, however, alumni are far-flung and conferences must be held both on and off the campus. Stanford and Harvard probably run the biggest off-campus alumni conferences.

Stanford has taken one-day conferences to San Diego, Los Angeles, and Seattle, in cooperation with local alumni clubs in those cities. Several teachers give lectures in their fields, and the president talks about the university today. As with many regular Saturday seminars, morning coffee, lunch, and a closing late-afternoon reception are included.

But when Stanford went to New York City in April 1984, the university gave alumni the chance to spend almost four days with Stanford. Twenty-six faculty members and the president participated. Here is how the poster-sized promotional brochure described the program:

STANFORD IN NEW YORK. Now more than ever before, Stanford is making news with its innovative programming and excellent quality of education. During four days this spring, East Coast Stanford alumni will have the chance to find out what the experts in many fields are talking about. From April 26 through April 29 [Thursday through Sunday], a substantial portion of the Stanford community will travel to New York City for the largest Stanford alumni program ever held. On Saturday, April 28, an Alumni Conference, "Life in the 21st Century," will give you an intriguing look at life beyond the year 2000. On the days surrounding the conference, each of Stanford's seven schools, the Hoover Institution, the Stanford libraries, and the Athletic Department will hold special events focusing on their achievements. During the evenings, receptions, dinners, and special class reunions will keep East Coast Stanfordites entertained. Join some of the best minds at Stanford this spring and find out what everyone is talking about.

The president even led a Sunday morning run through Central Park before the closing brunch.

Not everyone can handle this much program on the road. It is hard to believe that anyone can. But it happened, opening up new possibilities for other institutions.

Weekend Alumni Seminars. Weekend seminars differ little from weekend alumni colleges, except that institutions who offer both call the shorter ones seminars. Weekend seminars or alumni colleges offer enough time for a little touring, so a wide range of program types exists. At one end of the spectrum are programs with little academic content. They may, however, be cultural, as in Duke University's use of a travel agent to book hotel accommodations and tickets to cultural events during a weekend at the 1981 Spoleto Festival in Charleston, South Carolina. This program resembles the short, domestic alumni travel programs that some institutions sponsor because they reach younger alumni than do the expensive alumni colleges abroad.

Also in this category of recreational, less educational weekend alumni seminars was Yale's fourteenth annual Alumni College Special Program at Yosemite, which took no faculty members but did use instructor-guides from the Yosemite Institute. By "special program" Yale distinguishes between academic seminars or alumni colleges abroad and less intellectual programs—such as the Yosemite weekend, a mid-September biking weekend in Vermont, one-week ski trips to Switzerland, golf tours to Scotland, sporting vacations to Ascot in England, and a cruise on the Hudson River to and from the Yale–Army football game.

Duke's alumni office invites alumni to a ten-year-old annual Alumni College Weekend Seminar in the early spring at the university's Marine Laboratory in Beaufort, North Carolina. Laboratory faculty members and students do the teaching, with an occasional guest speaker, such as the state's secretary of natural resources and community development. Participants are introduced to five topics, then concentrate on one while spending considerable time on outdoor field trips. Here is a university taking advantage of a unique resource. The University of North Carolina at Chapel Hill also has a marine facility, the Institute of Marine Sciences at Morehead City, where the university cosponsors with the Institute a Friday afternoon through Saturday seminar using the Institute's faculty. Lehigh University offers a Wetlands Weekend at the Wetlands Institute, which Lehigh operates in New Jersey. Alumni do not fear an overly academic program: the brochure prepares them to get "wet and muddy."

In the fall of 1985, just about the time foliage color peaks, Duke University offered a Martha's Vineyard Alumni College Weekend with four faculty members, including dean of Continuing Education Judith Ruderman. The Thursday–Sunday interdisciplinary program was sponsored jointly by the alumni and continuing education offices, and focused on "Our Resourceful Earth: Learning to Make the Most of It." Princeton University also chose Martha's Vineyard for a weekend alumni college a year before Duke on the same dates; in that fall the 1984 presidential election determined the topic. Cornell University offered a spring weekend seminar with four faculty members on a natural resources theme at the Mohonk Mountain House on a two-thousand-acre estate in New York's Catskill Mountains.

A close cousin of this entirely off-campus mountain retreat was Lehigh's Alumni College Weekend Program on "The Appalachians and the Poconos: Evolution of a Folded Mountain Range" during color season in the fall of 1983, a program that took place on the Bethlehem, Pennsylvania campus and added bus tours to interesting geological sites. This resembles some alumni colleges abroad, which can begin with on-campus seminars prior to departure for distant lands.

Like Princeton, UNC-Chapel Hill studied politics in an off-campus seminar. Alumni visited several Washington, D.C., locations not available to the public, thanks to the alumni director, whose previous work had been for a U.S. senator. UNC also sponsored an outdoor alumni weekend in the mountains in mid-May of 1984. The focus was seasonal wildflowers, with teaching by the director of the North Carolina Botanical Garden, a research associate, and a photographer.

The University of Pennsylvania has run three-day alumni seminar weekends in Charlottesville to study Thomas Jefferson; in Newport, Rhode Island; and in New Orleans. For 1986 and 1987 Penn planned weekends in Chicago and in Monterey, California.

Occasionally two or more institutions will cooperatively sponsor a weekend alumni seminar. This more commonly happens with off-campus Saturday seminars or alumni colleges abroad.

PROGRAMS RELATED TO ALUMNI SEMINARS

Three adult education programs related to alumni seminars are Continuum, the National Issues Forum, and M.I.T.'s Enterprise Forums.

Continuum. Related to the small cooperative alumni seminars described above is the lifelong learning program, Continuum, for alumni/ae of about thirty colleges and universities who live in the Philadelphia area. An independent program housed at Haverford College, Continuum is almost certainly the most ambitious alumni continuing education project since Lowell Eklund tried to link major midwestern institutions back in the 1960s. Director Nan S. Havsy's nonprofit educational organization offers a wide range of noncredit alumni seminars. Some happen all in one Sunday afternoon, others run for several consecutive weeks on the same weeknight. Some take tours in the Philadelphia area; others visit a museum. Some are for whole families; most serve individual adult tastes. The organization also offers educational seminars for businesses and other organizations. In other words, Havsy is something like the director of alumni continuing education for thirty institutions' Philadelphia alumni.

The National Issues Forum. Syracuse University is one of dozens of colleges and universities across the country that sponsor the National Issues Forum. Available through alumni and nonalumni regional and on-campus seminars and based on the learning packages developed on three major topics a year by the Domestic Policy Association, the National Issues Forum is an adult learning program supported by the Kettering Foundation. In 1986, the topics were welfare, tax reform, and the Soviet Union. The alumni office at Syracuse subsidizes the program, making the cost to participants just $3 for study materials. At the end of the program year, the local discussion groups feed representatives into a national series of meetings at the Gerald R. Ford Library in Ann Arbor, Michigan, and in Washington, D.C., to convey discussion results to national policymakers. Some of the Syracuse discussion groups grow out of the university's alumni clubs.

M.I.T.'s Enterprise Forums. Enterprise Forums at M.I.T. bring engineering and entrepreneurial expertise together in case studies of real businesses in need of assistance. Alumni, faculty, and other persons with expertise form a panel to discuss in a public forum the challenges of young businesses that seek to capitalize on technological or engineering advances. Many owners of the businesses studied are M.I.T. alumni.

ALUMNI CLUB (CHAPTER) SEMINARS

Alumni club seminars (the generic term used here for club or chapter seminars) take advantage of club volunteers when mounting an alumni seminar in the field. Otherwise, the range of subjects, length of programs, and number of faculty or other teachers do not differ from other kinds of off-campus alumni seminars.

A variation on club seminars began in 1985 at the University of Notre Dame, where the Alumni Association inaugurated a series of alumni club seminars named in honor of longtime University president Theodore M. Hesburgh, C.S.C. Academic deans and the provost named the lecturers, providing an honor to the university's best teachers while ensuring alumni clubs the best lecturers. The plan projected programs in large and small, near and distant club areas, under single- or multiple-club sponsorship.

Most club seminars are different from almost all other alumni club programs. They require fairly large budgets, as well as expertise about academic subjects and teachers, and about creating an educational atmosphere, even in a hotel or conference center.

The challenge is worth meeting: club seminars can be highly successful. One university's alumni clubs found their social programs competing unsuccessfully with an academic office's seminars for alumni. At another institution, one alumni club exists almost exclusively to run the largest and most successful of the alumni club seminars. Usually, it is the other way around: strong clubs that always do a good job on social events also run the best seminars.

Club Seminar Handbooks. Club seminars require carefully trained volunteers, and institutions that put substantial responsibility in volunteer hands find club seminar handbooks essential. Often these handbooks both teach the fundamentals about running public programs, and outline the philosophy of alumni continuing education.

Here, for example, is the opening paragraph of the first section, "How to Plan an Educational Event," in the Vanderbilt Alumni Association's handbook, *The Vanderbilt Alumni Education Prospectus:*

> *Recognizing that education and learning processes do not end the day of graduation and that Vanderbilt University has an unusual resource in its faculty, the Vanderbilt Alumni Association offers unique learning opportunities to alumni through the Vanderbilt Club Program. The Alumni Association wants to maintain the intellectual relationship be-*

tween alumni and the University. Toward that end, each Vanderbilt Club should recognize its role as a major link in the alumni education process. Taking utmost care in planning each educational event and coordinating plans with the Office of Alumni Relations will have positive implications for the success of the Club's overall educational program, as well as other Club programs. Club leadership, with input from various Club committees and the Alumni Office, should consider topic, speakers, time and location, publicity and invitation, and budget in the planning process.

The handbook then briefly discusses these planning areas, before closing the introductory section with this summary:

The Alumni Office will print, address and mail invitations. It will also contact faculty speakers of the Club's choice to ascertain availability for a certain event and make travel arrangements for the speaker. The Alumni Office will pay for invitation mailings and the speaker's travel and accommodations.

The Club will select the location and specific time for an event, determine whom to invite, collaborate with the Alumni Office to decide topics and determine speakers, and specify all information to be included in the invitation within eleven weeks of the event. The Club is also responsible for setting a budget. All Club educational events should involve a telephone committee to encourage maximum participation.

Here is an optimum schedule to follow in planning:

16 Weeks Before Event	*agreements should be reached between the Club leadership and the Alumni Office concerning topics, dates, place, speakers, and format.*
11 Weeks Before Event	*final copy for invitation delivered to the Alumni Office for printing.*
7 Weeks Before Event	*invitation mailed from Vanderbilt University.*
4 Weeks Before Event	*local publicity begins and alumni receive invitations.*

The *Prospectus* lists the faculty and topics available, divided into "Fine Arts and Culture" (6 choices), "Current Issues and Trends" (15 choices), and "Science and Technology" (4 choices), then closes with "Additional Educational Resources" (Vanderbilt Centers for Research and performing ensembles from the

Blair School of Music). The entire handbook is just twenty-five pages, devoted primarily to short paragraphs describing the topics for which faculty are available. The Vanderbilt alumni officer in charge is listed inside the front cover.

Washington and Lee University's handbook is an efficient eight-panel pamphlet that announces the program, describes its purpose and the basic format for a seminar, and then presents fourteen teachers, their topics, and their photographs. The details of which responsibilities belong to the sponsoring alumni group and which to the alumni continuing education director are left for individual arrangement. The University assumes that these seminars will be under three hours long on a morning, afternoon, or evening; cost $35 per person or $50 per couple; and include suggested advance reading for each topic.

Other handbooks develop a longer argument for the value of alumni continuing education and the role of the sponsoring alumni clubs, give more details about actual seminar operation (a complete club seminar budget, for example), and include sample brochures from other clubs' seminars. Handbooks may encourage clubs to name an alumni continuing education officer, who would in turn set up a seminar committee. The role of this club officer, and of the committee, in choosing seminar topics and faculty should be spelled out. Many successful club seminars have developed from cooperative discussion between a university officer and an appropriate club volunteer, an arrangement that increases a club's commitment to its seminar.

The sample alumni seminar schedules above, which represent the combined suggestions from several schools' handbooks, show programs in different formats. Note that "discussion" may mean plenary or small-group settings.

The Future of Alumni Seminars

Three things seem likely to happen to alumni seminars. First, they will begin to incorporate the new electronic technologies, and the resulting efficiencies in cost and in professional and

Sample Alumni Seminar Schedules

One-day alumni club seminar		Abbreviated Programs	
9:00–10:00	Registration	9:30–10:00	Registration
10:00–11:00	First lecture	10:00–11:00	First Lecture
11:00–11:30	Coffee break	11:00–11:15	Coffee break
11:30–12:30	Second lecture	11:15–12:15	Second lecture
12:30– 2:00	Luncheon	12:15– 1:30	Luncheon
2:00– 2:40	First discussion period	1:30– 3:00	Closing panel discussion, summary
2:50– 3:30	Second discussion period		
3:45– 4:30	Closing panel discussion, summary		
4:30– 5:30	Cocktails	*Or:*	
		9:00– 9:30	Registration
		9:30–10:15	First lecture
		10:15–10:45	Break
		10:45–11:30	Second lecture
		11:30–Noon	Closing panel discussion

Weekend Alumni Seminar		Abbreviated Program	
Friday		**Friday**	
2:00– 4:00	Registration	5:00– 6:00	Registration
4:30– 5:15	Introduction	6:00– 8:00	Cocktails and dinner
5:45– 6:30	Cocktails	8:00–10:00	Introduction; lecture or film; discussion
6:30– 8:00	Dinner		
8:00– 9:00	Lecture or film		
9:00–10:00	Discussion		
Saturday:		**Saturday:**	
7:00– 8:00	Breakfast	(see standard 1-day program, above)	
8:30– 9:30	Lecture		
9:30–10:00	Coffee break		
10:00–11:00	Lecture		
11:15–12:15	Discussion		
12:30– 1:30	Luncheon		
1:30– 5:30	Free time		
5:45– 6:30	Cocktails		
6:30– 8:00	Dinner		

8:00– 9:00	Lecture or film	Evening Museum or Theater	
9:00–10:00	Discussion	Seminar	
		5:30– 6:00	Registration and cash bar
		6:00– 7:00	Heavy hors d'oeuvres, punch
Sunday:		7:00– 8:00	Lecture and
7:00– 8:00	Breakfast		discussion
8:30– 9:30	Lecture	8:00 ff.	Museum tour,
9:30–10:00	Coffee break		concert, play,
10:00–11:00	Lecture		etc.
11:15–Noon	Closing panel discussion, summary		

volunteer staffing (including faculty participation) will make alumni seminars available to more alumni.

Second, social and demographic factors will increase demand for weekend alumni seminars, so that eventually sponsoring institutions will not be able to meet the demand: they will run out of staff and faculty. Based on current trends, alumni seminars could become the most popular form of alumni continuing education over the next ten years—much more popular than on-campus alumni colleges or alumni colleges abroad. When this happens, more institutions will turn to volunteer alumni to design and run their own alumni seminars, in addition to expanding programs alma mater offers directly to alumni. In effect, colleges and universities will train alumni to be more self-directed learners, competent to identify topics, and able to use many educational resources (not just the faculty from the home campus) in their own on- and off-campus seminars.

Third, as seminars proliferate, sponsoring institutions will begin more clearly to distinguish between the purposes of on-campus and off-campus programs. The campus will become an even more precious educational environment than it is today, and when alumni can physically return, seminars will concentrate on educational goal-setting and motivation, close contact with the faculty, and skills-building for the use of new educational resources like computers, computer-driven educational packages, and computer library searches. Off-campus seminars will feature contract learning between alumni and their on-campus faculty contacts, and self-directed learning.

CHAPTER 6

PLANNING
ALUMNI COLLEGES ABROAD

An alumni college abroad (or alumni university abroad, if the sponsor is a university) takes university faculty and alumni on a group travel experience. Usually the program lasts two weeks, but some travel programs are as short as a weekend or last long enough to go around the world.

Educational travel programs also take alumni to places within the United States. The University of Pennsylvania has run two four-day weekend trips—to Newport, Rhode Island, and to Jefferson country in Virginia. The University of Michigan takes alumni on summer weekend tours to the Shaw and Stratford theater festivals in Canada. The university has also taken alumni to a major architectural show in Chicago and to Colonial Williamsburg, Virginia. River rafting trips have been popular at several institutions for over a decade.

Educational travel programs for alumni need different treatment than the alumni colleges and the alumni seminars. With alumni colleges abroad, program formats (the exact length and the use of time) are extremely varied, but the planning usually begins in one of three ways: an institution buys an itinerary from a travel agent and the faculty lives with it; or it modifies one of these standard itineraries; or it starts from scratch with an academic agenda and builds a unique program, often with the assistance of a travel agent.

Two handbooks have been written specifically about running educational travel programs for alumni. Stephen L. Barrett, executive director of the Alumni Association at Brigham Young University, edited *Passport to Successful Alumni Travel Programs* (1976, revised in 1983) for CASE. Every college or university officer responsible for alumni travel should keep Barrett near at hand. His monograph will be helpful whether one buys trips from travel agents or designs them alone. A second handbook, *The Trips and Tours Manual*, by Kenneth Ostrand of the University of New Orleans, concentrates on designing travel programs from scratch. Ostrand is especially good early in the handbook, where he discusses the cruise and travel industry and the demographic reasons why he believes alumni travel will become more popular as time goes on. Most of our references here will be from Barrett, who edited the written advice of fifteen experts.

Barrett believes that the circumstances of alumni travel are so complicated, the risks so important to understand, and change so frequent, that a disclaimer is appropriate. Here is his, to which we subscribe:

> . . . The material covered here represents the best experience available at this time on alumni travel, but we cannot guarantee that every statement will be in force when you make use of it. Federal and state regulations governing travel change often. We urge you to consult with the legal counsel representing your individual association or institution and with reputable tour agents before you make major commitments.

The Purposes of Alumni Colleges Abroad

Barrett and his contributors pooled their experience to produce a list of reasons why colleges and universities run alumni colleges abroad. Such a program, they said,

1. provides a continuing educational involvement with the institution
2. identifies and makes possible the cultivation of prospective donors
3. brings foreign alumni into contact with their college or university
4. develops positive relationship between tour participants
5. identifies and makes possible cultivation of prospective volunteer workers
6. stands on its own financially
7. builds good will for the university among tour participants and non-participants
8. provides fringe benefits for qualified staff members
9. makes sense for most institutions
10. can be enjoyable to everyone involved.

In addition, sponsoring institutions derive two fringe benefits from these programs. First, the faculty can use alumni colleges abroad to travel to distant parts of the world related to their research. And second, universities may claim a small but important contribution to international understanding when these programs put influential Americans in contact with citizens of foreign lands.

Planning Schedules and Cycles

The longer the program, the more advance notice alumni need to clear their calendars. Brochures announcing two- or three-week alumni colleges abroad should reach alumni six months to a year before the program takes place. Some institutions that offer many trips a year send a general announcement listing all programs before mailing the brochures for individual alumni colleges abroad. This gives alumni a look at the entire range of choices at once. Other institutions print the travel program list in the alumni magazine. But it is not uncommon to mail only the specific announcements as they are printed.

Sponsoring institutions will usually sign up with travel agents over a year in advance. Agents operate on this schedule in order to book airline seats, charter ships, and reserve hotel space, and many institutional partners with whom we might wish our alumni to travel also plan this far ahead. From a marketing point of view, it helps to share a list of next year's programs with participants in this year's alumni colleges abroad, since some alumni become perennial travelers with the university faculty.

Colleges and universities starting out in the alumni travel business may want to start small and grow incrementally, rather than offering twenty trips the first year, only to cancel several. Once an institution expands to more than one or two alumni colleges abroad in a year, it is advisable to provide a variety of program destinations, times of year, subjects studied, and prices.

Cooperative Alumni Colleges Abroad

Alumni colleges abroad work well with the combined alumni participant groups from two or more sponsoring colleges or universities. It is wise to be selective about traveling partners. Educational programs put into close quarters adults who will be discussing issues of importance. The advantages of putting people of reasonably similar educational backgrounds into these experiences together is not unlike the advantages of putting them in college together in the first place. The alumni of any of the institutions in the same league make good traveling partners. They share something from the start—a fondness for similar institutions.

Experience tells us that these alumni also like the same levels of educational activity in preparation for, and during, an alumni college abroad; and their faculty not only get along but may already know each other professionally. Finally, it is more important for an alumni college abroad than for an ordinary alumni travel program to maintain some control over the environment—to be able to reserve the ship's dining room as a lecture hall, to adjust the itinerary at a faculty member's request, and to put participants into a situation where everyone shares some travel goals. For all these reasons, it can be a good idea for a sponsoring institution to join up with a similar institution from the moment a program is conceived.

Most alumni colleges abroad provide for plenty of unstructured sightseeing, rest, and recreation, even when a continuing education unit is the sponsor. Still, the level of academic intensity can vary greatly. The University of California at Los Angeles Extension office sponsors The Cambridge/UCLA Program jointly with the University of Cambridge in England. This series of three-week programs provides serious, almost full-time academic work, and most participants earn credit. This much academic fare might be hard for most alumni offices to put together, unless their institutions regularly offer programs abroad for undergraduates in which a few alumni would be welcome.

Financing Alumni Colleges Abroad

Chapter 9 shows how some alumni colleges abroad can pay for themselves, while others provide revenue to offset the expenses of other alumni continuing education programs that normally need a subsidy, like the off-campus weekend alumni seminars.

Many large travel agents take the big up-front financial risks for promotion and hotel or ship reservations. The university's revenue is based upon a percentage of gross agency income, or is earned at so many dollars per participant. Normally one complimentary space for a staff or faculty member results from fifteen to twenty spaces sold to paying participants, but more spaces are negotiable. Institutions that use minimal agent services take more financial risk up front but produce more revenue for themselves, or they can use that revenue to keep alumni prices down.

Because of their fiscal health, alumni travel programs make

a good place for colleges and universities to start alumni continuing education. Only reunions are handier, but reunions are not a good place to generate net revenues. On the other hand, reunions and alumni travel programs identify potential donors to the institution, and in this sense both programs lead to financial benefits later on. Clemson University studied the giving records of alumni travel program participants compared to a control group of alumni who had never participated. The participants showed annual giving increases in the range of 20–130 percent compared to the control group, whose annual giving increased 26 percent (see Barrett, 1983, p. 86).

Organization and Staffing

A few travel agents, seeing an attractive market in educational alumni travel, have become more flexible about modifying their standard itineraries to suit particular faculty members from sponsoring institutions. This is good news, because a responsive travel agent can be invaluable to a college or university sponsoring alumni travel, even if the faculty want to lay out a proposed itinerary. The larger agents have staff specialists for airline, hotel, and cruise ship bookings, foreign operations, tour guiding, trip documentation, and emergency procedures for the safety of participants and sponsor. It is expensive in staff time and dollars for a university to duplicate this expertise. And if the university goes it alone, low registration means canceling the program, whereas the larger agents can afford to run a trip that is undersubscribed.

Stanford University, the University of Michigan, and Brigham Young University run very large travel programs. Stanford offers 35–40 trips a year, nearly all of them with faculty aboard. Peter Voll, whose travel staff includes ten full-time professionals, calculates that he has personally developed over 200 programs in his thirteen years at Stanford. He buys off-the-rack itineraries from good agents, but also develops his own programs. At most institutions alumni travel is part of one staff person's job, and in this circumstance a good agent is required.

Legal Risks

Alumni colleges abroad carry greater legal risks than any other kind of alumni continuing education, and sponsoring institutions need to stay on top of the issues. Barrett's handbook is helpful on questions surrounding institutional liability, the Internal Revenue Service, and the U.S. Postal Service.

Earle Blackmon's article in the Barrett handbook (pp. 48–58; Blackmon was director of services at the National Entertainment Conference in 1973) covers the following topics under travel liability: school liability, signing contracts, charters, trip leaders, broken legs and other headaches, waivers (including two case studies involving the death of a participant and the limits of participant responsibility), settlement of claims, brochure wording related to liability, liability insurance, and "Whom do you (the sponsoring school) represent?" Blackmon's point is that sponsoring colleges and universities take on considerable liability when sponsoring travel programs, but by being careful about what kinds of contracts they sign and by knowing as much as possible about travel agent services, they can limit their liability and reduce the likelihood of lawsuits and other trouble.

John Bisset summarizes the IRS and U.S. Postal Service questions in his essay, "Legal Considerations of Alumni Travel" (see Barrett, 1983, pp. 20–22):

> First, the IRS has clearly stated that the operation of a tour or travel program by a university alumni organization is not exempt from federal income tax since the income received is produced from a commercial service and not an educational activity. Second, the U.S. Postal Service has taken a rather dim view of non-profit associations using their mailing permit to promote "commercial activities" and, depending on regional jurisdictions, has forced some organizations to use a standard commercial bulk rate mailing permit as opposed to their non-profit permit. Third, there is the question regarding personal tax liability when an association executive accepts a "free trip" or a host from the organization accompanies a sponsored tour.
>
> The IRS has generally held that there are two technical means through which the value of the trip would be nontaxable. The first would be exclusion from income altogether. This would occur either where most of the recipient's time is spent performing duties for the employer, or

where the trip has been awarded as a gift instead of compensation. The second means of obtaining nontaxability is by virtue of using standard allowable business deductions from income. In this case, it must be demonstrated that the primary purpose of the trip was for business and not for pleasure.

Bisset wisely recommends that each sponsoring institution consult its own lawyers about these matters. The new tax law of 1987 makes this advice even more important. At this writing, early in 1987, we know some things that will change as a result of the new law. But the detailed regulations that will be written based on the new law will take a year or more to write, and therefore no advice here will substitute in the future for careful legal counsel.

The new law does make one change plain: it will be more difficult to write off business trip expenses. Starting in 1987, such trips must be entirely for business purposes. Deductions for unreimbursed charitable travel expenses will be disallowed if there is a significant element of personal pleasure, recreation, or vacation in the travel. Even travel expenses related to education programs will be harder to deduct. The travel that gets one to an educational program (travel to Paris to study at the Louvre) is allowed; but a wine tour through the Loire Valley is not allowed. In lay terms, educational travel expenses can no longer be deducted at all. On the other hand, a trip leader can deduct personal expenses while on the trip: a Boy Scout leader on a camping trip, or a continuing education dean at work on an educational travel program.

Participants in continuing education programs can deduct continuing education costs, but starting in 1987 these expenses can only be lumped under miscellaneous deductions, the total of which must exceed 2 percent of gross income before any of these expenses are deductible.

Nothing in the new tax law alters the fact that in 1987 the Congress was taking direct aim at abuses in the use of tax exempt status by universities to cut promotional costs when operating noneducational business enterprises like alumni insurance or group travel programs. In these instances, citizens operating small businesses in those fields have objected to unfair competition by the universities, and Congress is clearly on their side.

We have learned some other details about legal issues since Bisset wrote his article. With regard to the revenues from alumni travel programs, at least one IRS district has determined that such revenues are not "exempt," that is, they are taxable because travel is not the business for which a university holds tax-exempt status. On the other hand, the best legal advice (by no means conclusive because not tested in the courts) suggests that alumni colleges abroad, if sufficiently educational, might be considered by the IRS to be part of the business for which a college or university holds tax-exempt status, and those travel revenues might be tax-exempt.

The issue (if it comes to court) will be: How much education is enough on a travel program? It is impossible to say, at this point, but the best advice might be to follow Barrett and make continuing education the primary reason for offering an alumni college abroad. This would mean that the idea and the general itinerary for the program would begin with the expertise of a specific faculty member with regard to a particular part of the world. Advance reading materials would be mailed to participants before the trip, along with a reading guide or syllabus from the faculty. Teaching would take place nearly every day of the trip. And program revenues would be shown to offset the cost of putting on educational programs for alumni at the sponsoring institution. A college or university that operates alumni colleges abroad in these ways should do better in an IRS audit than the university that lost its IRS case because its alumni travel programs had no educational component to speak of.

Similarly, faculty members who do a significant amount of teaching on travel programs, administrative staff members whose official job descriptions include responsibilities before and during alumni colleges abroad, and even spouses of either group who are asked in writing to take on specified hosting functions during these programs, should do much better during IRS audits than any people whose relationship to the program is tangential. At least one institution did well in such an audit. The IRS withdrew its suit, in which it had claimed that participating faculty and administrative staff members should pay personal income tax on the retail value of the trips they accompanied on the theory that these trips were provided by their employing institutions in lieu of compensation. The institution in this case had specified in the official job descriptions or otherwise in writing the foreign travel duties of all these people as part of their employment. Even the spouses were given responsibilities that directly supported the employed spouses' work. Institutions that resist using valuable complimentary spaces in order to include faculty members on alumni travel programs need to look very closely at these issues, since the faculty members may keep the programs out of trouble. Colleges and universities should also be prepared to explain to the IRS that fundraisers who use complimentary spaces work hard on university business.

None of these procedures guarantees that a sponsoring institution will win a suit by the IRS. Alumni travel attracts attention because some institutions' gross revenues are in the millions of dollars. However, a sponsor can lower the risk of losing a case should one come up. The best protection to date seems to have lain in making alumni colleges abroad as educational as possible, even though most are noncredit programs, and to ensure that all staff and faculty have specific, significant duties. For lists of appropriate duties for hosts on these programs, see "Caring for Participants," by Frank Jones, executive secretary of the Indiana University Alumni Association (pp. 23–26 in Barrett's handbook), and Barrett's "Sample Tour Host Checklist" and "Brigham Young University Alumni Tour Director's Guidebook" (pp. 42–47).

One other IRS issue, not as frequently discussed, is whether alumni who pay for alumni travel programs can write off all or part of their fee as a tax-deductible contribution to the sponsoring college or university. At least one school's lawyer has advised against this, since for that institution no portion of the travel program fee was a voluntary contribution: part of the fee was for travel services (airfare, hotel, and other fees), and a smaller portion went to the sponsoring institution to cover expenses of the educational office that had sponsored the program, developed the curriculum, and paid the faculty. Another institution, following the example of large museums that sponsor group travel for patron-members, states in its brochures what portion of the fee is tax-deductible. The best advice is for sponsoring institutions to check with their own lawyers, since no two alumni travel programs are exactly alike; and for individual alumni to check with their own tax lawyers on the advisability of writing off all or part of the program fee.

A U.S. Postal Service issue related to alumni travel programs was discussed in Congress in 1986. The issue was whether the average taxpayer should subsidize university travel brochure mailings through the third-class mailing program for tax-exempt institutions. The Postal Service's local postmasters have the power to interpret applicable regulations, and no clear rules of conduct have been established. The focus of postmasters' questions has been the wording of an official postal form that accompanies third-class, nonprofit, bulk mailings to the post office. Form PS 3602 requires the university officer responsible for the mailing to sign a statement that reads:

> *The signature of a nonprofit mailer certifies that: (1) The mailing does not violate section 623.5, DMM; and (2) Only the mailer's matter is being mailed; and (3) This is not a cooperative mailing with other persons or organizations that are not entitled to special bulk mailing privileges; and (4) This mailing has not been undertaken by the mailer on behalf of or produced for another person or organization that is not entitled to special bulk mailing privileges.*

One institution's alumni association temporarily lost all subsidized mailing privileges because of brochures that were obviously printed by travel agents. The association's privileges were reinstated a few months later, when the postal service reclassified the association, not as an educational organization but as a charitable institution.

Nothing can guarantee to keep an institution out of court with the Postal Service over travel brochure mailings. The best advice is to reduce the risk in the following ways. First, the travel programs sponsored by a college or university, or its alumni association, should be educational. If they are not, the local postmaster could refuse nonprofit mailing privileges. Second, the brochures that promote alumni colleges abroad should be as inoffensive to the Postal Service as possible. One school satisfied its local postmaster by (1) showing the postmaster that the program was so educational as to be the institution's and not the travel agent's; (2) prominently displaying the sponsoring institution's name on the brochures while reducing almost to invisibility any reference to the travel agent, and making it clear that the agent only provided certain professional services with regard to travel arrangements; (3) using only the officially registered return address of the sponsoring institution; and (4) printing a statement in the brochures that they are the property of the sponsoring institution, and providing to the postmaster at mailing time a receipt showing that the school has paid for brochure printing. In addition, some postmasters could require that all travel reservations be sent to the permit holder and not to the agent; others seem unconcerned by this issue.

The goal here is to make any mailings of colleges and universities an honest representation of a truly educational activity. Even so, in 1987 Congress may specifically exclude most alumni travel brochures from the nonprofit mailing program. If it does, each sponsoring institution will want to review the new legislation to determine whether some alumni colleges abroad can still qualify.

Participants

Fred Harvey Harrington sees educational advantages in affinity group travel. He says that "some study tours . . . are just money-making ventures of the travel agency variety. Many are much better. . . . Results are best when the adults signing up are somewhat alike in interests and educational background, but not all friends in advance. Too much previous association leads to excessive socializing on the trip and reduces the intellectual activity" (Harrington, 1977, p. 114). University-sponsored alumni colleges abroad fit Harrington's preferences perfectly.

The best alumni continuing education programs include participants young and old, but most alumni on the longer foreign travel programs are older and wealthier than the average. Some schools have tried to attract younger alumni to travel programs by offering lower-priced trips of shorter duration. Frank Jones thinks young alumni like a recreational emphasis (ski tours sell to younger alumni), but such programs are not very educational. The most successful educational travel programs for younger alumni take place over long weekends in one domestic location, like Colonial Williamsburg or a city whose cultural resources serve the faculty well.

Topics

Topic and destination are directly related in many alumni colleges abroad. In this regard it is useful to know what areas of the world attract the most alumni interest. Stephen Barrett and Jack Maguire (formerly at the University of Texas) surveyed a random sample of one university's alumni in 1980 and found that roughly half were interested in the Eastern Mediterranean, Eastern United States, and Mexico or Latin America, while one-third were interested in Europe,* the South Seas, New Zealand, and Australia, and one-quarter were interested in Scandinavia, the Orient, and around-the-world programs (some alumni indicated one or more preferences). Air/sea cruises and family camping were the most popular travel program formats (see Barrett, 1983, pp. 5–6).

As we mentioned earlier, some institutions (Cornell is one) have attached alumni colleges abroad to on-campus alumni continuing education programs. Sometimes the predeparture seminar takes only part of a day.

A few institutions have offered continuing education units (CEUs) for participation in alumni colleges abroad. Normally

---

*Because of cultural, climatic, and access differences, travel directors and even some agents think of Scandinavia, Russia, and Europe (England, France, Spain, Germany, Switzerland, and Italy) as three separate destinations, even though all are part of the European Continent.

in these cases the difference between credit and noncredit status is whether a participant writes a paper for faculty evaluation. Another procedure is to provide participants with a certificate of participation which describes the educational activities associated with the alumni college abroad. The participant can then work out with an employer or other educational institution the credit value of the certificate.

The Importance of Education on Alumni Colleges Abroad

Robert Forman, executive director of the University of Michigan Alumni Association, writes:

> Our alumni travel program, the first and perhaps the most successful operated by any alumni association, includes a faculty member on most tours. That person is always an expert on some aspect of the countries visited and gives several lectures during the course of the trip.
>
> In addition, many of these tours are preceded by an enrichment seminar in our Alumni Center. Specialists in other aspects of the countries to be visited lecture to both those tour members who can come to Ann Arbor and others among the 1,000-plus persons on our Alumni Enrichment mailing list [letter to Steven L. Calvert, May 27, 1986].

By 1986 Forman was in his twenty-first year of alumni travel; during that time his alumni association had served 25,000 participants in 175 programs for gross revenues of $24 million. Given his experience, he provides important leadership to alumni and continuing education directors. Elsewhere he has stated:

> [A]lumni associations should be in the travel business because they can provide a dimension of service which most organizations cannot. Universities have great faculty resources. These people should be a part of our travel program. No alumni tour should operate under the auspices of an alumni association without an individual from the faculty or the administration of the university taking part. Furthermore, the job shouldn't be only that of a fellow sightseer. The assignment should include opportunities to provide seminars on location, on subjects of academic interest, whether they be directly related to the country visited

*or not. The faculty or administrator should be part of a program inviting
foreign alumni to meet the visiting group and to share in the educational
objectives of such travel. The alumni association representative should
be along, not only to insure the logistical and service comforts of the
trip, but to see that the educational objectives are indeed met. Travel
programs which do not include such educational services are not, in my
judgment, legitimate activities of alumni associations [Barrett, 1983,
pp. 68–69].*

To summarize: universities can provide their alumni with
extraordinary educational travel experiences, something a large
and expanding market cannot get anywhere else. Alumni colleges abroad also expand the university's horizons of influence
by putting educated adults in touch with other peoples of the
world under the direct guidance of faculty experts. In this sense,
they are potentially among the most important of university
programs.

CHAPTER 7

PLANNING MEDIA AND SPECIAL PROGRAMS

Building on unique strengths, college and university sponsors of alumni continuing education have developed a variety of programs outside the more traditional alumni college, seminar, and travel formats. Since most of these programs are still relatively experimental, we will only outline and not analyze them. Readers may find useful ideas among these examples, and the confidence to try them that comes from seeing them in place at sister institutions.

Print Media Educational Programs for Alumni

Print media, like the alumni magazines at many colleges and universities, and electronic media, from audiotape and videotape to television and TV-satellite conferences, provide the alumni of a few schools with continuing access to the intellectual life of alma mater.

Printed materials provided the earliest alumni continuing education program on record—Yale's three-year reading program, announced in 1913, through which alumni could earn the A.M. degree. The University of Michigan's encyclopedic history states that during the 1920s about 600 faculty-prepared reading lists reached 5,000 alumni. The Brandeis University National Women's Committee formed special study groups based on twenty-four reading lists prepared by the faculty in the early 1970s. Some alumni magazines offer reading recommendations from the faculty to alumni.

A few institutions with university presses start book clubs for alumni and offer them discounts. Notre Dame has an alumni book club, and its director of alumni continuing education has considered developing learning packages that will integrate some of these books with study guides and other educational materials.

Educational Programs Using Electronic Media

Alumni offices are working their way up through the electronic technologies in their attempts to keep in touch more effectively with alumni. Some of these efforts have educational purposes. Yale University bound a flexible plastic 45 RPM soundsheet into its March 1969 alumni magazine, and explained in the accompanying article that this technology allowed the presentation of an aural subject through a visual medium. The soundsheet, called "Music at Yale," showcased the quality and variety of musical activity at the university with excerpts from musical groups to which alumni seldom had access: the Yale Bach Society, the symphony and chorus, a performance on guitar, and more.

In 1986, Yale produced four videotapes for alumni, all but one on aspects of the university's intellectual life. "Yale's Undergraduate Colleges" described the residential life of the university and "New Haven Update" explored the city around the university (and scored public relations points with New Haven), while "The Inquiring Mind: Science at Yale" and "A Process of Understanding: The Social Sciences at Yale" featured two academic areas of the curriculum. The alumni association planned future videotapes on the arts and humanities and on "Engineering: A Yale Tradition." These videotapes were provided at alumni association cost to all alumni clubs, with additional copies available at the cost of reproduction to high school guidance offices, alumni interviewers of high school applicants, and other interested parties.

In 1986 Brown University sold over 150 copies of a videotaped lecture by a favorite faculty member for $35 per cassette. Stanford University has made videotapes for alumni, and the Massachusetts Institute of Technology produces videotapes on technical subjects for sale to alumni and others.

Tufts and Stanford universities offer audiotaped lectures and seminars to alumni. Stanford's catalog is extensive, and tapes are sold through a program called "The Audible Stanford: The 2½ × 4" Lecture Hall," a play on the older, ongoing "Portable Stanford" book program from the University Press.

A very few institutions have begun experiments with television. TV courses are not new to continuing education, but television in alumni affairs is still in its infancy. Interactive television via computers and satellite links kicked off major capital campaigns for large universities in the mid-1980s. These technologies hold great potential for alumni continuing education.

The ultimate goal of all this technology may be to support the educational projects of self-directed alumni learners. More about that in Part III.

Special Programs

Here are a small number of programs that either do not fit, or barely fit, the alumni continuing education field now, but that may become more important in the future.

ALUMNI TEACHING

During Mount Holyoke College's winter term in January 1985 an alumna offered a course on the lingering effects of the Vietnam era. This is the logical extension of institutions using graduates as guest lecturers in alumni seminars.

ALUMNI AUDITING

The American University, Yale, Columbia, and Barnard College all offer formal alumni auditing programs. Many other institutions allow alumni to audit classes on a less formal basis. The price seems to suggest the degree of formality. For example, Barnard charges nothing; others charge minimal or modest tuition. Normally, alumni auditors cannot earn credit.

ALUMNI-IN-THE-COLLEGE

Dartmouth has tried three different experiments in which alumni, parents, and spouses were invited to the campus for a one-week residential participation in regular undergraduate courses. Advance study materials warmed up the adults before they joined undergraduates for a week in the middle of the term, and special seminars for the adults (some run by the faculty, some by especially capable students) enriched the adults' experience during the week. In one of the experimental programs the week of adult participation immediately followed freshman parents' weekend, and two dozen parents stayed on.

ALUMNI CONTINUING EDUCATION FOR CREDIT

Williams invited a small number of alumni to enroll on the campus as full-time students during the short winter term of Williams's 4–1–4 academic calendar. Yale invites alumni to take full-length term courses for credit under a new program called Alumni College Term-Time.

PARENTS PROGRAMS

High-quality educational programs for parents are good for relations, especially where a large number of parents are alumni, too. There is a great similarity between Brown University's Friday–Sunday Parents Weekend each October, and Dartmouth's Alumni-in-the-College. It seems likely that parents will be treated more and more like alumni as the costs of paying for adolescent educations escalate and the bill-payers become more interested in what they are paying for. Many institutions already invite parents nearly every time they invite graduates to an alumni continuing education program.

EDUCATIONAL PROGRAMS FOR HIGH SCHOOLERS, UNDERGRADUATES, RETIRED ALUMNI, AND OTHERS

Duke, Johns Hopkins, and Washington and Lee universities are among the institutions sponsoring summer programs for high school students. Called Summer Scholars at Washington and Lee, these very talented students attend summer camps a month or more in length. The payoff: some participants are so impressed that they apply for admission.

Ohio University's Student Alumni Board offers undergraduates the chance to work with local alumni on a wide variety of community and campus service projects. Other colleges and universities also provide this kind of subtle and usually minimal alumni training for undergraduates. Related to career counseling seminars in which alumni advise undergraduates, these programs offer yet another opportunity for alumni to exemplify for students the values engendered by a continuing life of the mind.

The New School for Social Research in New York City, The University of California at Berkeley, Harvard, Brown, and a few

other institutions have supported self-directed adult learning
for individuals and groups through programs like the Harvard
Institute for Learning in Retirement. These programs provide
almost no direct academic support. They get learning groups
started, provide access to university libraries and other educational resources, and leave the rest to the participants. Learning and teaching go hand-in-hand: participants take turns in
the roles of teacher, lecturer, and discussion leader. At Brown,
participants may enroll in the regular curriculum. It should not
be long before a college or university designs such a program
specifically for alumni.

CAREER AND CONTINUING EDUCATION COUNSELING

Many institutions serve alumni as well as undergraduate
and graduate students from their career and graduate education
offices. Rutgers University's alumni federation offers Recareer-
ing Workshops. Notre Dame's Alumni Association adds an
Alumni Clearinghouse, a computer-based system to link alumni
looking for jobs with alumni ready to hire. The University of
Arizona and Princeton University are trying out computer bulletin boards that alumni can use with personal computers at
home or in the office. To the extent that these services increase
their capacity to guide alumni toward continuing education resources, they will become more closely related to alumni continuing education.

With so many alumni continuing education program formats
to choose from, it is time to look at the academic content appropriate for each. Volunteers and directors will find it helpful
to know what themes have worked for other institutions in
alumni colleges, alumni seminars of many kinds, and alumni
colleges abroad.

CHAPTER 8

CHOOSING FACULTY AND CURRICULUM

"How do we choose a topic for an alumni continuing education program?" "Who does the choosing?" This chapter will answer these two questions, but it is worth emphasizing here that the best programs result from flexible planning in which any idea coming from volunteer alumni, the faculty, administrators, and even undergraduates receives serious consideration. Once a subject area has been selected, developing the exact topic and faculty treatment can be the result of faculty thought alone; but again, involved volunteers and administrators often lend a helpful hand. Volunteers have a pretty good sense of what will sell to fellow alumni, and experienced administrators have learned much about what works and what does not work.

Regardless of who gets involved in topic selection and development, once a sponsor has chosen the right program format for a given alumni setting (on campus, off campus, short programs or long ones, sedentary or traveling), it is time to decide what to teach.

Setting can determine faculty or curriculum or both. For example, an alumni college abroad in China immediately narrows our focus for the curriculum. More often, though, an alumni continuing education program director finds an opportunity to put alumni and faculty back together in a setting that offers some flexibility with regard to faculty and curriculum. This chapter will offer some general suggestions for making these choices but will also list dozens of specific topics that have proven successful in a variety of program formats at institutions across the country.

Guidelines from Adult Development and Learning Theories

College and university presidents and trustees, alumni directors, continuing education deans, certain other institutional officers, and innumerable adult volunteers who help higher education by guiding adult involvement in so many ways, know a good deal about adult development and learning. The success of their continuing education curriculum, their alumni and development programs, and many other activities speaks to their intuition about adult needs. Some of these professionals and volunteers have gone beyond experience and intuition to study the research of Daniel Levinson on life structure, Jane Loevinger on ego development, David Kolb on learning styles; Eric Erikson and George Vaillant on stage theories of adult development; Cyril Houle, Alan Knox, and K. Patricia Cross on general adult education theory; Malcolm Knowles on andragogy;* and Jerold Apps on applying theory to practice in adult education. We commend the reader to these writers as we consider topics for alumni continuing education programs.

Implicit in the strategy of discussing program formats before content is an acknowledgment that several barriers can prevent adults from participating in alumni continuing education programs. The most experienced directors know the primary im-

*Yugoslavian adult educator Dusan Savicevic gave Knowles the term andragogy in 1967 to describe the learner-centered (as opposed to teacher-centered or institution-centered) adult education model that Knowles had been developing since about 1940.

portance of accessibility, and make programs accessible by designing location, duration, and price with their alumni always in mind.

Location is crucial, and this is different from most other kinds of continuing education. Deans of continuing education experiment with delivery systems that make learning accessible to anyone; but location for them is still a minor problem by comparison with the director whose market is spread around the country, or around the world. Simply put, a university cannot involve many alumni in education if it offers its dispersed alumni one on-campus alumni college. Alumni continuing education must be offered as a varied and movable feast, able to reach alumni where they live.

Successful programs also fit busy alumni lives. Since most of these programs take a liberal arts approach, rather than serving professional needs, they compete for recreational time: evenings, weekends, and vacations. The shorter a program's duration, the more alumni can consider attending. For younger alumni, program duration can be as important as location. In fact, duration is related to location, since it takes time to reach a distant program. This important combination of time and place makes weekend alumni club seminars the most popular form of alumni continuing education at institutions that sponsor them.

Price keeps most alumni from participating in alumni colleges abroad, which can cost a couple $2,000–20,000. But price sensitivity matters less in alumni colleges, less still in shorter seminars. Chapter 9 will discuss price sensitivity in alumni continuing education programs.

Choosing Curriculum Before Faculty

Every college and university has faculty stars, and some of them attract participants almost without regard to a program's topic. On the other hand, a good topic improves with the right faculty member; but a bad topic cannot be saved no matter who does the teaching. Therefore, it is slightly more important to find a good topic when planning a successful program. Let us discuss how to do that, before talking about the selection and proper support of the faculty.

THE STRENGTH OF THE LIBERAL ARTS IN ALUMNI CONTINUING EDUCATION PROGRAMS

Each sponsoring institution should play from its strengths. This is especially true of programs for alumni, because alumni know those strengths—and weaknesses—from experience.

Alumni also have strengths and weaknesses. For example, institute graduates are stronger (as a whole) on technical subjects than liberal arts graduates. And no matter what the sponsoring institution, alumni continuing education must pitch its programs at the generalist, because alumni are as diverse a group as the undergraduates. When these programs reach substantial size they can begin to target segments of the alumni body and to offer seminars for graduates in specific fields. Most programs have not reached these proportions and should aim at the alumni body as a general audience. For this reason, the liberal arts account for an overwhelming number of successful topics, and most institutions with successful programs offer a strong faculty in the arts and sciences.

Quite apart from the fact that liberal arts programs succeed because they reach most alumni of most institutions, sponsors should feel some obligation to keep graduates in touch with the liberal arts. Fred Harvey Harrington reminds us that "whatever is said, whatever course preferences adults have, liberal education must not be set aside. It is fundamental to the weighing of values, and cannot be neglected even in the most practical age" (1977, p. 111). To survive in our changing world, we all need technical updates and specific skills from time to time. But what about those needs we have because we ourselves change? For these needs the liberal arts provide the strength that comes from a perspective outside ourselves, a reflection upon our most closely held values, and enduring truths which anchor even our changing selves in a changing world.

Notice, in our lists of successful topics for alumni continuing education programs, how often the program directors and volunteer leaders have found a route through contemporary themes to the most enduring questions about human nature. Notice how often a study of the Middle Ages seeks to explain the characteristics of modern men and women; how often the Middle East explains something in the heart of all humankind. The best alumni continuing education programs do not explore modern investments, or personal computing, although these subjects sell seats. The best programs offer the best thinking of the best faculty on subjects that engender deep thought about crucial human issues.

THE IMPORTANCE OF INTERDISCIPLINARY PROGRAMS FOR ADULT LEARNERS

Many of the topics listed on the following pages feature one teacher's expertise. This practice results more from budgetary pressures than any theory of adult education. The best programs find ways to finance the interdisciplinary study that meets adult learners' needs. As Malcolm Knowles says,

> Children have been conditioned to have a subject-centered orientation to most learning, whereas adults tend to have a problem-centered orientation to learning. This difference is primarily the result of the difference in time perspective. The child's time perspective toward learning is one of postponed application.
>
> The adult, on the other hand, comes into an educational activity largely because he is experiencing some inadequacy in coping with current life problems. He wants to apply tomorrow what he learns today, so his time perspective is one of immediacy of application. Therefore, he enters into education with a problem-centered orientation to learning [1978, p. 58].

Milton Stern, from the perspective of the University of California–Berkeley with its tens of thousands of adult learners, states the case with equal force while pointing explicitly to interdisciplinary study:

> [Adult learners] are more rewarding, more challenging, and more critical than undergraduate students. . . . The adult student, not pursuing a degree—and most of them do not—is eclectic in the humanities, inter-

ested . . . in specific aspects of a subject but not usually in its totality, interested in limited sequences of courses and different from the graduate student of the humanities who although he may have a passionate thirst for knowledge, is really apprenticed to a learned trade in the humanities. . . . The passionate pilgrims among adult students are just about as frequent as among the younger . . . [but] it is the rare adult who will submit himself or herself eagerly to the typical disciplinary approach of humanities subject matter. The adult student is an interdisciplinary animal by nature . . . and it is of utmost importance to understand this in programming and teaching [Milton Stern, 1979, pp. 2–5].

In short, the best curriculum for alumni continuing education has proven to be interdisciplinary liberal arts programs.

How to Teach Adult Learners in Alumni Continuing Education

No matter what the format for an alumni continuing education program, two aspects of methodology have proven important. One is the use of discussion, usually following faculty lectures. The other is the use of advance and follow-up reading to expand the effectiveness of short programs.

Discussion, whether in small groups or in plenary sessions following lectures, makes participants out of passive learners. Discussion increases a seminar's effectiveness, because active learning surpasses passive learning. More than this, adult participants bring a wealth of experience to discussion, and the best programs bring this out.

In alumni continuing education programs, adult learners are back on a familiar campus but do not seek grades or credit. These circumstances reduce two common barriers to free intellectual interchange, and increase the effectiveness of discussion as a methodology. We can reduce inhibitors further when forming discussion groups by separating family members and good friends; this reduces long-established pecking orders.

Reading lists can be attached to alumni continuing education programs. The extra work for the faculty and program administrators is minimal, and the reading greatly expands the effectiveness of the teaching. Advance and follow-up reading put more education in reach of alumni participants, urging them to become better self-directed learners who can make brief faculty contact last for months. This will become important as alumni continuing education expands to the point where faculty time at the podium becomes a limiting factor. There are limits, too, however, on how much reading can be assigned in conjunction with different program types. Even a long alumni college cannot expect registrants to get through Stendhal's *Red and Black* and Tolstoy's *War and Peace*. Each school should experiment with these limits for its own alumni. Use follow-up surveys to determine who read what. Adults are like other students; some will read everything assigned, others much less. Faculty goals should be high, but within reason.

These two methodologies increase the educational value of any continuing education program. They also increase the alumni relations effect on participants in alumni continuing education: the more time participants spend thinking about alma mater's educational programs the better for the participants and for their institution.

THE DEPTH CHARGE PRINCIPLE

Beyond these two methodologies, alumni continuing education at its best provides continuing education by the same method that fine teachers have always used, and which James A. Epperson, the academic director of Dartmouth's Alumni College from 1976 to 1978, called the depth charge principle. Near the end of his twelve-day Alumni College in 1976 called "Dis-Connections: Changing Relationships in American Life," Epperson found himself under attack by frustrated participants who claimed his program had further disconnected them, and who demanded that he re-connect them. Epperson explained that he taught by the depth charge principle. He made up the phrase, but probably took his cue from a passage in Robert Pirsig's novel, *Zen and the Art of Motorcycle Maintenance* (pp. 183–84), assigned reading for that alumni college:

> The atmosphere was explosive. Almost everyone [in the classroom] seemed as frustrated and angered as [Phaedrus] had been by the question.
>
> "How are we supposed to know what quality is?" they said. "You're

supposed to tell us! Then he told them he couldn't figure it out either and really wanted to know. . . .

"It's not my job to re-connect you," Epperson told his alumni students that day. "That is your job. My job is to send intellectual depth charges into your souls. They will go off later on, when you will deal with them in your own way." That is effective continuing education.

When alumni continuing education programs use something like Epperson's depth charge principle, it will not matter that the delivery system is short-term noncredit programming or that participants take part during weekends, evenings, or vacations. Ivan Illich reminds us in *Deschooling Society* that our term, school, derives from the Greek word for leisure.

Curricula Aimed at Specific Age Groups of Alumni

Alumni continuing education can take advantage of adult development theory to offer programs of special interest to different age groups. Financial seminars, which attract midlife and retirement-age alumni, have been popular. So have preretirement seminars. Reunion seminars are perfect occasions for these age-specific programs, but institutions whose alumni live nearby can offer such topics almost any time of year on the campus.

These are skills-building programs aimed at age groups that need those specific skills. We can use this knowledge both ways: If we want to provide a seminar for a twentieth reunion class, we can find out where this age group's interests might lie, and provide an appropriate program. Or, we can take a subject we want to offer and predict who will come. In skills-building seminars, an awareness of adult development stage theory can predict our success (and avoid disasters) in southern Florida or the Southwest, where many retired alumni live, or in the major cities where our younger alumni settle early in their professional careers.

We can make good predictions about who will come to liberal arts programs, too. Alan Knox has reported that programs "dealing heavily with philosophy and religion attracted participants with a median age of 45, those dealing with the arts a median age of 40, and those dealing with political affairs a median age of 35. . . . In philosophy and literature, the peak occurs later. . . . In old age there tends to be an increase of interest in topics that emphasize connections between the individual and the rest of mankind through time and space. Examples of such topics include history, genealogy, philosophy, religion, and societal issues" (Knox, 1977, pp. 205, 373). The young are at an age when these concerns do not naturally reach their peak of strength. Alumni colleges, which so often feature such themes, draw an older crowd of alumni.

Lest we think that young men and women of business will flock to management seminars, Harrington, in a chapter on the increasing importance of continuing professional education, quotes Peter Drucker to the contrary:

> [A]s they acquire experience, professionals recognize the value of approaches they neglected when in college. As Drucker (who is worth listening to) says, "many subjects are better learned by experienced older men. Management is one of them." Overall planning (especially planning for change), generalization, understanding complex systems, and seeing the big picture fall into the same category. "Continuing education may be where the true generalist will come into being" [1977, p. 84].

Knowles (1962, p. 278) urges us to take the changing life tasks of adults into account when developing our curricula. He reminds us how different are the needs of adults starting careers or raising families from the needs of older adults in midlife or retirement.

The Classroom for All Ages

William Perry's stages of ethical and intellectual development, or Lawrence Kohlberg's stage theory of moral development (reported in Cross, 1983, pp. 176–84), remind us that much of what a college education instills keeps on challenging adults at all stages of life, and probably needs revitalization by frequent academic exercise. In this sense, alumni continuing education finds itself in a position of real advantage and purpose, because programs can tune up intellectual, moral, and ethical as well as professional or general living skills. Alumni continuing ed-

ucation can and should expect to put young and old alumni
together in a classroom where the classics will be discussed,
for the need to tune the ethical and moral sensitivities of adults
crosses all age boundaries. Writing is another area in which
alumni of all ages can work together.

To summarize, adult development and learning theory can
predict the success or failure of many alumni continuing education programs in the planning stages. We should be aware
of these theories and use them where we can. But the nature
of the liberal arts and interdisciplinary study makes them less
susceptible to prediction than age-specific, skills-building seminars.

As difficult as it may be to attract younger alumni to these
programs, we must strive to do it. For all the benefits of mature
adult experience, younger alumni contribute an idealism, a
freshness about our most pressing human issues; and indeed
older adults frequently object when younger alumni are missing
from alumni colleges and seminars.

The challenge appears most noticeably with alumni colleges
abroad, but even here we must accept it. Younger participants
have a way of naturally encouraging older alumni to get the
most out of a travel program abroad. This effect can be seen
when grandparents take grandchildren on alumni colleges
abroad, or when younger faculty members or administrative
hosts bring along their children. The most enthusiastic dinner
table conversations come from older adults who have just spent
the afternoon keeping up with teenagers or younger alumni in
explorations around a foreign city or town. Especially for well-
traveled older alumni, there is extraordinary value in seeing a
beautiful but familiar cathedral, work of art, or landscape anew
through the eyes of a much younger fellow traveler.

Successful Topics for Alumni Continuing Education Programs

Volunteers and professionals who plan alumni colleges,
seminars, alumni colleges abroad, and special programs like
knowing what subjects have succeeded for other institutions.

What follows is a list of successful topics by program format.

Two caveats. First, try topics you can do well. You must have the right faculty, no matter what your format. Second, while some topics work only in one program format, others are more adaptable. For example, updates on the situation in the Middle East have worked in seminars from an hour or two to alumni colleges almost a week long. On the other hand, "The Middle Ages" requires a considerable time frame.

Readers will recall that some institutions' alumni colleges are shorter than others'. Therefore, rather than listing topics that have worked in various alumni colleges, and then listing similar topics for alumni seminars of nearly the same length, it makes more sense to consider together all topics that work in alumni continuing education programs of similar length, whether they are called alumni colleges or alumni seminars.

Two exceptions. Topics appropriate for alumni colleges of one week or longer will be listed as such, since no one refers to these longer programs as seminars. In some cases several topics come from the same alumni college in the same year, because schools like Cornell offer a choice of one-week themes. When one school's several topics are listed together, notice the attempt at a balance of subjects: no one has studied China, the Soviet Union, and the Middle East in the same year. We will also list the alumni college abroad topics separately. (Sponsoring institutions are given in parentheses, so that readers interested in more information will know whom to call. Occasionally similar topics have been clustered.)

TOPICS FOR SHORT PROGRAMS (HALF-DAY, EVENING, OR ONE-DAY)

If Karl Marx Returned Today (Stanford)

Learning While Writing My 28th Book (movie script from novels as second draft) (Stanford)

The New Families (Stanford)

Living Clocks (evolutionary, physiological, and environmental biorhythms) (Stanford)

Historicism: Boon or Burden (impact of historical inspiration on modern art) (Stanford)

Right Turn, Wrong Turn: Adolescents Make Choices (Stanford)

The Arms Race (Stanford)

Conceptual Block-Busting (innovative problem-solving) (Stanford)

Business Careers and Ethical Values (Stanford)

Exploring the Human Brain (Stanford)

The Business of Show Business (Brown)

The Vatican Collection: The Legacy of the Popes (Ohio Wesleyan, Brown)

Renoir: A Major Retrospective Exhibition at the Museum of Fine Arts (Brown)

A Conversation with Alex Haley (Brown Commencement Forum)

Explorations in Space (Brown Commencement Forum)

The Silent Generation Reconsidered: Women of the '50s (Brown Commencement Forum)

Why Do Americans Hate the News Media? (Brown Commencement Forum)

Jerusalem: Present and Future (Brown Commencement Forum)

Swimming in the Mainstream: Black Life in Corporate America (Brown Commencement Forum)

Folly in Government (on Vietnam) (Brown Commencement Forum)

The Medical Consequences of Nuclear War (Brown Commencement Forum)

A Half Century of Commitment to Social Justice (Brown Commencement Forum)

Ernest J. Gaines Reading (Author of *The Autobiography of Miss Jane Pittman*, reading from his latest novel, *A Gathering of Old Men*) (Brown Commencement Forum)

Dimensions: Sculpture and Beyond (Brown)

Saving Yesterday and Building Tomorrow (architectural preservation) (Brown)

Views of Earth: The Johnson Space Center (Brown)

Kaleidoscope: The Plants of Northern Ohio (Ohio Wesleyan)

Outsiders and Insiders in American Culture (history) (Ohio Wesleyan)

Reaganomics Revisited (Ohio Wesleyan)

Creativity and the Human Experience (Ohio Wesleyan)

Topics on Faith in Modern American Life (Notre Dame Reunion Seminars, a day and one-half each June)

A Day on Capitol Hill (Georgetown)

Salt Marshes of Rhode Island (Brown, field trip with lecture and box lunch)

Shakespeare: His World, His Stage, His Audiences (at the Folger Library and Theater) (Georgetown)

Learning to Live with Computers (Indiana)

How the Newer Tax Laws Affect You in 1985 (Indiana)

What's New about Aging? (Indiana)

Assertive Discipline for Parents (Indiana)

Documentary Photography in America (Indiana)

Germany Forty Years after the Holocaust (Indiana)

Hoagy Carmichael: The Stardust of His Songs (Indiana)

Criminal Process and the Supreme Court: Are the "Good Guys" Winning? (Indiana)

World Hunger (Indiana)

Happy Birthday, Bach (Indiana)

Happy Birthday, Handel (Indiana)

Poetry of James Whitcomb Riley (Indiana)

South Africa under Fire in the United States (Indiana)

Drugs and Infectious Diseases (Indiana)

Adolescent Peer Socialization (Indiana)

El Greco's Toledo: A Slide Tour of Spain's Imperial City (Indiana)

Masculinity and Femininity in Dance, Mime, and Theatre: Perceptions of Performers and Audiences (Indiana)

Parks and Gardens, a World-Wide Phenomenon (Indiana)

The Golden Age of Radio (Indiana)

Future U.S. Trade Strategies: The Albanian or the Hong Kong Solution? (Indiana)

The Environment: Quality of Life in the '80s and '90s (Wisconsin-Madison)

Biotechnology: What's in the Future for Life on Earth? (Wisconsin-Madison)

Television Literacy: Changing Values in the Information Age (Indiana)

How NOT to End Inflation (Indiana)

Bible as Literature (Indiana)

Whose Word Is God's Word and How Do We Know? (Vanderbilt reunion lecture)

Reflections on Our Lives in Families (Vanderbilt reunion lecture)

Living in Faith with Uncertainty (Vanderbilt reunion lecture)

Educating Gifted and Talented Children (Indiana)

Magic and Religion: The Beginning of Mormonism as a Case Study (Indiana)

Ballet as a Performing Art (Indiana)

Contemplating Nuclear Catastrophe: Can We Live Sanely in the Shadow of the "Unthinkable"? (Indiana)

Life Insurance (Indiana)

Cardiopulmonary Resuscitation (CPR) (Indiana)

The Beat Goes On: Rock and Roll from Elvis to Prince (Indiana)

Immigration and America (Indiana)

The Adolescent in Literature from *Romeo and Juliet* to *The Catcher in the Rye* (Indiana)

Religious Influences in the Public Schools (Indiana)

Some Contemporary Abuses of Religion (Northwestern)

The Courts and Pro-Life (Williams pre-football seminar)

Family Communication: Cohesion and Change (Northwestern)

The Middle East (Indiana)

Poland and Recent Events (Indiana)

Central America Today (Northwestern)

An Introduction to the Heavens (with Planetarium Tour) (Indiana)

Teen Sexuality: A Matter of Choices (Indiana)

Fear of Crime as a Policy Problem (Indiana)

Winning: A Challenge for Women (Indiana)

The Future of Welfare States? (Indiana)

Quarks: How Do We Know They Are Really There? (Indiana)

Business in Your Life (Alabama)

Personal Health (Alabama)

State Issues (Indiana, Alabama, Wisconsin, SMU)

Art and the Individual (Alabama)

How to Read a Portrait (Ohio Wesleyan)

"The Ladies in Waiting" by Valazquez, the Favorite Painting of Intellectuals (Williams pre-football weekend seminar)

From Food to Philosophy: Meaning in Still Life Painting (Wisconsin-Madison)

How Musical Questions Influence Scientific Research (Northwestern)

The Oracle at Delphi: Myth and Legend (Ohio U)

Economic Myths and Realities (Wisconsin-Madison)

Wills and Estate Planning (Ohio U)

Organized Chaos: The Nature of Chaos and Its Patterns (Ohio U)

Beyond Freedom of Education: The Search for Classroom Excellence and Reform (Ohio U)

Midlife Seminars (Middlebury reunions)

Marionette Theater (family event by Tufts University)

Walking Tours of Boston (Tufts)

Cordon Bleu Cooking (Tufts)

New Perspectives on the Living World (Tufts)

The Russians (Ohio U; Northwestern; Commencement Seminar at University of North Carolina-Chapel Hill, hereafter UNC-CH). NOTE: UNC-CH's weekend seminars became so popular that evening seminars seem to have been discontinued.

Moscow Graffiti as Signposts of Social Change (Northwestern)

Beijing Graffiti (Dartmouth)

From the Taj Mahal to the Alhambra: Arab Contributions to the World (Wisconsin-Madison)

One-author one-work evening seminars (contemporary writers: John Irving, Walker Percy, Norman Cousins, Milton and Rose Friedman, southern fiction, others) (UNC-CH)

The Post-Modernist Controversy in Fiction (Northwestern)

Freud and the Twentieth Century (UNC-CH)

Socrates: Living the Examined Life (UNC-CH)

The Darkness at the Core: Hitler and the Twentieth Century (UNC-CH)

Hitler Fifty Years Later (Williams pre-football seminar)

The Cherry Blossom and the Honda: Contemporary Japan and Its Traditional Roots (also expanded into one-week Vacation College) (UNC-CH)

Professional Ethics—Legal, Medical, and Journalistic: A Case Study (ethical questions from morality to accountability about heart transplants) (Northwestern; repeated later the same year)

The Institutionalization of Care: The Death of Community (Northwestern)

Stress and Life Cycles (Northwestern)

Eating Disorders: Anorexia Nervosa and Bulimia (Wisconsin-Madison)

More Than Fun and Games: The Meaning of Sports in American Life (Northwestern)

Spiritual Survival in the Twentieth Century (UNC-CH)

Makers of the Modern Mind (UNC-CH)

Makers of the American Mind (UNC-CH)

Images of the City ("Images of the City and the Anti-City Bias: The Cultural Geography of the City in the United States" and "Alternative Views of Cities in Europe and Non-Western Societies") (Ohio Wesleyan Saturday seminar; Northwestern with different title)

Vigilantism and Self-Defense (Northwestern)

The Changing Family (Northwestern)

Time Management for the Two-Career Family (Illinois)

Understanding War (UNC-CH)

Debate on the Economy (Rutgers)

Managing Your Money (Northwestern)

Theater Programs (Rutgers)

Symphony Programs (Rutgers)

Glee Club Programs (Rutgers)

TOPICS FOR WEEKEND PROGRAMS (THREE AND FOUR DAYS)

Nature's Balances (Cornell, Mohonk Mountain House seminar)

Mountain Wildflower Weekend (UNC-CH)

The Appalachians and the Poconos: Evolution of a Folded Mountain Range (Lehigh, fall program)

Yale in Yosemite (Yale, perennial in May)

Wetlands Weekend (Lehigh in New Jersey Wetlands)

UNC and the Sea (UNC-CH)

Marine Lab Alumni College Weekend Seminars (Duke, perennial in April)

Washington Weekend (UNC-CH)

Our Resourceful Earth: Learning to Make the Most of It (Duke on Martha's Vineyard, fall)

The Presidency in 1984: Challenges for the Future (Princeton on Martha's Vineyard, fall)

Stress and Burnout (Brown in California)

A Weekend with Mr. Dickens (UNC, Greensboro Chapter)

Choices (Pomona weekend for alumnae and women undergraduates)

Work, Play, and Recreation (Lehigh)

Dreams: Freud & Jung (Notre Dame)

Drawing: Anyone Can Learn (Notre Dame)

Art & Music Live: A Weekend in the Country (Connecticut College)

Religion and Politics: From Constantine to Reagan (Yale)

Ethics and the Individual (Smith)

A World of Gardens (Smith)

Values, Experience, and the Individual: What If? (Lehigh)

The Humanities in the Modern World (UNC-CH)

Teaching Values: The Problems of Moral Education (UNC-CH)

Human Rights and the Law (UNC-CH)

Modern Art, Film, and Literature: The Search for Meaning (UNC-CH)

The Gin Game and Modern Drama (UNC-CH)

Islam and Its Modern World (UNC-CH)

Human Welfare and Social Services (UNC-CH)

The Culture of Narcissism (UNC-CH)

Myth, Marriage, and Salvation (UNC-CH)

Poland: Decline and Fall of the Russian Empire? (UNC-CH)

Civilization in Crisis: The 14th and the 20th Centuries—An Exploration of Barbara Tuchman's *A Distant Mirror* (UNC-CH)

Distinguished Faculty Seminars (UNC-CH)

American Foreign Policy in a Dangerous World (UNC-CH)

The Demise of the Welfare State in America? (UNC-CH)

American Architecture and American Values (UNC-CH)

Central America: Political Earthquake Zone? (UNC-CH)

Human Values and the Nuclear Arms Race (UNC-CH)

Great Authors (Pinter, Wilde, Shaw, Shakespeare, Dickens, Moliere, others: Wilde and Shaw were most popular) (UNC-CH)

Mark Twain (UNC-CH, Dartmouth, Notre Dame [*Huckleberry Finn*])

What Photographs Have Done to Us (UNC-CH)

Sports and American Values (UNC-CH)

The Old Testament: Old and New Interpretation (UNC-CH)

Myths of the Ancient Traveler: The Greek Tales of Mystery, Exploration, and the Imagination (Cornell Reunion Week)

The Greeks: The Cursed and the Blessed (UNC-CH)

The Elusive French (UNC-CH)

The Soviet Union (Yale)

China (UNC-CH, Yale)

Paris: Capital of Artistic, Historical and Literary Revolutions (Yale)

The Madonna and Modernism: Renaissance and Modern Art in Contrast (UNC-CH)

Justice, Social Change, and the Third World (UNC-CH)

Women and Power (UNC-CH)

The Black and the White: Understanding South Africa (UNC-CH)

New Light on a Brilliant Morning: Impressionism and Post-impressionism (UNC-CH)

Evil (UNC-CH)

Complications: Moral Issues in Contemporary Health Care (UNC-CH)

American Foreign Policy and the Lessons of Vietnam (UNC-CH)

Seeing with an American Eye (UNC-CH)

Myth and Reality (very popular) (UNC-CH)

State Politics (North Carolina by UNC-CH)

Oceans and Ice: Ithaca's Geologic Past (Cornell Reunion Week)

Promise or Peril: Recombinant DNA (Mt. Holyoke)

Evolution: What Difference Does It Make? (UNC-CH)

Raleigh's England (very popular) (UNC-CH)

Middle Class Guilt (very popular) (UNC-CH)

Love, As You Like It (UNC-CH)

Capitalism and Christianity (UNC-CH)

The End of the World (UNC-CH)

Family Life in America Is Changing (Rutgers)

Inflation and the American Psyche (Rutgers)

Outdoor Weekend Trips (Canoe Trip, Delaware Water Gap; Pocono Weekend; Pinelands Flora, Fauna, and Folklore) (Rutgers)

New Directions for Society in the 1980s (Rutgers)

The Media as a Social Force: Its Influence and Responsibility (Rutgers)

Conference on Design (Stanford)

Ethical Issues in Medical Practice (Notre Dame)

TOPICS FOR WEEKDAY OR WEEKEND SERIES (2–8 HALF-DAY OR EVENING PROGRAMS)

Community Issues in Politics, Education, Culture (Brown, 3 City Hall Luncheons, spring)

Principles of Modern Medicine (Alumnae of Northwestern, 10 weekdays, fall)

Alchemy for the 21st Century: Water, Air, Earth and Fire (M.I.T., winter)

Certainties and Surprises in Presidential Elections (Tufts)

Presidential Election Series (Rutgers)

The Apocalypse (Georgetown). NOTE: Georgetown's series take place during its one-week alumni college.

Barbara Tuchman's *A Distant Mirror* (Georgetown)

Shaping Faith in the Modern World: The Jesuit Tradition of Prayer (Georgetown)

Justice in the Book of *Job* (Georgetown)

The Ethics of Intervention (U.S. Foreign Policy) (Georgetown)

Common Folk in the Era of the American Revolution (Georgetown)

Impressionism (Georgetown)

The Painting of George Innes (Georgetown)

Art Deco in Washington (Georgetown)

Chicago and New York: The Capital of American Architecture (Alumnae of Northwestern, 10 weekdays, fall)

The Contemporary Intellectual World (Important developments in philosophy, theology, literature, and the sciences) (Georgetown)

U.S. Constitution Bicentennial (Georgetown)

Graham Greene: Two Novels (*The End of the Affair; The Quiet American*) (Georgetown)

Faith and Reason: A Happy Marriage? (St. Thomas Aquinas' five ways of demonstrating the existence of God) (Georgetown)

Mad about the Raj: Forster's *A Passage to India* and Scott's *Staying On* (India under British Rule) (Georgetown)

A Portrait of Jesus (the difficulty of finding the historical Jesus) (Georgetown)

Following in the Footsteps of Alexander the Great (Brown)

George Washington: A Hero for All Seasons (Brown)

The Legacy of Thomas Jefferson (Georgetown)

The U.S. in Vietnam: Was It a Just War? (Georgetown)

The Tradition of Ignatian Spirituality (St. Ignatius Loyola) (Georgetown)

The Social Responsibilities of Business (Georgetown)

American Art in the Mid-Nineteenth Century (Georgetown)

Eighteenth-Century American Architecture and Decorative Arts (Georgetown)

The Catholic Church and Politics in Nicaragua and El Salvador (Georgetown)

The 1920s: America Before Roosevelt and Before Reagan (Georgetown)

Daily Life in Eighteenth-Century London (Georgetown)

Shakespeare's Comic Vision (Georgetown)

Aristotle on the Good Life (Georgetown)

Christ in Contemporary Theology (Georgetown)

The Medieval Cathedral (Georgetown)

Imagination and Reality: Ways of Human Understanding (Georgetown)

The Immigrant Experience in America (Georgetown)

What Is Christianity? Paul's Answer (Georgetown)

Cats (the Broadway hit musical) (Georgetown)

Eros: Ever Ancient, Ever New (love and sexuality in Plato's 4th century B.C. Athens and in contemporary American society) (Georgetown)

1984: Orwell and History (Georgetown)

The Spirit of Plato's Philosophy: The Art of Asking a Question (Georgetown)

The Civil War in the Shenandoah Valley (including Gettysburg battlefield tour) (Georgetown)

A Way of Seeing: An Introduction to Field Ornithology (Georgetown)

"Such Sweet Thunder": Shakespeare's Vision of Love (Georgetown)

Stanford's Great Authors Lecture Series (for example, Shakespeare on Stage) (Stanford)

Revolution in the Earth Sciences (Colby College)

The 1960s: Expectations, Confrontations, Liberations (Georgetown)

American Interior Design and Decorative Art in the 18th Century (Georgetown)

The Art of Antoine Watteau (Georgetown)

The Art of James McNeill Whistler (Georgetown)

Life and Culture in Tudor England (Georgetown)

The Gospel of Mark (Georgetown)

Existentialism: Values in Question (Georgetown)

The Great Depression: America's Response to Hard Times in the 1930s (Georgetown)

Twentieth-Century Germany (Alumnae of Northwestern, 10 weekdays, fall)

American Literature and the Great Depression (Georgetown)

Fiction Now (Alumnae of Northwestern, 10 weekdays, fall)

The Infinite Variety of Theatrical Experience (Alumnae of Northwestern, 10 weekdays, fall)

The Plays of Henrik Ibsen (Georgetown)

Socrates: The Man and the Paradox (reading the *Euthyphro*, the *Apology*, and the *Crito* for what they tell us today) (Georgetown)

The Visual Arts in the Islamic World (Georgetown)

Popular Rule in America (the American idea of democracy) (Georgetown)

The American Bishops' Pastoral Letter on War and Peace (Georgetown)

Urban Planning in America (Georgetown)

Continuity and Change in the American Political System (Georgetown)

Personal Financial Planning (Illinois)

Planning Your Retirement (Illinois)

How to Start Your Own Business (Illinois)

The Changing American Family (Colby College)

Techniques of Effective Communication (Colby College)

The American Identity: Male and Female Visions (Colby College)

TOPICS FOR ALUMNI COLLEGES
(ONE WEEK OR LONGER)

Archaeology & the World of the Bible (Johns Hopkins); NOTE: JH always devises alumni colleges in "the history of ideas" format.

The Bible: In the Beginning and Now (UNC-CH)

Religion and Public Education (UNC-CH)

The Making of the American: An Unfinished Agenda (JH)

Hail, Holy Land: The Idea of America (Dartmouth)

The American Dream (Dartmouth)

America Evolving (Penn State)

Who's on First? Baseball and American Culture (Cornell)

Historical Geology: Chasms in Earth, Time and Perspective (JH)

A Visitor's Guide to the Universe (Cornell)

Evolution: Change through Time (Penn State)

Concepts of Progress (JH)

Myth: From Prehistory to Posthistory (JH)

Lest the Old Traditions Fail: Myth, Heroic Legend, and the Challenge of Change (Dartmouth)

The Persistence of Myth (Northwestern)

Quest for Balance: Needs, Resources, Values (Ohio Wesleyan)

Man vs. Nature: Who's Ahead? (Dartmouth)

Visions and Nightmares: Conflicting Images of Human Nature (Northwestern)

1984: Being Human in a Brave New World (Wellesley)

Wholeness in a Fractured World (Ohio Wesleyan)

The Modernist Revolution: Breakdown or Breakthrough (Northwestern)

Lessons from the Past: The Worlds of 1886 and 1986 (College of Wooster [Ohio])

Over Here, Over There: Artists Abroad in England and America (Duke)

The Making of the Self (Northwestern)

Geology and Life in Montana's Beartooth Mountains (Franklin and Marshall, Princeton)

Energy for the 21st Century (University of the South)

Pluralism in the Americas (Washington and Lee)

Faces of Change: Contemporary Black America (Cornell)

American History: Domestic and Foreign Challenges (University of Virginia)

The Reagan Era after Reagan (Cornell)

The Right to Dissent: Individual Freedom vs. Social Responsibility (Northwestern)

Freedom and Authority in America (Dartmouth)

Law: Who Needs It? (Dartmouth)

The Brain (Cornell)

Psychology: Inner Depths and Outer Limits (Cornell)

Origins of Modern Consciousness: Wagner, Nietzsche, Freud, and Kafka (Cornell)

The Future of Freedom and Dignity: The Ethical Challenge of the Life Sciences (Smith, Mount Holyoke, Amherst, University of Massachusetts, Hampshire College)

Human Values and the Health Care System (UNC-CH)

Society and Health (Washington and Lee)

Genetic Engineering (Whitman)

Scientific Frontiers (Washington and Lee)

The New Biology (Brown)

Adult Development: Beginning in the Middle (Illinois)

The Minds of Men and Robots (Lehigh)

Technology and American Life (University of Chicago)

The Machine in the Garden: Science, Technology & Culture (Dartmouth)

The Limits of Economic Growth (Whitman)

Freedom (University of Washington)

Society in Search of Values (Ohio Wesleyan)

The Crisis of Values in a Changing World (Dartmouth)

Preparing for Life in the 1970s (Dartmouth)

Dis-Connections: Changing Relationships in American Life (Dartmouth)

Men and Women: What's the Difference? (Dartmouth)

Men and Women in the Movies (Lehigh)

Sex and Sensibility: Men, Women, and Love in the Western World (Northwestern)

Where Have All the Heroes Gone? (Dartmouth, UNC-CH)

Hot and Cool: The American Jazz Tradition (Cornell)

The Arts: Return to Realism (Illinois)

The Arts in Our Lives (Brown)

The Modern Arts and the Modern World (UNC-CH)

The Creative Frontier: What's Happening in the Arts (Cornell)

The Inner Frontier: People and Their Institutions (Cornell)

Interpretations of Contemporary Religious Life (UNC-CH)

Popular Culture and American Values (UNC-CH)

Society and the Media (Washington and Lee)

Espionage and Intelligence (Cornell)

The Soviets (Princeton)

The Soviet Union and Détente: The Past as Prelude to the Present (Wellesley)

The Soviet Union: Rut, Reform, or Revolt? (Stanford)

Russian Past—Soviet Present (Brown)

Russia and America: Perception and Reality (UNC-CH, Cornell)

The Russian Temper (Cornell)

China: Politics, History, and Culture (Illinois)

China: Its Heritage and Its Promise (UNC-CH)

The Ways of Cathay: China Past and China Present (Cornell)

China: Beyond Confucius and Mao (Wellesley)

The Cherry Blossom and the Honda: Contemporary Japan and Its Traditional Roots (UNC-CH)

Japan: The Robot and the Lotus (Stanford)

Understanding the Third World (Wellesley)

The Middle East: The Image and the Reality (UNC-CH)

A Portrait of Egypt (Cornell)

South Africa: Crisis and Challenge (Cornell)

Workshop on Alaska (University of Alaska)

What Makes the South Southern? (UNC-CH)

North Carolina: Its History, Its Culture, Its People—A Reassessment (UNC-CH)

The Greeks (UNC-CH)

Classical Athens (Washington and Lee)

Periclean Athens (Yale)

The Romans (UNC-CH)

The Nature of Empire (Dartmouth)

The Spirit and the Flesh: Exploring the Middle Ages (Wellesley)

The Quest for Perfection: A Modern Pilgrimage through the Middle Ages (Dartmouth)

The Renaissance: Forms, Reforms & Revolutions (Dartmouth, UNC-CH, The University of the South)

The Napoleonic Era: The Emergence of the Modern World (Dartmouth)

Beethoven and the World of the Romantics (Wellesley)

Music in the Age of Romanticism (Cornell)

Elizabethan England: Court and Country (Washington and Lee)

Victorian England: The Lasting Legacy (UNC-CH)

The World of Upstairs, Downstairs: Edwardian England, 1901–1914 (UNC-CH)

The Civil War: America Asunder (UNC-CH)

The Twentieth Century (Dartmouth)

Reassessing the 60s: Where Have All the Flowers Gone? (UNC-CH)

Coming Together, Coming Apart: America in the 1960s (Cornell)

Great Writers, Etc. (Washington and Lee)

Government in America: On Our Backs? On Our Side? (UNC-CH)

Illuminations on Foggy Bottom (U.S. Foreign Relations) (Brown)

The Gilded Age: America from 1865 to 1914 (UNC-CH)

Film and Fiction (Yale)

The Play's the Thing: Perspectives on Theater (Cornell)

War & Peace (Dartmouth)

The Last Humans? (Rensselaerville Institute)

TOPICS/DESTINATIONS FOR ALUMNI COLLEGES ABROAD

The Americas

Bermuda (Lehigh taught geology and ecology in 1980)

Mexico/Yucatan (Mayan culture)

Peru and the Andes (Dartmouth, Brown, Stanford have taught cultural history, 1982 through 1986)

Peru and the Galápagos (Darwin)

Sea Cloud (four-masted tall ship; Dartmouth has taught American literature of the sea; African-American history of the slave trade; Mayan culture; Stanford has taught marine geology in the Caribbean; Yale has taught history and culture in the Eastern Mediterranean)

South America (Peru; Amazon; major cities in Brazil and Argentina)

The British Isles

The British Isles (circumnavigation; Princeton taught art, architecture, natural history, and literature; Dartmouth added history to literature; Notre Dame focused on English, Scottish, and Welsh universities to study cultural history)

Elizabethan England (Washington and Lee taught Court & Country)

Cambridge, England (Yale's program featured Tudor Art and Architecture, English Baroque, the Age of Hogarth, the Grand Tour, Reynolds and Gainsborough, the Beginnings of Landscape Painting, Gothic Revival and the Pre-Raphaelites)

Scotland golf tours (Lehigh, Yale)

Continental Europe

Rhine River (Yale taught Reformers on the Rhine: A Century That Changed the World)

Vienna (Brown taught music)

Danube River (cruise; Dartmouth taught the Habsburg dynasty, art, and music)

Rhône River (cruise; Dartmouth taught French and Western European cultural history from the Renaissance)

Italy (circumnavigation; Brown taught Italian Renaissance history, politics, and culture)

Venice and the Shaping of the West (Princeton)

Holland and Belgium (waterways cruise; Brown taught history)

Middle Europe (Berlin, Leipzig, Prague, Vienna; Brown taught German cultural history; Holyoke taught music)

Scandinavia (Brown taught the Vikings, Scandinavian history and contemporary affairs, art and culture in 1985; Holyoke taught art and literature in 1985)

The Baltic (usually including Leningrad; Dartmouth taught cultural history and religious history in 1983)

Soviet Union (Cornell Wintersession Trip to Leningrad and Moscow; credit available)

Russia (Stanford, Brown, and Dartmouth have taught cultural history in the northern cities, and along the Volga River)

Africa

Great Trade and Spice Route to Africa and the Far East (Yale taught prehistoric cultures, contemporary international affairs)

Kenya, Africa (Stanford has taught the wildlife; Dartmouth cultural history and geology)

Senegal (Mount Holyoke taught literature and civilization; took a French professor and faculty member Shirley Chisholm)

Egypt (cruises or land-based trips)

Eastern Mediterranean

Eastern Mediterranean (Greek Isle cruises teach Greek and Turkish cultural roots; Ancient Civilizations cruises may add Hebrew cultural history)

Southern Pacific and the Far East

Sea Islands (Stanford taught culture, and added astronomy during the Halley's Comet period in winter 1986)

Bali and Java

Tahiti and the Society Islands (Lehigh)

China

Japan

DOMESTIC TRAVEL PROGRAMS

New England and the Sea (Williams at Mystic, Connecticut)

New England Cruise (Eastern Provinces of Canada and New England; Yale)

A Naturalist's View of Cape Cod (Williams)

Newport, Rhode Island (University of Pennsylvania taught Three Centuries of American Splendor)

Virginia (University of Pennsylvania taught at Charlottesville and Monticello: Thomas Jefferson and His Eighteenth-Century World)

Mississippi cruises

The Three Cultures of the Southwest (one week in Santa Fe; Brown)

Grand Canyon (Stanford)

Alumni College in the Rockies (Williams)

Baja California Sur (Stanford; Cornell taught The Desert and the Sea)

California Delta Cruise (San Francisco to Sacramento) (Stanford taught Gold Rush history)

Alaska (Dartmouth taught geology, literature, native culture)

Hawaii (Princeton taught The U.S. and the Pacific Powers: Partnership or Rivalry?; Cornell taught natural history)

St. Croix (Cornell taught a Natural Ecology and Marine Biology Winterlude)

The Faculty

With format, location, and topic in mind, it is time to hire and pay the faculty; and to decide whether to award credit, continuing education units (CEUs), or certificates of participation to participants. Institutions with academic directors turn over faculty hiring to them.

HIRING THE FACULTY

Whether an institution hires a different faculty director for each program (as Harvard does), or an administrator hires the faculty after consulting academic leaders (as does Ohio Wesleyan University), fine programs usually start one of three ways.

An attractive topic may surface in the minds of administrators, faculty members, or the alumni themselves, and the best faculty members are hired to teach it. The idea may come from the media, imitation of other schools' successful programs, or a clear knowledge of subjects the sponsoring institution teaches best.

A charismatic and especially effective teacher might offer a subject from his or her primary research field, a secondary academic passion, or an avocational area of expertise. Some schools are known for expertise in particular academic fields, and many good faculty members or teams can repeat subjects in those fields again and again.

A place, event, or artifact may be turned into a seminar featuring an appropriate teacher. Chapter 4 offered several examples of off-campus, one-week alumni colleges that take advantage of special places, like Martha's Vineyard, New Jersey's

Pine Barrens, or a marine laboratory off the coast of North Carolina. The arrival of "The Treasures of Tutankhamun" at a major museum near the campus exemplifies an event on which to build a seminar. Artifacts that may become the focus of a seminar include works of art, architectural monuments, and restored period furniture or jewelry.

PAYING THE FACULTY

Professionals expect to be paid for their work, and when a faculty member is asked to teach, he or she expects to be paid. Alumni offices also ask faculty members to talk about the state of the institution at alumni clubs. That is often considered a community service, and an honorarium is not required, although expenses are usually covered. Some colleges and universities ask the faculty to teach alumni continuing education programs for free, as if these were community service performances. The risk is that these institutions may occasionally receive service in kind: a canned presentation or old lecture, lightly dusted. The best faculty members will develop an excellent new piece for the occasion, but even most of these would feel better about an honorarium. We do not want to start off on the wrong foot with the faculty as we build an alumni continuing education program. Alumni get real education from these programs, and they will pay reasonable tuition for it. Part of that tuition should end up in faculty pockets.

How much to pay the faculty varies a great deal. Some institutions pay a token amount, others remunerate well. Some set flat rates, others peg honoraria to faculty salaries (the Harriet P. Arnold chairholder will cost a program more than this year's newest assistant professor). Different, equally qualified professionals will give different advice on this subject. We cannot go wrong to pay small but meaningful honoraria, on the theory that we are more likely to get fresh material, delivered with enthusiasm. It seems slightly preferable to pay the same fee no matter who does the teaching. Since only the best faculty should appear in alumni continuing education programs (because of their public relations impact, among other reasons), in the end most of your faculty budget will turn up in the right pockets.

The range of honoraria paid to a faculty member for teaching in an alumni continuing education program in 1986 was generally $200–$1500 per week. For short seminars, the range was from $100–$500 per day. There is still an element of community service in alumni continuing education teaching, and honoraria levels can be set just low enough so that no one forgets, but not so low as to offend either the faculty or the alumni.

The total compensation to faculty who teach in alumni continuing education is the sum of their honoraria plus benefits package contributions tied to compensation and the other advantages of participation described in Chapter 2: the opportunity to teach with new colleagues in interdisciplinary programs; the freedom to try new techniques and new materials, which would not be approved so easily for the regular curriculum; the chance to teach interesting adult students; and the opportunity to travel to off-campus seminars and alumni colleges abroad. Added up, these are extremely attractive circumstances under which to teach. Alumni continuing education programs seldom fail to attract the right faculty members if program directors assemble the right combination of rewards.

William Oostenink, professor of biology, organized an alumni college at Colgate University that operated almost entirely on the freely given energy of a few faculty members for five years in the late 1970s and early 1980s. Oostenink had been heavily involved in volunteer speaking engagements at Colgate alumni clubs. He was also keenly aware of the value of two Colgate summer programs that provided access for adults to the Colgate faculty: one a program for high school teachers funded by the National Science Foundation, the other an IBM seminar begun in the late 1960s. Oostenink and a few colleagues studied these three concepts and developed Colgate's alumni college. The athletic department cooperated by providing a children's program. Coming almost entirely from the faculty, Oostenink's alumni college was a special accomplishment in which he took great pride.

Oostenink is by no means alone. Many faculty members at a variety of institutions across the country, once involved in alumni continuing education, come to value it highly and share their feelings with colleagues and alumni alike. As among past participants, their enthusiasm is the best promotion for the program.

Charles T. Wood, Daniel Webster Professor of History at Dartmouth College, taught his first summer alumni college in 1967 as a discussion leader, served as academic director and lectured in three more alumni colleges in 1973–1975, and altogether has been a lecturer or discussion leader in dozens of alumni colleges, club and other alumni seminars, and three alumni colleges abroad. His own words offer a fitting conclusion to this discussion of the faculty's role in alumni continuing education programs:

> *Probably most faculty members become involved in Alumni Continuing Education because of the pay, but we stay involved because of the excitement. The truth is that our regular teaching brings us into contact with students who, no matter how bright, lack experience. In turn, this deficiency means that those whom we normally teach have no more than theoretical grounds for challenging our interpretations and concepts, those models of reality on which an academic understanding of reality is typically based. And, much as we may resent having our thoughts challenged in specific cases, we know that it is through such student doubts that we improve our insight.*
>
> *Those participating in Alumni Continuing Education may have lost many of the purely academic skills enjoyed by our regular students, but they bring to the task a variety of understanding based on what those students can never have: experience. As a result, teaching the truly mature provides a kind of stimulation quite different from that of normal classes. Vast ranges of human thought, so baffling to the young undergraduate, are no longer so for older students, and the challenges mounted come less from theoretical objections than from knowledge gained after years of practical living, often of a kind that we faculty members have never had. It has the effect of keeping us honest—and on our toes.*
>
> *Over and beyond that, Alumni Continuing Education liberates faculty even as it liberates participants. It allows us to transcend the narrow scholarly confines of our individual disciplines because its very nature*

and purpose encourages us to speak to those issues that are truly important in the disciplines we profess and not just to their scholarly minutiae. In addition, insofar as programs in continuing education are frequently interdisciplinary in focus and team-taught in format, they provide an opportunity not just to learn from friends, but also to find out (often after many years) exactly what it is that they really do. So to colleagues I say: "Try it, you'll like it!" [text provided to Steven L. Calvert on June 17, 1986].

Curriculum Planning

Once the faculty have been hired, someone must be responsible for quality control over initial curriculum planning, the way a program is described in promotional brochures, the execution of the program itself, and followup evaluation. This is the sponsoring unit's job, not the faculty's.

Teachers hired for their first alumni continuing education program may appreciate guidance on the best length for lectures (thirty to fifty minutes), the right balance of lecturing and discussion (more than half discussion), the appropriate level of sophistication for this audience of generalists (Sallie Riggs suggests a level between a *New York Times* article and a professional paper that avoids jargon but never talks down to adults), and the amount of advance and followup study (one 300-page book per program day). Advance preparation by alumni should be considered optional, and teachers in the program should keep in mind that (like undergraduates) some participants will have done it all and others none of it.

Offering Credit, CEUs, and Certificates of Participation

Most alumni continuing education programs are strictly noncredit. Papers and tests are missing, a fact that some programs highlight in their promotional materials. There are a few exceptions, but sponsors walk a thin line between offering an exciting intellectual challenge and expecting too much work from adults who may be attending to get a break from work.

ALUMNI COLLEGE
August 4–15, 1985

Certificate of Participation

To Whom It May Concern:

This is to certify that **JOHN DOE** attended Elvira Alumni College 1985 from August 4 through August 15 at Elvira College in Oak Ridge,Tennessee.

This year's program, entitled "Lest the Old Traditions Fail: Myth, Heroic Legend, and the Challenge of Change," offered participants the opportunity to immerse themselves in the historical, cultural, religious, and literary backgrounds of several civilizations—western and non-western, ancient and modern—in order to investigate two issues. The first issue was how to understand the simultaneous similarities and differences among myths, legends, stories, and other cultural artifacts from different cultures in different places and times throughout human history. The second was to understand the ways in which these myths and legends undergo change through time and different cultures in order to perform their functions in human societies.

Participants were sent to read in advance Sigmund Freud's Moses and Monotheism; Hugh A. MacDougall's Racial Myth in English History: Trojans, Teutons, and Anglo-Saxons; N. Scott Momaday's The Way to Rainy Mountain; J. R. R. Tolkien's The Hobbit; selections from Richard Wilhelm's Confucius and Confucianism, James R. Walker's Lakota Myth, Karl Kroeber's Traditional American Indian Literatures, and The Bible; and the following essays or articles: "The Canon of Yao" and "The Canon of Shun" from Clae Waltham's Shu Ching, Book of History, Derk Bodde's "Myths of Ancient China" from Samuel Noah Kramer's Myths of the Ancient World, Robert G. Henricks' "The Hero Pattern and the Life of Confucius," three short selections from The Golden Legend of Jacobus de Voragine (translated and adapted by Granger Ryan and Helmut Ripperger), Robert A. Oden's translations of The Gilgamesh Epic and of "Atrahasis: The Babylonian Legend of the Flood" (the oldest flood narrative), and later Moses legends.

Fifty-five hours were devoted to the academic program: 32.5 hours of classroom lectures, 10 hours of small seminar discussions and one 1.5-hour faculty panel discussion, 10.5 hours of feature films directly related to the Alumni College theme, and a half-hour tour of the university Library exhibitions developed especially for Alumni College and its theme.

Elvira College regards participation in Alumni College as the equivalent of a three semester hour course, although it does not offer credit toward any degree for participation in Alumni College.

This Certificate has the force of an official transcript.

[signed]

George Baltimore, Ph.D., Director
Alumni Continuing Education
August 15, 1985

Attachment: Alumni College 1985 Schedule of Events

241

When the continuing education department or another academic unit sponsors or cosponsors the program, credit or continuing education units (CEUs) may be available: Duke and the University of North Carolina at Chapel Hill offer CEUs. Most alumni offices or alumni associations have difficulty getting authority to grant credit or CEUs. In addition, credit and CEUs require record-keeping and transcript services that might place an unwanted burden on an alumni association. The continuing education office usually has this machinery in place.

Still, alumni colleges that provide six or seven hours a day of academic effort owe participants some symbol of their achievement. One solution is to give them, automatically or on request, a certificate of participation, enumerating faculty contact hours or otherwise defining the program's academic activity. This kind of certificate has earned teachers advancement in primary and secondary school districts, and one participant earned five course credits toward her bachelor's degree at another institution for each of two alumni colleges. A sample certificate is provided on page 241.

Brigham Young's Stephen L. Barrett believes that alumni colleges abroad that include faculty teaching should offer credit. As the number of schools offering top-notch alumni continuing education programs increases, those that offer credentials could find themselves with a competitive advantage over those that do not, especially where different institutions offer the same package in the same area. On the other hand, if a concern for credentials begins to dominate alumni continuing education, the program will begin to lose its identity among the other continuing education programs.

CHAPTER 9

FINANCING A COMPLETE ALUMNI CONTINUING EDUCATION PROGRAM

How do we pay for alumni continuing education? Alumni continuing education can be nearly cost-free, even when it pays for new staff to run the programs. Before the institution gets to that point, however, several financial matters will be of interest to professionals in continuing education or alumni relations. This chapter assesses the financial implications of such programs for sponsoring colleges and universities, touches on several sensitive areas, reviews financial arguments for and against alumni continuing education, discusses how to finance individual programs, and recommends strategies for funding a complete menu of educational programs for alumni. We will present sample budgets for an alumni college, an alumni seminar, alumni colleges abroad, and the overall alumni continuing education program.

Financing Alumni Continuing Education: The Big Picture

Continuing education is big business, and getting bigger fast. The Census Bureau reported in 1985 that most college students were 22 or older; and that in the preceding fifteen years the percentage aged 25–29 increased from 11.4 to 14.2, and among those aged 30–34 it almost doubled to 9.9 *(Washington Post)*. Providers outside higher education—including corporate class-rooms—already sell more adult education to this expanding market than do colleges and universities.

Many academic institutions, in response, now contract to provide continuing professional and other adult education pro-grams to business and industry. M.I.T.'s Enterprise Forums bring alumni and faculty expertise to bear on the start-up busi-ness problems of young technology-based companies owned by alumni and others. The Stanford Alumni Association's Con-tinuing Education Executive Programs serve alumni and others who want business-oriented courses pitched at a level the gen-eral manager or investor can understand. These programs are taught by arts and sciences faculty rather than teachers from the Stanford Business School, which offers its own professional education seminars.

ALUMNI CONTINUING EDUCATION'S VALUE-ADDED EFFECT ON DEVELOPMENT

If K. Patricia Cross (1981) is right that one-third of all adults pass through a formal continuing education program each year, and we remember that adults who seek education are those who have had the most already, then we know that America's continuing education classes are filled with college and uni-versity alumni. The basic assumption behind alumni continuing education is that alumni will return to the institution they know and trust when they need more education. Adults bring tens of billions of dollars annually to continuing education. Evidence shows that, when alumni come for alumni continuing educa-tion, they bring more than tuition dollars: their support for alma mater increases and so the university gets tuition dollars and increased philanthropy. At its best, the relationship is mutually supportive, for alumni get much in return: a sense of continuity with their past, a sense of belonging to an institution that is of personal value to them, ties with old friends, and access to a lifetime of education.

The value-added effect of alumni continuing education on college or university fundraising must be clearly understood for everything else in this chapter to make sense. The only serious obstacle raised by institutions not offering alumni continuing education is the cost of developing or maintaining programs. However, any institution putting up this barrier should keep in mind that the long-term financial effects on sponsoring institutions are surprisingly good. Therefore, concerns about any short-term costs of alumni continuing education are shortsighted.

G. Michael McHugh, formerly director of Cornell's Alumni University, has had direct experience with the long-term financial benefits of alumni continuing education:

> *In the final analysis, institutional advancement is what we're all about. As I see it, the alumni college represents one of the purest and most altruistic forms of advancement. Consequently, to me it is a cardinal sin to ever, ever talk about fundraising at an alumni college. The good will your program generates will ultimately pay big dividends, so never try to justify your existence on future alumni giving. That will lead to all the wrong reasons for your existence.*
>
> *Ultimately, perhaps in as long as 10 years, you will be as pleasantly surprised as I was at Cornell to discover that major gift income from only a few participating alumni far exceeded the cumulative cost of the program. Five people cited CAU as one of the major reasons for their gifts—which totalled well over a million dollars. So, I repeat: Don't play the numbers game to justify your program. Simply do it—and do it with style, with grace, and with confidence that you are providing your best [McHugh, 1984, p. 27].*

FOUR VIEWS OF THE ALUMNI CONTINUING EDUCATION BUDGET

Once this value-added effect is understood, we can look confidently at the budget for alumni continuing education in four ways: (1) the annual budget taken alone; (2) institutional funding as an investment in alumni relations; (3) outside funding; and (4) the long-term effects on fundraising. Each view helps to make the programs affordable to virtually every institution. Together, they make a strong case that every institution should offer alumni continuing education.

The Annual Budget. Once a college or university has several kinds of alumni continuing education programs, it can look not only at individual budgets to see if they pay their bills, but it will also see that some programs can help to fund others. The major program types offer more or less predictable budgetary results. Of course, in any program, the budget can be volatile, unpredictable. There is no certain way to predict how many customers will buy a product, but over time a clear pattern has emerged.

The big, on-campus, summer alumni colleges can break even, not including some indirect costs, like salaries, telephone charges, and depreciation on office equipment. Many of them need one to five years to develop a clientele, especially if they are the first kind of alumni continuing education the alumni have ever seen. After that, alumni colleges that develop a market and survive can pay all direct costs. A few cover staff time; one or two could cover telephone calls, office supplies, and depreciation on the buildings used for teaching.

Alumni seminars on the campus can break even, usually not counting some indirect costs. Most off-campus seminars attracting at least 150 participants break even; seminars with more than 200 participants make money. Smaller off-campus seminars at some distance from the institution and therefore requiring faculty air travel may require a small institutional investment.

Alumni colleges abroad can make enough money to fund the rest of the alumni continuing education menu. They do this at several institutions now. Other colleges and universities do not put this much fiscal pressure on alumni colleges abroad, and continue to fund other alumni continuing education programs from institutional budgets. Alumni colleges abroad that have suffered losses may have done so because they did not use a travel agent who takes the front-end financial risks, and bet their own up-front investments on the chance for large profits. No college or university needs to take these risks, because good travel agencies are not hard to find.

Special programs run the fiscal gamut. A major concert with a seminar might make enough money to fund a small undergraduate scholarship. Most of the early experiments in videotaped educational programs for alumni still look like investments on the books because they have not yet created their own market and do not recover the high television production costs.

Small institutions with small alumni or continuing education staffs may manage only a few alumni continuing education programs a year. If finances are tight, the early programs might be reunion seminars and alumni colleges abroad. Other on-campus seminars with a high potential for large audiences would come next, followed by a short summer alumni college. The last programs to mount, but those that will produce the largest number of alumni contacts, are the off-campus seminars. Schools that have all these program types will find that, in general, the travel programs and a few large-revenue seminars will pay all the other bills.

One important detail about the annual budgets of alumni continuing education programs: they are not actually annual budgets at all. Directors should help their institutions to define these programs as having at least two-year lifespans, to allow for adequate prior planning and final accounting after the programs have taken place. Only some shorter seminars can live comfortably within one fiscal year. It can be confusing and waste valuable staff time when dozens of program budgets have to be closed out and reopened or rolled over when they cross arbitrary fiscal boundaries bearing no logical relationship to program life.

Institutional Funding as an Investment in Alumni and Public Relations. As part of an institution's overall alumni and public relations strategy, alumni continuing education costs nothing. Planners can make a fundamental mistake if they misunderstand the carefully constructed world of institutional advancement. Alumni relations is not a business. It has no bottom line. The bottom line comes after the fundraising has been done. Professionals often use an agricultural metaphor to explain the relationship: alumni relations plows the ground and plants the seeds before development fertilizes the developing harvest and then reaps the rewards.

Businesses have bottom lines, and their goal is to make money. So, they charge whatever the market will bear for their goods and services. The goal of alumni relations is not to make money. The goal of alumni relations is participation by alumni in university life. When that job is done well, alumni appreciation for the university's role in society results in devotion and dollars.

As part of alumni relations, alumni continuing education's goal is also participation. It is therefore counterproductive to charge what the market will bear, because that philosophy raises prices and keeps some potential alumni participants away. Many institutions understand this and invest in alumni continuing education programs that attract participants through moderate fees.

Not everyone thinks this well about alumni continuing education's budgets. The revenue potential of a service like education can be very tempting. The fundamental problem with this approach is that, once alumni participants have paid what they know is full price for a profitable educational service, what will motivate them to increase their annual giving, their contribution to the next capital campaign, or their bequest to the university? In effect, they have already made a contribution (although it may not have been tax-deductible and cannot be matched), but through a short-sighted annual budget concern it will become nothing like the gift the development office had in mind.

Outside Funding. Alumni continuing education can attract foundation and corporation funding. The University of Michigan received a grant from the Carnegie Corporation in 1929 to explore and then establish off-campus alumni courses. Oakland University developed alumni education with Kellogg Foundation support in the 1960s. Alumni offices have developed temporary partnerships with local businesses in support of alumni seminars. One sponsoring alumni club solicits donations from local corporations to support its winter seminar. In return, the corporations send participants free to the seminar.

Private donors have supported alumni seminars. One alumni club annually solicits a list of guarantors who will pay seminar bills if tuition revenue falls short. Another seminar resulted from a specific one-time gift of an alumnus.

Ultimately, colleges and universities may want to ask their development officers to find support for alumni continuing education. There are donors for whom this is an attractive opportunity. Because the field is new, some of these donors will also be new to the institution.

The Long-Term Effects on Fundraising. As G. Michael McHugh has suggested, alumni continuing education can produce evidence that these programs attract far more new money to the institution than the total amount of investment the programs require. Stanford's study in the early 1970s showed that participation in educational programs ranked second only after service in senior volunteer positions as a predictor of significantly increased alumni giving.

In general these programs behave just like other educational programs: practical skills courses pay, while the liberal arts often need a little support. We must not forget, however, that this kind of bookkeeping does not take into consideration the ancillary fiscal benefits which can make program deficits seem more like prudent investments. We have not counted the tens of thousands of dollars that pour into faculty pockets, almost always on an overload basis; and into service departments for dining, housing, building maintenance, police, and the bookstore. Nor have we counted the increased alumni giving which Stanford found in its study, for, as Robert Cooper reminds us in his 1979 *Currents* article, it is easier to raise money from involved alumni.

SUMMARIZING THE VIEWS ON FUNDING ALUMNI CONTINUING EDUCATION

Fred Harvey Harrington pays close attention to questions about funding adult education, especially the noncredit liberal arts programs most closely associated with alumni continuing education. He believes that only continuing professional education can make a profit, but that colleges and universities nevertheless have a responsibility to provide adults with continuous access to the liberal arts without prejudice against them for being adults: "Typically . . . the adults who enroll in American colleges and universities have a harder time rounding up the money for fees than do young undergraduates, most of whom have parental support and better access to scholarships and loans than do adults" (1977, p. 190). Harrington finds that most adult education programs are far more price-sensitive than degree-granting programs for younger learners, and so there is increased danger of shutting out participants if alumni continuing education tries to behave like a business with its own bottom line. Harrington cannot understand why anyone talks about adult education "paying its own way":

> Why should adult education pay its own way? Undergraduate, professional, and graduate education do not pay their way. In public colleges and universities younger students are asked to provide only about a quarter of what it costs to educate them. . . . Those enrolled in privately controlled institutions may provide as much as half. But for obvious reasons students will not be expected to shoulder the entire burden. In helping individuals develop, higher education contributes to the economy and the society. Society is therefore expected to and does make a substantial contribution through government subsidies and private philanthropy [1977, p. 190].

In the specific case of the liberal arts in the marketplace, Harrington urges that

> administrators must give attention to the money question. Liberal education for adults lacks the basic financial support that practicing professionals, business executives, and trade union officials are glad to provide for continuing career education, or that cooperative extension enjoys inside the government. A college or university that is serious about noncredit education for adults should, therefore, shift a little money in that direction. All institutions have some free funds, even in these hard times. Another approach is to tap some of the profits from continuing professional education. Still another is to give liberal education for adults a certain priority in fund raising. This field does have appeal

to donors, for the general public is beginning to recognize that dividing life into years for education, work, and leisure is wrong. All should be present always [1977, p. 119].

Developing Budgets for Specific Alumni Continuing Education Programs

Budgets for alumni colleges look different from budgets for alumni seminars, which in turn differ from alumni college abroad budgets. It will therefore be useful to look at one budget of each type.

AN ALUMNI COLLEGE BUDGET

All alumni continuing education budgets are relatively simple. They do not handle complicated issues like depreciation; only computer alumni colleges deal with capital equipment. They do include faculty and other salaries, and salaries automatically cause contributions to the institution's benefits packages to be charged against the alumni college budget.

Alumni colleges, because they are residential, on-campus programs, produce relatively large and lengthy budgets. Items that appear on these budgets but seldom on small seminar budgets are food, lodging, and transportation. An alumni college budget line item for entertainment may disguise a special event that is just as complicated to budget as an entire off-campus seminar. Once we understand an alumni college budget, the budgets for other programs will be easier to read.

Shown on pp. 252–53 is a hypothetical budget for a twelve-day summer alumni college for 250 participants. Notice the main categories of expenditure, and the proportionate amounts spent in each category. For example, revenue derives entirely from participant tuition. Usually, this would not be true for the first few years of many alumni colleges, where the budget would be subsidized by the institution.

Food and lodging, which amount to pass-through charges

Sample Alumni College Budget (Simplified)

Code	Item	Amount	Sub-Total	Note
0300	General Revenue		−$150,000	("–" indicates income)
	0–999 Sub-Total Revenue		−$150,000	(SEE TUITION NOTE*)
1110	Directors	750		(only Academic Director)
1120	Tenured Faculty	10,000		(4 lectures @ $2,500)
1130	Tenure-Track Faculty	14,000		(14 discussion leaders)
1420	Student, Nonenrolled	700		(student workers)
1570	Police, Extra	100		(banquet security, etc.)
1810	Lecturers Fees	600		(guest lectures @ $150)
1860	Other Fees	1,000		(gallery talks, assistants)
1910	Fringe Distribution on 1120	3,093		(@ 12.5%, for example)
1920	Fringe Distribution on 1570	25		(@ higher staff fringe rate)
	1000–1999 Sub-Total Compensation		30,268	
2020	Supplies	1,500		(paper, notebooks, etc.)
2190	Photographic Prints	50		(faculty promo photos)
2250	Photocopying	50		
2310	Books & Publications	8,500		($40/couple, plus faculty)
2700	Rental & Leases	500		(evening program films)
	2000–2999 Sub-Total Supplies & Equipment		10,600	
3410	Travel	100		(charter bus: events/tours)
3600	Entertainment	2,500		(general, social)
3610	Banquets & Receptions	12,250		(opening, closing events)
3620	Food Service	37,250		(participants, faculty, staff)
3700	Rooms	42,000		(180 resident participants)
	3000–3999 Sub-Total Travel & Entertainment		94,100	
4000	Miscellaneous	957		

4410	Prizes & Awards	100	(valedictorians, faculty)
4510	Promotion/Advertising	7,000	(brochure design, printing)
4600	Postage	3,500	(brochures, books, other)
4800	Mailroom Services	500	
4900	Media Department Charges	500	(show films, microphones)
	4000–4999 Sub-Total to Other Department	12,557	
5100	Purchased Services, Internal	500	(slides, social hours, other)
5600	Internal Printing	400	(participant notebooks)
	5000–5999 Sub-Total Purchased Services	900	
6530	Moving/Delivery Service	75	(mailings to post office)
6540	Other Maintenance Services	1,500	(set-ups)
	6000–6999 Sub-Total Buildings & Grounds	1,575	
	1000–6999 TOTAL EXPENSE	150,000	
	0–999 TOTAL REVENUE	−150,000	
	ACCOUNT TOTAL	0	(break-even budget)

*TUITION

Resident Adults	150 @ $700 =	$105,000	
Day Students	70 @ $450 =	31,500	
Young Alumni/ae	30 @ $450 =	13,500	(" = " free room, meals)
TOTAL TUITION REVENUE:	250 participants @	$150,000	

from other campus service centers (and therefore provide no funds for the director to spend on the academic program), account for almost two-thirds of the budget. Younger alumni and older alumni on fixed incomes, who find the total program charge a problem, cannot afford the residential aspect of an alumni college. A few will stay with nearby friends and commute to alumni college. Families occasionally camp nearby.

Because younger alumni grow up to be older alumni, and therefore represent the future of the alumni college, it makes sense to subsidize their participation while they are less than fifteen years out of college. Many of them will establish the habit of alumni college participation. Remember, though, that as two-profession couples enter the years when previous generations began coming to alumni college, they have more trouble taking simultaneous vacations from their jobs. As a result, alumni colleges are becoming programs primarily for fifty- to ninety-year-olds.

Many of the expenses for this twelve-day alumni college could be halved if this were a five- or six-day program. Tuition, on the other hand, could be more than half the figures shown. Notice how much is spent on promotion (some programs spend up to 25 percent of the gross budget on promotion) and on the faculty. It does not pay to skimp in these areas. Not all alumni colleges include books mailed in advance to registrants, but several institutions think it important, especially if they care about the continuing aspects of their alumni continuing education.

When G. Michael McHugh was at Cornell, he set tuition by using what he called the 80 percent rule. That is, when setting tuition he totaled expenses for an estimated number of participants, then took 80 percent of that number of participants and divided the smaller number back into the expenses. The result was financial protection for a program that was healthy but just missed selling out. While at Brown, Sallie Riggs used a pricing system that first found the tuition that would cover expenses for 100 participants (where 100 was the higher of two estimates of participation), refigured the tuition for 80 participants, and then set tuition at a level slightly above the midpoint between these two amounts. An alternative is to figure all predictable fees, set tuition, then add a small amount as a financial cushion against lower enrollment or unexpected costs. Once a budget has been established that works, new budgets can be estimated from year to year by increasing the expense side using the Wholesale Price Index or Consumer Price Index and adjusting tuition accordingly.

The example above is a theoretical budget, although based on real experience. Different institutions' alumni college budgets do better or worse than break even. Where more than one office wants to sponsor the alumni college, these offices share profits or losses.

No matter what an institution's commitment to break-even or subsidized budgets, some programs fail to attract enough participants to avoid what Sallie Riggs calls a mid-course correction. That is, when registration moves too slowly to reach a low but acceptable level based on originally budgeted expenses, but cancellation is not indicated, the director can redesign the program slightly through the budget. He or she can take out a less important film here and a badly undersubscribed afternoon workshop there, and can scale back variables like printed materials and the miscellaneous line item often put into budgets for this very purpose.

PRICE SENSITIVITY OF DIFFERENT PROGRAM TYPES

To make an alumni college's budget as healthy as possible, planners need to know how price-sensitive different alumni continuing education programs can be. Otherwise, they may try to squeeze too much revenue out of the program, and raise tuition until alumni resist participation. The shorter an alumni college and the less expensive it is, the more price-sensitive it becomes. Where expenses (excluding room and board) suggest a tuition of $200 for a three-day alumni college, the director will justifiably agonize over adding $25 per person to tuition in trying to balance the budget. It may be necessary to combine cost-cutting with tuition hikes. On the other hand, a three-week alumni college abroad to China priced at $5,000 might just as well be priced at $5,500. The automobile industry works the same way: manufacturers make the most money on high-ticket models.

AN ALUMNI SEMINAR BUDGET

Seminar budgets are usually much smaller and simpler than alumni college budgets. It is possible to attach a seminar to an expensive cultural event, thereby running the apparent budget (much of it composed of pass-through fees to a museum or other service providers) into large figures. A faculty seminar on Verdi's *Aida*, followed by a performance at the Metropolitan Opera, would produce a budget dominated by the cost of opera tickets. But most break-even seminars pay only for faculty, promotion, and lunch, based on revenues from a tuition between $5 (for complicated programs with attendance in the hundreds) and $25 per person.

Off-campus seminars are more expensive, because they include travel costs for faculty and often for staff. It may also be necessary to rent space, although many colleges and universities provide free seminar space to sister institutions. Another campus also provides the right atmosphere for an off-campus seminar.

The budget below is for a Saturday seminar (9:00 A.M. to 4:30 P.M.) a thousand miles from the campus, using two faculty members. The faculty need overnight accommodations for two nights, plus meals and incidental expenses. No staff travel is necessary because volunteers at the sponsoring alumni club will run this program on seminar day. But promotion is expensive: direct-mail postcards first, and then brochures sent to the 2,000 alumni and parents of undergraduates within driving distance of the seminar. A sister institution provides the site at minimal cost, but there are charges for audio-visual set-up, and for coffee and luncheon at the faculty club. The postseminar reception is a cash bar that pays for itself (but keep these receptions short, and provide coffee for drivers).

SAMPLE BUDGET FOR AN ALUMNI CLUB SATURDAY SEMINAR

Code	Description	Amount	Sub-Total	Note
0300	General Revenue	-$2,500		(100 participants @ $25)
0900	Reimbursements	- 1,935		(college subsidy)
	0–999 Sub-Total Revenue		-$4,435	
2190	Photographic Prints	10		(faculty brochure photos)
2020	Supplies	25		(name badges, etc.)
	2000–2999 Sub-Total Supplies & Equipment		35	
3410	Travel	1,200		(2 faculty)
3620	Food Service	850		(luncheon, coffee break)
3700	Rooms/Meals/Other	500		(faculty expenses)
	3000–3999 Sub-Total Travel & Entertainment		2,500	
4600	Postage	1,025		
4800	Mailroom Services	75		
	4000–4999 Sub-Total to Other Departments		1,100	
5510	External Printing	600		(postcard, brochure)
5710	Rental of Space	150		(set-up, P-A system)
5720	Rental of Equipment	50		(slide projector)
	5000–5999 Purchased Services		800	
	1000–6999 TOTAL EXPENSE		4,435	
	0–999 TOTAL REVENUE		-4,435	
	ACCOUNT TOTAL		0	(break-even budget)

Since a good turnout would be 100 participants and tuition is price-sensitive, the sponsoring institution's alumni office budget contributes a subsidy roughly equal to the costs for faculty travel and expenses—costs always covered by the alumni office when university speakers appear at an alumni club function. Tuition covers all local costs and the faculty honoraria. The sponsoring alumni club will collect all tuition initially and pay the faculty directly. This has two advantages. The faculty will see the whole honorarium, and the institutional seminar account escapes an automatic debit for fringe benefits. In effect, the faculty are hired by the alumni club as outside consultants. The club may return to the university any funds that remain after local bills have been paid.

Saturday seminars close to or on the campus can pay all costs (including faculty honoraria and fringe benefits) from reasonably priced tuition, because faculty travel is by private automobile, overnight accommodations are unnecessary, and some promotion can be by inexpensive campus flier (no postage), poster, and newspaper advertisement. This can sometimes be done with tuition as low as $5, especially if 100–200 people attend.

Another way to increase the likelihood that a seminar will pay all the bills, even at some distance from the campus, is to use the full weekend format. The total price for these programs is more like that for a short alumni college and, for its market (older alumni, in most cases), less price-sensitive. Therefore, certain miscellaneous costs can be covered out of increased tuition. To reduce the age of participants and increase the market, an alumni office might subsidize tuition, at least for young alumni, or might avoid high-priced resort housing.

BUDGETING AN ALUMNI COLLEGE ABROAD

Few colleges and universities design and plan their own alumni travel programs without substantial help from a travel agent. For most institutions, this would not even be advisable, since it requires special expertise not available on the alumni office staff, lots of staff time, and considerable front-end financial risk. Therefore, we will look here only at a much simpler budget that reflects a sponsoring university's plans for an academic program based upon an itinerary developed initially by a travel agent. The itinerary, while modified by the agent to suit the faculty's needs, is the responsibility of the agent and therefore the large costs for travel, hotels, meals, transfers, and travel directors show up only on the agent's budget. Colleges and universities interested in planning their own travel programs from scratch and building complete budgets may want advice from experienced alumni travel directors at the University of Michigan, Stanford University, or Brigham Young University alumni associations.

The budget for the academic program on an alumni college abroad includes revenue, faculty honoraria, staff planning costs, preparation and distribution of academic materials for advance study by registrants, promotional expenses, and staff travel abroad to direct the program.

It is a good idea to keep careful track of expenses, including staff time, incurred by alumni colleges abroad, since these expenses can be written off against revenue. It remains to be seen whether excess revenue from alumni colleges abroad may be used to offset expenses not covered by revenues from other alumni programs, especially other alumni continuing education programs.

In any event, it is important that educational programming drive alumni college abroad planning if sponsoring institutions are to gain some measure of protection from IRS and Postal Service scrutiny. The budget for an alumni college abroad will reflect the seriousness of the academic enterprise: faculty honoraria and travel expenses will appear, as will the cost of preparing and providing advance study materials to registrants. The budget may also reflect the cost of purchasing the promotional brochures to announce alumni colleges abroad, even if much or all of this expense is reimbursed by the travel agent after the program, along with reimbursement for faculty travel expenses, preparation of study materials, postage, staff time, and more. No one can be sure at this point whether it is better practice for the university to receive all payments for travel programs, keep an amount that will later pay the university's bills, and pass the larger amount through to the travel agent, or whether the college or university should let the agent provide the clerical service of processing registration and payment checks and then obtain reimbursements and participant revenues from the agent after the program has taken place. In all these cases, good record-keeping is essential. Institutions that are in the alumni travel business do not often sign contracts that expressly state the responsibilities of university and agent, but they probably should.

Budgeting alumni colleges abroad has become so idiosyncratic that no single budget sample will be terribly helpful. Instead, a simple listing of important budget elements with an idea of their magnitude for a two-week cruise program should provide the tools with which each institution can build its own budgets.

Faculty Honoraria. The amounts of honoraria vary greatly, from zero to thousands of dollars. A reasonable practice used by some institutions is to approximate the fee that would be paid for a given set of lectures and discussions were the program to take place on the campus rather than abroad. For example, if a summer alumni college lecturer gets $250 per lecture (or day with the program), and the alumni college abroad calls for four lectures plus discussion, a reasonable honorarium would be $750–1,500. Do not forget to budget for fringe benefits, including automatic contributions to retirement funds.

Academic Materials. Participants are more likely to read materials sent to them than materials merely recommended, especially as academic books become increasingly difficult to find. (Tax laws force books out-of-print so quickly that sponsoring institutions have begun getting copyright permission to reproduce readings for program registrants.) All costs of these materials should be budgeted, from the cost of copyright permissions to book prices, photocopied maps, the faculty's reading and study guides, and postage to mail them. If the faculty buys books, slides, maps, teaching aids, or other materials to help them prepare lectures, these expenses should all be charged to the program budget. As with an alumni college, $20–$40 per week in books and materials is about right.

Promotional Materials. Whether the sponsoring institution designs and prints its own brochures locally or purchases brochures modified for them from a travel agent's basic design, the costs of the brochures themselves, shipping them to the university, and the postage and handling to mail them to alumni should all appear as expenses on the budget. Schools with 40,000–80,000 alumni can expect brochures and postage to cost anywhere from $5,000–15,000.

Staff Costs. Some institutions charge staff officer and assistants' time against the specific travel programs, including time spent accompanying and working on the programs themselves, and all expenses incurred by them while fulfilling those duties. Agents usually award complimentary spaces for staff or faculty at about the rate of one space per fifteen or twenty sold tickets. Travel costs to the university are thereby kept to a minimum. A complicated alumni college abroad might take as much as 10 percent of an officer's and a secretary's annual effort: $3,500 or more.

Revenue and Reimbursements. Alumni colleges abroad should not cost an institution money, unless an agent goes bankrupt. Even that disaster can be moderated if all program deposits go into a holding account to be drawn upon only for that specific program; otherwise agents will sometimes roll deposits for one program over into other accounts to cover costs there, and if the worst happens, everybody's money turns up missing. Revenue to the college or university can be budgeted as a percentage of total program earnings or can be based upon a fixed dollar figure per participant. Either way, some monies coming to the sponsoring institution will be true revenue, earned by attracting participants to the academic program; other monies will reimburse front-end costs the agent contracts to provide whether the trip takes place or not. Each institution should carefully consider its own fiscal practices and applicable laws when developing its procedures regarding revenue and reimbursement for alumni colleges abroad. The care taken in bookkeeping should reflect the fiscal magnitude of these programs.

An Overall Alumni Continuing Education Budget

Below is a well-balanced overall alumni continuing education budget, assuming a goal of breaking even on direct costs, with the university contributing personnel, office space, equipment, and supplies. This budget might take a different shape if the sponsoring unit needed more revenue.

An important issue raised by such a budget is where to recover the staff and office expenses. Most alumni offices do not recover them; they invest in programs as a way of life, with university monies backing them up. Independent alumni associations might subsidize alumni continuing education out of revenues from dues, the life insurance program, or the proceeds from a merchandizing campaign. The key question about alumni continuing education for many independent and dependent alumni operations is not what it costs in absolute dollars, but what it costs per participant contact. The answer is that it costs less than virtually all other alumni programs, such as the volunteer club and class officers' weekends, reunions, or presi-

AN OVERALL ALUMNI CONTINUING EDUCATION BUDGET

PROGAM	EXPENSE	REVENUE	BALANCE
Summer Alumni College	$75,000	−$75,000	$0
On-Campus Seminars (3)	9,000	−7,500	1,500
Reunion Seminars/ Forums (3/6)	4,500	−2,500	2,000
Off-Campus (Alumni Club) Seminars (8)	35,000	−20,000	15,000
Alumni Colleges Abroad (4)	48,000	−68,000	−20,000
PROGRAM DEVELOPMENT/ VIDEO, ETC.	5,000	−3,500	1,500
TOTALS	$176,500	$176,500	$0

dential speaking tours to alumni clubs. In continuing education offices, the balance of programs may need to shift in favor of revenue-producers, if all indirect costs must be paid from alumni continuing education revenues alone.

Upon reaching the point where alumni continuing education offers a large menu of programs like those in the hypothetical budget above, an institution eventually will ask: Do we continue to assign the individual programs to different staff members, or is it time to appoint a director of alumni continuing education? Some institutions will concentrate the particular talents required by these programs in one or more specialists. Others may choose to involve several or even all staff members in alumni continuing education planning, so that they work directly with the faculty. This option has the advantage that everyone on the staff experiences the institution's academic strengths first-hand while planning contributions to the intellectual lives of their alumni constituents.

Part Three

The Intellectual Residence of Alumni

CHAPTER 10

ALUMNI CONTINUING EDUCATION AND THE FUTURE OF ADULTS AND UNIVERSITIES

Toward a Coherent Lifelong Relationship Between Adults and Universities

How can we fine-tune our colleges and universities to support a population of lifelong learners, and at the same time increase support for higher education? Many new perspectives on the relationship between adults and universities will be needed.

Alumni continuing education can help. Already, at institutions that use it to advantage, it improves the quality of alumni relations and the effectiveness of continuing education. It makes alumni relations a true partner in the institutional enterprise of education. It helps continuing education achieve continuity in adults' intellectual lives. Its greatest potential, however, lies in the perspective alumni continuing education gives to the overall lifelong relationship between adults and universities.

267

Think of the many adult roles in our colleges and universities today. Adults are teachers, administrators, alumni volunteers, board members, patrons, parents of students, and students themselves. A host of professions serve these adult relationships, but they function separately, occasionally at odds. Because adults will soon be the most important age group to our universities, we must develop a more coherent relationship between them.

The new model will consider the latest studies of adult development to determine those times of life when adults most need the university, and also those times when adults are best able to contribute something back to the university. When we integrate these lists of needs on both sides, we will begin to see what a lifetime of involvement in an intellectual community might look like. Then, by building closer collegial relationships among the professions that relate adults to universities, we can add coherence and make more of precious university resources.

No single model will do. Individuals who care about the university and professionals charged with running it will find what works for each institution. This chapter will only try to ask a few of the pressing questions and then suggest the role alumni continuing education might play in providing some answers. As readers ponder these questions, they might begin to consider what contribution alumni continuing education could make toward answers. In other words, what difference might it make if alumni held permanent membership in the intellectual life of their alma maters?

WHAT IS THE ROLE OF VOLUNTEER ADULTS IN THE EDUCATION OF UNDERGRADUATE AND GRADUATE STUDENTS?

We have regents, trustees, visiting committees, visiting nonacademic faculty members, internships, out-placement, and other less formal roles for volunteer adults who can contribute to the quality of undergraduate and graduate education. How might the university involve these volunteers more closely?

How might absentee trustees be involved more effectively? What new roles might be created, and how might they be organized, supervised, and paid for? Should more adults come into the campus or even the classroom? What kinds of mentoring might adults perform and for whom? How might adults contribute to greater relevance between what students study and the skills they will need in careers? How can adults bring their lifetime of experience into the intellectual questing of much younger college students, and how can we foster and perpetuate the rigorous academic skills and idealistic perspectives of younger students? What effect can or should adults have on the extracurricular lives of younger students?

HOW MIGHT ALUMNI RELATIONS BETTER REPRESENT THE QUALITIES AND NEEDS OF THE UNIVERSITY TO ALUMNI, AND ALUMNI OPINIONS AND NEEDS TO THE UNIVERSITY?

Do we need a new definition of an alumnus or alumna to reflect a lifelong relationship? What are the important non-academic and volunteer programs for the future relationships between adults and universities? Which educational programs should the alumni office run, cooperate in running, or cede to other offices? How might professionals and volunteers best be prepared for their different roles in the university? How might younger students best be prepared for these roles?

HOW MIGHT THE FUNDRAISING PROFESSION BETTER SERVE THE NEEDS OF UNIVERSITY AND PATRON ALIKE?

What is the best way to prepare an adult for philanthropy? How much does a donor need to know about the use of gifts? Where does the responsibility for gift use begin and end for the donor and for the university? What are the advantages and disadvantages of close involvement by donors, even if they are alumni? Do we know who does not support the university and why? Can we find new ways to identify the interests of non-donors so as to involve them in university life?

HOW MIGHT CONTINUING EDUCATION BE REDESIGNED TO PROVIDE LIFELONG CONTINUITY AND TO USE THE EDUCATIONAL RESOURCES IMPLICIT IN AN ADULT'S LIFELONG EXPERIENCE?

Through what courses, seminars, public events, peer and mentoring activity, and individualized counseling and training might young students learn to be lifelong learners? What skills do adult learners need and how can they develop them? What can adults of different ages bring back to younger learners?

HOW MIGHT ENHANCED PROFESSIONALISM IN ALUMNI RELATIONS AND CONTINUING EDUCATION IMPROVE THE RELATIONSHIP BETWEEN ADULTS AND UNIVERSITIES?

Who will redefine these professions, where redefinition will help? Where will the new professionals come from? How might adults gain a clearer understanding of their lifelong roles in the university? Who will oversee a new, coherent relationship among education professions such as alumni relations, fund-raising, continuing education, undergraduate and graduate school deaning, career and education counseling, athletics, governance, and more?

WHERE DO COLLEGE AND UNIVERSITY RESPONSIBILITIES END?

How might the concept of lifelong membership in an educational institution improve the quality of decision-making by national, regional, and local leaders? Must a university's influence in the nation and the world rest solely on the hope that its degrees confer lasting wisdom? If our colleges and universities do not exercise continuous, beneficial influence upon decision-makers, who will?

The Baby Boom Effect

These and other questions need answers now, because adults will soon be the most important age group in university life, and our universities will be shifting their focus in response. The largest group of adults, whose relationship to our universities should become a major focus of our attention, are people born between 1946 and 1964. They began reaching age forty in 1986; the last in this group turn forty in 2004.

The baby boom effect is already being felt in our universities. The U.S. Census Bureau statistics show average college ages up among young adults in their mid-twenties, and the proportion of older students is up significantly already in every age group and particularly among adults in their thirties.

Consider also the baby boom's babies. Assuming that these children are born to thirty-year-old parents, those babies began arriving in 1976 and will keep coming through 1994, reaching college at ages 17 to 25 between 1993 and 2019. If we compare the dates for the baby boomers' return to college with the dates when their own children first attend, the overlapping period begins in 1993 and lasts until 2004. That gives colleges and universities almost no time to prepare for a new situation: the simultaneous decision of parents where to send their children to college and where to get their own continuing education.

Under these new circumstances, any university that does not offer continuing education to its alumni by 1993 could begin losing those baby boom parents and their children. By 1993 parents will be paying from $10,000 to $100,000 for each child to receive a baccalaureate degree. Multiply this amount by a larger-than-normal college population (the so-called ripple effect) scheduled to arrive between 1993 and 2004 and it becomes clear that universities cannot afford to ignore the continuing education needs of their own alumni.

There are several ways universities can signal serious interest in educating their alumni and other adults. For families put in financial binds by a multigenerational need for education, universities could provide family plans, or even sell lifelong learning insurance, instead of the educationally irrelevant straight-life policies now sold by many alumni associations.

Universities that see what is coming and gear up a lifetime commitment to their students are going to get the students of both generations at once; those that do not, will not. At stake are billions of tuition dollars, the lifeblood of most institutions. And, in an ironic twist on today's alumni shutting off annual giving when admission is denied to their children, the phenomenon may begin to reverse its course: adults shutting off alumni giving to those universities that accept their children but take no responsibility to serve them.

University Responsibility for American Higher Education

Only by taking seriously the responsibility for lifelong education can universities maintain their role as leaders in American higher education. The alternative might be the takeover of continuing education by the private sector. Such an alternative fails in two ways. It hurts our universities by usurping their role in American life. But it also offers adult learners little hope of educational continuity.

Alumni continuing education suggests that universities accept responsibility for the lifelong education of alumni. This keeps a large proportion of continuing education in the hands of the universities, where much of it belongs; and it addresses the issue of continuity in a lifetime of education. Individual adults may from time to time avail themselves of the particular resources of other colleges and universities or nonacademic providers but they will identify their lifelong intellectual residence as the undergraduate alma mater—the institution that first introduced them to the world of higher education, trained them to be competent adult learners, and offered them periodic and lifelong counseling and intellectual renewal. That is the perspective alumni continuing education contributes toward the future of higher education.

Applying Alumni Continuing Education

UNIVERSITY LIFE FOR A FUTURE ALUMNUS

Adults come in contact with many university offices, among them the admissions office, deans, faculty, coaches, extracurricular organizations, academic and career counselors, the alumni office, perhaps a graduate school and its alumni office, and the university publications and fundraising offices. When alumni add continuing education and volunteerism or employment at alma mater, the result can be a bewildering variety of relationships. The variety is fine. The trouble comes from the competition of all these offices, which probably do not consult each other.

With public funds for education shrinking and adult demands upon universities expanding, adults and universities need a more rational relationship. The individual adult needs to keep well informed about his or her educational home in order to take best advantage of its services. On the other hand, universities become increasingly dependent upon the support adults can give, provided they are properly motivated.

By applying what we know about adult development, we can decide which university offices can benefit most from their relationships with adults of different ages. We must begin to apply this knowledge, especially to our own graduates.

Very young alumni may have no use for the educational resources of alma mater. Fresh out of college, they have little need of refresher courses. The balance of theory over practice in their recent intellectual lives ripens them for concrete experience in the world of adult life and work. On the other hand, the youngest graduates may need career counseling and seminars on personal finances or the roles of adults starting marriages and families. Young alumni make extremely useful interviewers for the admissions office, since their recent university experience helps them to answer applicant questions and to ask their own questions aimed at searching out the best young people for the university of today. The career office can use young alumni as speakers on career days to instruct undergraduates on choosing and starting careers, living in a new city, and financing housing and transportation.

Only nearer middle adulthood can alumni help to place undergraduates in meaningful summer jobs or serve on departmental visiting committees as their own careers near a peak of power, knowledge, energy, and effectiveness. At this point alumni for the first time become interesting to fundraisers. While alumni in middle adulthood are busy and therefore hard to involve in time-consuming volunteerism, they are particularly effective when they do become involved. They make superb alumni chapter, class reunion, or special project leaders. They also enjoy the peak of their personal spending, and may purchase expensive university services, such as life insurance; some of them take advantage of alumni travel programs. Those facing mid-career changes may return to the university part-time or full-time for new degrees or personal enrichment.

Near the ends of their careers and in early retirement alumni often exhibit a peak of what George Vaillant (in *Adaptation to Life*) calls generativity. They become deeply involved in volunteerism, some may extend themselves to make the gift of a lifetime to the university, and a few enroll in bequest or life income trust programs. With a wealth of experience behind them, they serve effectively on top-level boards and visiting committees and advise boards and presidents in areas of their expertise. Some work in university offices on a volunteer basis after retirement. These alumni are prime candidates for noncredit continuing education. Among alumni continuing education programs, alumni colleges abroad become especially popular.

The better an institution understands its adults, the better it can design its services and its methods of finding the adult resources it needs. Continuing education offices understand that philosophical or religious issues attract older adults more than do economic or political issues, and can market its programs accordingly. This knowledge can affect the design of the program itself: an ethics seminar will work better in a discussion format if older adults with relevant life experience participate, whereas a lecture or question-and-answer format may be more appropriate for undergraduates or younger alumni.

A thoughtful annual fund director may make his programs more effective in the long run by emphasizing participation (no matter what level of giving) of younger alumni, who have less disposable income and less perspective on the value of the education they have received. A twenty-fifth reunion class near the peak of its professional power and earning potential should have a higher dollar goal and may receive more attention than the fifteenth- or thirty-fifth-year class.

One goal of selecting the right time of life to offer a university service to a graduate or to request some service in return is to create a balance of giving and receiving that satisfies and pleases both the institution and the adult. It may not do to pursue a simple plan of investing in relations programs for younger alumni before switching to more earnest (and one-sided) requests for help later in their lives. If our goal is satisfying lifelong relationships between adults and universities, then the relationship for each adult should carry the rewards of giving and taking at every period of life.

In this goal, the university needs the cooperation of every office that needs or serves adults. Without the special relationships fostered by the career office, what can the university give that recent graduates need? Without the admissions office and its interviewing program, what can the youngest graduates give of great value to the university? Without a bequest program, what can alumni of modest means contribute of financial benefit? Without continuing education, how can volunteers on boards and visiting committees understand the current academic enterprise well enough to give wise counsel?

A lifelong relationship with a complex institution like a college or university should be filled with refreshing challenge and change, surprising and timely benefits. It should have balance and strength. It should be as good at all points for the adult as for the university. As we approach the next century, with knowledge exploding and the world we live in changing several times in a human lifespan, this relationship between adults and universities must be strong and healthy, for it will have to withstand pressures that we can only begin to imagine today.

FOUR PROPOSED ADDITIONS TO THE RELATIONSHIP BETWEEN ADULTS AND UNIVERSITIES

Educators should be thinking of new ways to enrich the relationship between adults and universities. We might: (1) reshape student life to develop lifelong learners; (2) teach lifelong learning skills to undergraduates and alumni; (3) develop a coherent lifelong relationship between adults and universities; and (4) develop an alumni sharing program. Each college or university will give specific shape to these areas. Here are some suggestions.

Reshape Student Life to Develop Lifelong Learners. No school surveyed in the research for this book had a specific plan for encouraging its students to make continuing education a permanent part of their lives. Most assumed that one result of a top-quality undergraduate experience or graduate program was the habit of learning. This is about as true as the myth that students learn how to write by submitting a few papers in for-credit courses. Purposeful learning during adulthood is both a habit and a skill.

Eventually continuing education must be encouraged from the top of a college or university administration. Presidents who identify it as a necessity of modern life can set a campus climate in which students know that learning outside their curricular lives is not only allowed but encouraged or even expected. The faculty and administration will be encouraged to promote and teach in extracurricular educational programs.

Perhaps, in order to foster the habit of continuing education among undergraduates, a university will find ways of protecting time in a student's life for this kind of activity. The concept of T-points shows up in some individual courses: for extra activity in the course a student earns T-points, which will raise a final grade. T-points might be offered for approved continuing education activity and students could apply them toward grades in related courses or toward cumulative grade point averages.

The faculty would not merely approve the plan but design it. The goal would be to start adolescents into the habit of making time for learning in their busy lives. Jerold Apps, discussing the differences between childhood and adult education, prefers to focus on a continuity linking one to the other, and strikes this same chord about the importance of teaching younger students to be competent older ones:

> The middle ground on this issue seems to be a recognition that learning is continuous throughout life and that educators should strive to tie together and relate the education which is directed toward young people with that which is directed toward adults. Since today's child is tomorrow's adult, have we prepared the child for a life of learning? On the other hand, have we so divided the education of children and adults that today's child has to begin all over again, when he or she becomes an adult, to learn what learning is and how one goes about it? [1979, p. 169].

The advantage of taking alumni continuing education seriously should be obvious enough. Any institution, remembering that its students will be its students for life, will pay more attention to the ways in which undergraduates internalize the lifelong learning habit.

One way to reduce the discrepancy between the learning lives of undergraduates and that of most adults is to encourage extracurricular courses, lectures, and intellectual events as an attractive feature of regular undergraduate life. The key concept is attractive. Colleges and universities wrestle with the problem of relating students' extracurricular lives to their lives in the classroom, reaching for ways to make dormitory, fraternity, and sorority life more purposefully educational and less purely social or even escapist, and also looking hard at the intercollegiate and intramural athletic programs to make sure they play an educational role in student life. Part of the answer may be a university-wide effort to make resources and adult participants available for afternoon and evening continuing education programs in which undergraduates are motivated to participate. At some institutions, extracurricular, noncredit learning is encouraged in a "miniversity" program, where undergraduates design, staff, and hire faculty for noncredit courses from ballroom dance and auto repair to religion, music appreciation, and current issues in Latin America.

Teach Lifelong Learning Skills to Undergraduates and Alumni. Here again, no such programs turned up in the research, although several institutions believed that their students absorbed some lifelong learning skills either in the regular undergraduate classroom or by observing the relationship between work and the intellectual lives of the faculty. This may not be enough anymore. We cannot graduate whole generations of adequately prepared lifelong learners by accident. Here are a few suggestions for preparing them more purposefully.

1. Offer an undergraduate course on adult education.   This course, or sequential pair of courses lasting one academic year, would involve several faculty members and deans from departments around the university. Several benefits would result. Backing for institutional approval would have a headstart with so many deans and teachers involved. Because teachers from the sciences, social sciences, and humanities would be involved, any student could justify electing the course, since it could prepare them for lifelong learning in his or her profession in addition to its intrinsic pleasure. Some participating faculty members would not be familiar with adult education history, skills, and procedures, and would be true participants themselves. This might prompt changes in the ways they teach their other courses, so that the idea of lifelong learning in their subject would show up elsewhere in the curriculum. Fred Harvey Harrington goes much further, suggesting that every college or division in the university should have an assistant dean for adult education and public service, and that through joint appoint-

ments each academic department should have "an adult education presence at the working level" and not merely in its administration (1977, pp. 178–179).

The course itself could contain many elements already taught in continuing education courses at the graduate level. Some familiarity with the history of adult education here and abroad would provide an important perspective, showing students that the notion of education ending with adolescent schooling began in this century. The course would cover adult development theory—not only general physical and mental development but also moral, ethical, and philosophical development. Students would study exemplary lifelong learners as role models: Cyril Houle's *Patterns of Learning* might therefore be on the reading list. So might great biographies (Albert Schweitzer's *Out of My Life and Mind*, or Henry Adams's autobiography), and a classic *Bildungsroman*, like Goethe's *Young Man Werthe;* Shakespeare's *Antony and Cleopatra, Hamlet*, or *King Lear;* Melville's *Moby Dick* or Richard Henry Dana's *Two Years Before the Mast;* or even Dickens's romantic *David Copperfield*, or, in a metaphysical setting, the compressed adult education of Ebenezer Scrooge in *A Christmas Carol.*

Such a course, no matter what its readings and faculty, should aim at producing competent self-directed learners who have the skills to identify an educational need, to find and organize educational resources into a learning project that addresses that need, to organize their lives so that they can carry out the learning project, and to look back upon the project afterward knowing how to assess its success or failure to achieve the required goals. If the course were designed as a sequence, the first part could concentrate on adult learning theory (why and how adults learn), and the second could focus upon practical learning projects—identified, orchestrated, carried out, and evaluated by the students. Some projects should require group work, others should be carried out individually, to give students familiarity with as many true-to-life learning techniques, technologies, settings, problems, and solutions as possible.

If this goal is met, students who become self-directed learners will become teachers as well. This will be no mean feat, since our entire university education system omits any regular method for teaching the faculty to teach, let alone the students. The conscious teaching of continuing education to students will probably have the tangential effect of making the faculty more aware of how they teach and how they might improve their teaching.

2. Teach adult education in extracurricular settings.   Other "teachable moments" must be found in university life to teach purposefully the habit and skills of continuing education. Convocation and freshman week, commencement and senior week, all provide occasions when university leaders can point out the importance of continuing education to all members of the university. These are also times to point out university programs that provide access to education for nontraditional adult students.

Continuing education and other faculty members can develop handbooks that amount to self-taught mini-courses on the techniques and importance of continuing education. Such a handbook might contain the continuing education course, its topics and readings, in compressed form. Audio-visual materials could accompany the handbook.

3. Provide catch-up adult education courses.   Once self-teaching materials are available, they can be made available not only to current students but also to former students through alumni programs. The handbook and other materials can be advertised in the alumni magazine. Alumni seminars can teach some of the same materials to adults that the regular course teaches to students. For distant alumni, videotape or audio-cassette materials can substitute for live interaction between faculty and alumni. Individual alumni or alumni through their organizations may begin to request these kinds of continuing education services from their institutions.

4. Create a lifelong learning center.   Malcolm Knowles (1962, p. 347) envisions lifelong learning centers, where adults can find guidance and materials for their learning projects. He imagines these centers as an alternative to a sometimes overly structured university continuing education program, but universities themselves might set up flexible learning centers on

the campus to serve alumni and other community adults. Such centers could also be the origin of extracurricular educational courses, programs, and activities for younger undergraduates.

Develop a Coherent Lifelong Relationship Between Adults and Universities. The third proposal is that all offices that now relate adults to the university coordinate their efforts. Wake Forest University introduces high school counselors and parents of potential applicants to the university through a program called Life at Wake Forest, Admissions to Grave. This is on the right track.

Linda Carl (1986a) suggests that alumni associations should add the new role of educational broker to their traditional alumni services, because the associations already have such a strong relationship with alumni. By brokering, she means tracking all educational and cultural opportunities at the university and getting alumni involved in them. Ernest McMahon would expect the dean of alumni college to keep track of educational opportunities at other universities as well, and to refer alumni to any place where their needs could be met (1960, p. 52). These suggestions by Carl and McMahon would lend more coherence to the university's many educational offerings.

The idea of brokering has merit, with two caveats: (1) brokering is not enough and an alumni association should also be directly involved in providing alumni continuing education, so that alumni will think of the association as a credible source of educational advice and counsel; and (2) brokering itself has a spotty history, having failed in its only major national effort despite visionary leadership from James Heffernan of Syracuse University. Heffernan set up the short-lived National Center for Educational Brokering, a network of independent education brokers, on the theory that higher education was so institution-based that someone should provide client-centered advice to adults with continuing education needs. Somewhere in the effort to find enough qualified independent brokers, and probably hampered by the costs of organizing the effort, the system broke down. The function of client-centered brokering still needs to be fulfilled, however, and perhaps Carl is right that alumni associations can fulfill it.

One way the alumni association, the alumni office, or the continuing education office can provide this service is to build a strong organizational bridge to the university's counseling office. In addition to career and graduate education counseling for students, many of these offices provide general education counseling whenever students or alumni come or call in for advice. Since education counseling is a profession in its own right, there is no reason why the alumni association should duplicate that expertise rather than referring alumni to the existing counseling office. Perhaps this could result in two-way brokering, the alumni office referring alumni to the counseling office, which in turn might refer alumni back to alumni continuing education programs.

Offices can help each other. At some point, however, senior university officers will need to get involved to initiate coherent, institution-wide planning for the lifelong relationship between alumni and the university.

Alumni Sharing. Ernest McMahon suggested in 1960 that the dean of alumni college would recommend educational services at alma mater or at any other institution that offered what the graduate needed. Lowell Eklund tried this at ten midwestern universities in the early 1960s but ran out of foundation funding before the experiment caught on.

Eventually, the concept of alumni sharing should take hold. No university can be everything to each graduate. Each school has its specialties. Furthermore, geographical proximity may always be attractive to some adult learners, including alumni. The important thing is that alma mater take responsibility for the lifelong education of alumni, no matter where they live and no matter where they find the education they need. Brokering may be part of the answer.

One alternative would be a program of alumni sharing, in which an institution would invite all nearby college graduates of similar institutions interested in sharing alumni to participate in its educational programs. Before the invitation was sent, the alumni directors of the cooperating institutions would contact their own alumni in that locale and alert them to the upcoming opportunity. After that, those alumni would be welcome in the local institution's alumni continuing education and other programs, and they would know it because of the initial gestures by their own alma mater.

In this arrangement, the local institution would accept responsibility for a mailing list of nearby college graduates and would give its mailing lists for other regions of the country to other institutions in the alumni sharing program. It might be possible to allow these shared alumni access to other local university services and programs as well, such as career counseling. Access to a variety of cultural, athletic, and social alumni programs would offer a rewarding sense of participation.

Would alumni sharing affect alumni support for alma mater? Shared alumni should gain an increased sense of respect for alma mater, which would lead to increased alumni volunteer and financial support. At the same time, these alumni should come to appreciate the local institution more highly as well and begin to support it, increasing the value to the local university in community relations. Each institution in the program would gain these same advantages. Alumni sharing is not a way to give up one's own alumni; it is a way to serve them better, while bringing new nearby adults into the university community. The strength this program would give to American higher education across the board can only be imagined.

Conclusion

The future of alumni continuing education and of its role in redefining the lifelong relationship between adults and universities is the responsibility of institutions and individual alumni alike. College and university regents, boards, presidents, vice-presidents, faculty, the directors and deans of continuing education and alumni relations, and, perhaps most important, the students and alumni themselves, must work together to define the universities' needs for support through adult involvement, on the one hand, and adults' educational, cultural, social, and recreational needs, on the other. If these two agendas can be brought together effectively, the relationship will benefit everyone.

American higher education, such an important foundation for our representative democracy, must include its millions of alumni in planning for the future. Each institution will begin with its own alumni, on whose support it depends. What lies ahead may be a redefinition of what it means to be an alumnus or alumna; perhaps the new term we want is Milton Stern's members of the university. The charge upon each of us is to define what it means to be a member of the university of the future and to live up to that vision.

The seventy-five-year-old concept of alumni continuing education can contribute to our new definition of university membership. In applying that concept, colleges and universities may choose from a wide range of possibilities. Some institutions may modify existing programs to make alumni feel welcome in the institution's intellectual life. Loyola Marymount University in Inglewood, California, refers to its President's Day as a homecoming for the mind, a conscious adaptation of an alumni event that has been almost entirely social and athletic in the past. Other institutions may make substantial changes in the way they conceive of continuing education, alumni relations, admissions and commencement, career counseling, undergraduate extracurricular life, and more.

On their part, the alumni and other adults in the university family may take their new university roles lightly, continuing to support alma mater in modest ways and with good feeling; or they may jump wholeheartedly into a rich relationship in which their college or university becomes truly their lifelong intellectual residence. This is what one college president imagined over three-quarters of a century ago:

> It has become a really serious question for the college man of today, where he shall keep his intellectual residence. With many a man it is as serious, to himself at least, as the question where he shall keep his political residence. What better place than his college—his not because it is better than another's but because he knows it. Returning there from time to time he can see with the eyes of a man what he may have missed

seeing with the eyes of a boy. There he may put himself in contact with some of the impracticable things which he does not find among the practicalities with which he is most familiar. There he may touch some of the most vital things which concern living men [an open letter from Dartmouth College President Emeritus William Jewett Tucker to the Boston Alumni Association, January 1913].

Tucker spoke of his all-male institution. Today we include all men and women who welcome a new relationship of giving to and benefiting from alma mater throughout their lives. If this book can help us to approach that goal, it will have served its purpose.

Appendix

Resource List: Experienced Professionals in Alumni Continuing Education

Amherst College
Kent Faerber   413-542-2313
Secretary of the Alumni
  Council
Amherst College
Box 37
Amherst, MA 01002

Black Hills State College
Charles M. Schad   605-642-6446
Director of External Affairs
Kenneth Engelhardt
Director of Continuing
  Education
Black Hills State College
Spearfish, SD 57783

Brigham Young University
Stephen L. Barrett   801-378-2514
Director, BYU Alumni
  Association
Ida Smith   801-378-6745
Coordinator, Alumni Continu-
  ing Education
Alumni House
Brigham Young University
Provo, UT 84602

Brandeis University
Sallie K. Riggs   617-736-4212

Vice-President for Communica-
  tions and Public Relations
  (formerly Associate Vice-
  President for University
  Relations, Brown University)
Brandeis University
Waltham, MA 02254

Brown University
Robert A. Reichley   401-863-
  2453
Vice-President for University
  Relations
William Slack   401-863-2474
Associate Director for
  University Relations
Brown University
Box 1920
Providence, RI 02912

The College of Wooster (Ohio)
Sara L. Patton   216-263-2000
Vice-President for
  Development
Frank Knorr
Director of Development
(former Director of Alumni Re-
  lations who started the al-
  umni college)

287

Marjorie H. Kramer
Executive Director of Alumni
  and College Relations
Jeffrey Todd
Director of Alumni Relations
Wooster, OH 44691

Columbia University
Robert Pollock   212-280-2441
Dean, Columbia College
208 Hamilton Hall
William Oliver   212-280-8439
Executive Director for Alumni
  & University Relations
Box 400, Central Mail Room
Jack Murray   212-280-5541
Director of Alumni Affairs &
  Development
100 Hamilton Hall
Columbia University
New York, NY 10027

Cornell University
Robert MacDougall   607-256-
  4987
Director of Extramural &
  Summer Sessions
B12 Ives Hall
Ralph Janis   607-255-6260
Director, Cornell's Adult
  University
626B Thurston Avenue
Cornell University
Ithaca, NY 14850-2490

CASE (Council for
Advancement and Support
of Education)
John Hall   202-328-5914
Vice President for Alumni
  Administration
11 Dupont Circle, Suite 400
Washington, DC 20036

Dartmouth College
J. Michael McGean   603-646-
  3082
Secretary of the College
Blunt Alumni Center
Steven L. Calvert   603-646-2454
Director of Alumni Continuing
  Education
Associate Director of Alumni
  Affairs
Adjunct Assistant Professor of
  English
308 Blunt Alumni Center
D. Randall Spydell   603-646-
  3757
Project Officer in Continuing
  Education
201 Wentworth Hall
Dartmouth College
Hanover, NH 03755

Duke University
Laney Funderburk, Jr.   919-684-
  5114
Director of Alumni Affairs
Barbara Booth
Director of Alumni Travel &
  Continuing Education
614 Chapel Drive
Duke University
Durham, NC 27706
Judith Ruderman   919-684-6259
Director of Continuing
  Education
Bishop's House
Durham, NC 27708
Linda Carl   919-684-5578
Office of Cultural Affairs
Box 22146 DS
Duke University
Durham, NC 27706

Harvard University
James Quitslund   617-495-5731
Continuing Education
Associated Harvard Alumni
Wadsworth House
Cambridge, MA 02138

Idaho State University
Jennifer Fisher   208-236-2121
Director of Alumni Relations
Idaho State University
Pocatello, ID 83209

Indiana University Alumni Association
Frank B. Jones   812-335-5394
Executive Secretary
Gayle Stuebe   812-335-1711
Director of Indiana
  Mini University
Bloomington, IN 47405

Iowa State University
George H. Ebert   515-294-5033
Program Manager/Conferences
Office of Continuing Education
102 Scheman
Iowa State University
Ames, IA 50011

Johns Hopkins University
William Evitts   301-338-7963
Director of Alumni Relations
Marguerite Ingalls
Assistant Director of Alumni
  Relations
Steinwald Alumni House
Johns Hopkins University
3211 North Charles Street
Baltimore, MD 21218

Lehigh University
Donald Bott   215-861-3135
Executive Director, Alumni
  Association

Janet Tucker
Assistant Executive Director,
  Alumni Association
Leslie A. Brown
Assistant Executive Director,
  Alumni Association
Lehigh University
Alumni Memorial Building 27
Bethlehem, PA 18015

Loyola Marymount University
Dennis J. Branconier   213-642-3065
Director, Alumni Relations
Mark Zangrando   213-642-3065
Assistant Director, Alumni
  Relations
Loyola Marymount University
Rancho Palos Verdes, CA
  90274

McMaster University
Kenneth Fredrick   416-525-9140
  x2499
Director of Alumni Affairs
Alumni Memorial Hall
McMaster University
Hamilton, Ontario
  Canada L8S 4K1

Massachusetts Institute of Technology (MIT)
William Hecht   617-253-8204
Executive Vice-President, MIT
Joe Martori   617-253-8230
Associate Secretary of the
  Alumni Association
Robert Blake   617-253-8243
Regional Director for the West
MIT Alumni Association
MIT Alumni Center
Cambridge, MA 02139

Middlebury College
Hugh W. Marlow   802-388-3711
   x5202
Director of Alumni Relations
Forest Hall
Middlebury College
Middlebury, VT 05753

Mount Holyoke College
Carolyn Berkey   413-538-2300
Executive Director
Rosemary Matchak
Associate Executive Director
Kim Poolman   413-538-2652
Assistant Executive Director
   for Programs
Mount Holyoke Alumni
   Association
Mount Holyoke College
South Hadley, MA 01075

New York University
Mark Kalish   212-598-7937
Director of Alumni Relations
Kathleen Connick   212-598-2710
Assistant Director
New York University
22 Washington Square North
New York, NY 10011

Northwestern University
Don Collins   312-491-5255
Associate Provost
Jane Eesley   312-491-8550
Coordinator for Special
   Programs
Northwestern University
Rebecca Crown Center
633 Clark Street
Evanston, IL 60201
Ray Willemain   312-491-7660
Director of Alumni Relations
Northwestern University
Evanston, IL 60201

Ohio University
W. Barry Adams   614-594-5128
Director of Alumni Relations
Kristen Koeller
Administrative Intern
52 University Terrace
P. O. Box 869
Athens, OH 45701-5128

Ohio Wesleyan University
Laura Newman   614-369-4431
   x659
Director of Alumni Relations
Ohio Wesleyan University
16 University Avenue
Delaware, OH 43015

Pennsylvania State University
William Rothwell   814-865-6516
Executive Director of the
   Alumni Association
105 Old Main
Pennsylvania State University
University Park, PA 16802

Pomona College
Lee Harlan   714-621-8110
Director, Alumni Relations
The Seaver House
305 N. College Avenue
Claremont, CA 91711

Princeton University
Daniel N. White
Director of the Alumni Council
MaryMargaret Halsey   609-452-
   5815
Associate Director of the
   Alumni Council
The John Maclean House
Box 291
Princeton University
Princeton, NJ 08540

Reed College
Caroline H. Locher   503-777-7589
Alumni Director
Florence W. Lehman
Archivist and Alumni Director
 Emeritus (24 years)
Reed College
Portland, OR 97202

Rutgers, The State University of New Jersey
Mary Ruth Snyder   201-932-7061
University Director of Alumni
 Relations
Madeline A. Scott
Senior Alumni Relations
 Officer
Rutgers University Alumni
 Federation
172 College Avenue
New Brunswick, NJ 08903

Southern Methodist University
Gary A. Ransdell   214-692-3006
Executive Director
Office of Alumni Relations
Southern Methodist
 University
Dallas, TX 75275

Stanford University
William Stone   415-723-2021
Executive Director
Marian Player
Director of Continuing
 Education
Jenée Zenger
Assistant Director of
 Continuing Education
Beverly Smith
Associate Director of the
 Alumni Association

Peter R. Voll
Director of Travel/Study
 Programs
Stanford Alumni Association
Bowman Alumni House
Stanford, CA 94305-1618

Tufts University
Ronald C. Brinn   617-381-3526
Director of Alumni Relations
Tufts University
Medford, MA 02155

University of Arizona
Kent D. Rollins   602-621-7576
Director of Alumni
University of Arizona
Tucson, AZ 85721

University of Chicago
Carol Linné   312-753-2176
Executive Director of
 Alumni Affairs
Ruth Halloran   312-753-2178
Associate Director of
 Alumni Affairs
University of Chicago Alumni
 Association
Robie House
5757 Woodlawn Avenue
Chicago, IL 60637

University of Colorado, Boulder
Rich Emerson   303-492-8484
Director of Alumni Relations
Nancy Levitt
Assistant Director for Special
 Events
Koenig Alumni Center
Boulder, CO 80309-0459

University of Delaware
Patricia Kent   302-451-8841
Program Specialist in
 Continuing Education

University of Delaware
Newark, DE 19716

**University of Illinois
(Chicago Campus)**
Dorothy DiIorio   312-996-8535
Director, Chicago Campus
University of Illinois Alumni
  Association
4400 S. Peoria Street
Chicago, IL 60607

University of Michigan
Robert G. Forman   313-763-2452
Executive Director, Alumni
  Association
University of Michigan
  Alumni Center
200 Fletcher Street
Ann Arbor, MI 48109

**University of North Carolina
at Chapel Hill**
Warren Nord   919-962-1123
Director, Program in the
  Humanities
Division of Continuing
  Education
209 Abernethy 002a
University of North Carolina
Chapel Hill, NC 27514

University of Northern Iowa
Elly Leslie   319-273-2355
Director of Alumni Relations
University of Northern Iowa
Cedar Falls, IA 50614

University of Notre Dame
James Pollicita   219-239-6000 /
  800-348-5060
Director of Alumni Continuing
  Education
University of Notre Dame
  Alumni Association

201 Main Building
Notre Dame, IN 46556

University of Oregon
Philip J. Super   503-686-5656
Executive Director
University of Oregon
  Alumni Association
Eugene, OR 97403-9990

University of Pennsylvania
David G. Burnett   215-898-4819
Director, College of General
  Studies
Rhea Mandell   215-898-6940
Program Director
112 Logan Hall/CN
Michel Huber   215-898-7811
Director of Alumni Relations
John Hayden   215-898-7811
Assistant Director of Alumni
  Relations
E. Craig Sweeten Alumni
  Center
3533 Locust Walk/CQ
University of Pennsylvania
Philadelphia, PA 19104

University of Tennessee
David M. Roberts   615-974-3011
Associate Vice President
University of Tennessee
Suite 600, Andy Holt Tower
Knoxville, TN 37996

University of Virginia
Dean of Continuing Education
  804-924-0987
Dan Murdaugh   804-924-0987
Director, Summer on the Lawn
Arthur Green, Jr.   804-924-0987
Program Specialist, Summer
  on the Lawn
104 Midmont Lane

University of Virginia
Charlottesville, VA 22903

University of Wisconsin
Gayle Langer   608-262-2551
Associate Director, Wisconsin
  Alumni Association
650 North Lake Street
Madison, WI 53706

Vanderbilt University
William Meadows 615-322-2929
Director of Alumni Relations
117 Alumni Hall
Vanderbilt University
Nashville, TN 37240

Washington and Lee University
Robert Fure   703-463-8723
Director of Summer Programs,
  and Director of Alumni Continuing Education Programs
36 Washington Hall
Washington and Lee University
Lexington, VA 24450

Wellesley College
Anne Mitchell Morgan   617-235-0320
Executive Director

Wellesley College Alumnae
  Association
Wellesley, MA 02181

Wesleyan University
John Driscoll   203-247-9411
Director of Alumni Relations
Wesleyan University
Middletown, CT 06457

Williams College
R. Cragin Lewis   413-597-2151
Director of Alumni Relations
Williams College
P. O. Box 38
Williamstown, MA 01267

Yale University
Eustace D. Theodore   203-432-1940
Executive Director, Association
  of Yale Alumni
Nina Glickson   203-432-1944
Associate Director for Pro-
  grams, AYA
Jadwiga Sebrechts   203-432-1936
Associate Director for Educa-
  tion & Communications
901-A Yale Station
Yale University
New Haven, CT 06520

BIBLIOGRAPHY

ADLER, MORTIMER. "The Disappearance of Culture." *Newsweek*, 21 August 1978, p. 15.

APPS, JEROLD W. *Problems in Continuing Education*. New York: McGraw-Hill, 1979.

ARLETT, ALLAN. "Putting Capitalism to Work: Serve Your Alumni–and Make a Profit Too!" CASE *Currents*, December 1975, pp. 8–10.

ASLANIAN, CAROL B., AND BRICKELL, HENRY M. *Americans in Transition: Life Changes as Reasons for Adult Learning*. New York: College Entrance Examination Board, 1980.

BAILEY, STEPHEN K. "Political Ecology of Continuing Higher Education," *Proceedings of the 43rd Annual Meeting*. Knoxville, TN: Association for Continuing Higher Education, 1981, pp. 3–11.

BARRETT, STEPHEN L. "Add More Education to Your Travel Program." CASE *Currents*, May 1979, p. 33.

——. "Continuing Education for Alumni." CASE *Currents*, April 1976, pp. 18–19.

——, ed. *Passport to Successful Alumni Travel Programs*, revised ed. Washington, DC: Council for Advancement and Support of Education, 1983.

BENNE, KENNETH D. "Adult Education in a University." *Journal of Higher Education*, vol. 27, nos. 8 and 9 (November and December 1956).

BENNETT, WILLIAM. *To Reclaim a Legacy*. Washington, D.C.: National Endowment for the Humanities, 1984.

BERGEVIN, PAUL. *A Philosophy for Adult Education*. New York: Seabury Press, 1967.

BLIWISE, ROBERT J. "Greetings from the Cape." *Duke*, vol. 72, no. 4 (May–June 1986), pp. 36–39.

BOSANQUET, BERNARD, ed. *The Education of the Young in "The Republic" of Plato*. Cambridge: At the University Press, 1901.

CALVERT, STEVEN L. "Legitimizing the Bastard: The 'Natural' Child of Higher Education—Alumni Continuing Education," *Proceedings of "The Role of Non-Credit Programs in Higher Education: Administrative Issues,"* Kansas State University's National Issues in Higher Education Series, vol. 7, Fall 1982, pp. 54–63.

———. "A New Professionalism & the Future of Alumni Relations." Keynote address at Council for Advancement and Support of Education's District III Annual Conference, Atlanta, GA, 10 February 1986.

———. "Seminal Thinkers in the History of the Alumni Continuing Education Movement at Dartmouth College, 1913–1970." Unpublished report at Dartmouth College, Hanover, NH, April 1981.

———. "Planning Meaningful Reunions," in *Handbook of Institutional Advancement*, A. Westley Rowland, General Editor. San Francisco: Jossey-Bass, 1986, pp. 450–459.

CAMPBELL, DUNCAN D. *The New Majority: Adult Learners in the University*. Winnipeg: University of Alberta Press, 1984.

CARL, LINDA. *The Alumni College Movement*. Washington, DC: Council for Advancement and Support of Education, 1978.

———. "Arranging Alumni Education." *CASE Currents*, March 1986a, pp. 38–40.

———. "Strengthening Alumni Ties through Continuing Education," in *Handbook of Institutional Advancement*, A. Westley Rowland, General Editor. San Francisco: Jossey-Bass, 1986b, pp. 426–439.

CARNEGIE COMMISSION ON HIGHER EDUCATION. *Toward a Learning Society: Alternative Channels to Life, Work, and Service*. New York: McGraw-Hill, 1973.

CASTRO, JANICE. "Cultivating Late Bloomers: Smith's Ada Comstock Scholars Give More Than They Take." *Time,* 21 November 1983, p. 52.

———. Conference reports: (1) Evening College and Extension Administration as a Profession. Chicago, 1957; (2) New Dimensions of University Responsibility for the Liberal Education of Adults, Daytona Beach, FL, 1956.

CENTER FOR THE STUDY OF LIBERAL EDUCATION FOR ADULTS. *New Directions in Liberal Education for Executives,* March 1958.

———. *New Directions in Programming for University Adult Education,* 1957.

———. "Professional Preparation of Adult Educators: A Symposium," December 1956.

CENTRE FOR EDUCATIONAL RESEARCH AND INNOVATION. *Recurrent Education: A Strategy for Lifelong Learning.* Paris: Organisation for Economic Co-operation and Development, 1973.

———. Recurrent Education: Trends and Issues. Paris: Organisation for Economic Co-operation and Development, 1975.

CLEARINGHOUSE BULLETIN. "Alumni Institutes at Washington University." Reprint by the Center for the Study of Liberal Education for Adults, December 1958.

COMMISSION ON HIGHER EDUCATION AND THE ADULT LEARNER. Reported in *Chronicle of Higher Education,* 5 December 1984, n.p.

COOPER, ROBERT G. "Slicing the Big Marshmallow: Finding Your Market Identity in the Field of Continuing Education for Alumni." CASE *Currents,* September 1979, pp. 24–27.

CRIMI, JAMES E. "Adult Education in the Liberal Arts Colleges." Center for the Study of Liberal Education in Adults, September 1957.

CROPLEY, A. J., ed. *Towards a System of Lifelong Education: Some Practical Considerations.* Advances in Lifelong Education, vol. 7. New York: Pergamon Press and UNESCO Institute for Education, 1980.

CROSS, K. PATRICIA. *Adults as Learners.* San Francisco: Jossey-Bass, 1981

———. *The Missing Link: Connecting Adult Learners to Learning Resources.* New York: Future Directions for a Learning Society, The College Board, 1978.

———, AND MCCARTAN, ANNE-MARIE. *Adult Learning: State Policies and Institutional Practices.* ASHE-ERIC Higher Education Research Report No. 1. Washington, DC: Association for the Study of Higher Education, 1984.

————, VALLEY, J. R., AND ASSOCIATES. *Planning Non-Traditional Programs: An Analysis of the Issues for Postsecondary Education.* San Francisco: Jossey-Bass, 1974.

CUMMINGS, JACK B. "A Dozen for Alumni." CASE *Currents,* January 1976, pp. 11–12.

CUMMINGS, PETER. "Alumni Serenade: A Medley of 17 Off-Campus Activities to Have Them Singing Your School's Praises." CASE *Currents,* February 1983, pp. 34–35.

D'AMROSIO, JOHN. "A Study of Alumni Programming Goals at Units of the State University of New York." Unpublished Doctoral Dissertation, 1978.

DANIEL, CARTER A. "Notes for a Dissenting Commencement Address." *Chronicle of Higher Education,* vol. 18, no. 11 (7 May 1979), p. 56.

DARTMOUTH ALUMNI MAGAZINE. "The Alumni College" (report on its beginnings at Lafayette College in 1929), vol. 22 (November 1929), pp. 7–8.

————. "Back to the Books: Eleven-Day Alumni College Offers Recharge for Liberal Arts Batteries" (announcement of Dartmouth's first modern-day "Alumni College"), February 1964, p. 16.

————. "Dartmouth Lectures in Manchester," vol. 11, 1918–1919, pp. 293–294.

————. Hanover Holiday Plus Alumni College" (projections for first program for June 1937), vol. 29 (May 1937), pp. 15–16, 22.

————. "Noted Speakers Announced for Dartmouth Lectureships," vol. 13 (1920–1921), pp. 374–375, 439–440.

DARTMOUTH COLLEGE, TRUSTEES PLANNING COMMITTEE OF. *Report of the Committee on Alumni Relations, Sub-Committee on Intellectual Interests and Activities.* Hanover, NH: Dartmouth College, May 1958, pp. 1–19.

DIEKHOFF, JOHN S. "The Alumni University." *Journal of Higher Education,* vol. 28, no. 7 (October 1957).

DRAVES, BILL. *The Free University: A Model for Lifelong Learning.* Chicago: Follett Publishing Co., 1980.

DUEITT, SUE B. "American Higher Education Alumni Programs—A Goals Analysis." Ann Arbor, MI: University Microfilms International, 1975.

EBERT, GEORGE H. "The Certainty Method: Its Application to the Iowa State University Alumni Continuing Education Seminars." Paper presented at the Adult Education Research Conference, 17 April 1974, Chicago.

———. "Participation Factors and Educational Needs Associated with the Iowa State University Alumni College Education Seminars." Unpublished Doctoral Dissertation, 1972.

EISENBERG, GERSON G. *Learning Vacations.* Baltimore: Eisenberg Educational Enterprises, 1977.

———. *Learning Vacations.* Princeton, NJ: Peterson's Guides, fourth ed., 1982.

EKLUND, LOWELL. "The Alumni University—Education's 'New Frontier.' " Reprinted from *Adult Education,* Spring 1961.

———. "The Oakland Plan." *Alma Mater,* no. 5, November 1964, pp. 16–17.

———. "The Oakland Plan for the Continuing Education of Alumni." Reprinted from *Adult Leadership,* November 1966.

———. "University Extension Before 1915." *The NUEA Spectator,* June 1976, vol. XL, no. 24, pp. 6–8.

E. P. E. 15-minute Report. Editorial Projects for Education, vol. 16, no. 6 (1 December 1978), p. 4.

EMERSON, RALPH WALDO. "The American Scholar." *Selected Prose and Poetry,* second ed. Introduction by Reginald L. Cook. New York: Holt, Rinehart & Winston, 1969.

EPSTEIN, JOSEPH. "The Noblest Distraction." *Commentary,* August 1981, p. 55.

ERIKSON, ERIK. *Identity and the Life Cycle.* New York: W. W. Norton, 1980.

———. *The Life Cycle Completed: A Review.* New York: W. W. Norton, 1982.

EURICH, NELL P. *Corporate Classrooms: The Learning Business.* Princeton, NJ: Carnegie Foundation for the Advancement of Teaching, 1985.

FERGUSON, MARILYN. *The Aquarian Conspiracy: Personal and Social Transformation in the 1980s.* Los Angeles: J. P. Tarcher, Inc., 1980.

FORMAN, ROBERT G. "Alumni Relations: Moving into the Mainstream." CASE *Currents,* May 1979, pp. 6–9.

FREDRICK, KENNETH. "An Affair of the Mind." Paper presented to the annual conference of the Canadian Association for University Continuing Education, Ottawa, June 19, 1986.

FRIEDAN, BETTY. *The Feminine Mystique.* New York: Dell Publishing Co., 1974.

GABOR, STANLEY C. "The Adult Learner in Continuing Education." *Continuing Higher Education,* vol. 30, no. 1 (Winter 1982), pp. 2–7.

GARDNER, JOHN W. *Excellence: Can We Be Equal and Excellent Too?* New York: Harper & Row, 1961.

———. *Self-Renewal: The Individual and the Innovative Society.* New York: Harper & Row, 1963, 1964.

GARTNER, ALAN; GREER, COLIN; AND RIESSMAN, FRANK, eds. *After Deschooling, What?* New York: Harper & Row, 1973.

GOULD, SAMUEL B. "Quality in Adult Education." Address to the Association of University Evening Colleges. Louisville, KY, 17 November 1958.

———, AND CROSS, K. PATRICIA, eds. *Explorations in Non-Traditional Study.* San Francisco: Jossey-Bass, 1972.

GREEN CHAIR GROUP. *Predicting Distant Education in the Year 2001: Final Report.* Washington, DC: National Home Study Council, 1982.

GROSS, RONALD. *The Lifelong Learner: A Guide to Self-Development.* New York: Simon & Schuster, 1977.

———, HEBERT, T., AND TOUGH, A. *Independent, Self-Directed Learners in American Life: The Other Eighty Percent of Learning.* Washington, DC: Postsecondary Education Convening Authority, 1977.

HALL, JAMES W. "Let's Find a Way to Evaluate Experimental Learning." *Chronicle of Higher Education,* 5 November 1979, p. 56.

HARPER, NANCY. "Calling Adventurous Alumni to White Water, Black Sea." CASE *Currents,* June 1976, pp. 10–12.

———. "Turn Off TV, Tune in a Book." CASE *Currents,* February 1977, pp. 29–30.

HARRINGTON, FRED HARVEY. *The Future of Adult Education: New Responsibilities of Colleges and Universities.* San Francisco: Jossey-Bass, 1977.

HEFFERNAN, JAMES M.; MACY, FRANCIS U.; AND VICKERS, DONN F. *Educational Brokering: A New Service for Adult Learners.* Syracuse, NY: National Center for Educational Brokering, 1976.

HESBURGH, THEODORE M., C. S. C.; MILLER, PAUL A.; AND WHARTON, CLIFTON R., JR. *Patterns for Lifelong Learning.* San Francisco: Jossey-Bass, 1974.

HILL, HERBERT. "Those Early Days of Alumni College." *Dartmouth Alumni Magazine*, March 1971, p. 15.

HOPKINS, ERNEST MARTIN. "The Critical Period for the American College," *Educational Review*, February 1910, pp. 165–175.

————. "The Future of the American College" (1916 Inaugural Address on assuming the presidency of Dartmouth College). *Dartmouth Alumni Magazine*, vol. 9 (1916–1917), pp. 9–17.

HOULE, CYRIL O. "Community Educational Services as an Emerging Function of Higher Education," *The Community Responsibilities of Institutions of Higher Learning*, Norman Burns and Cyril O. Houle, eds. Chicago, IL: University of Chicago Press, 1948.

————. *The Design of Education*. San Francisco: Jossey-Bass, 1972.

————. *The Inquiring Mind*. Madison: University of Wisconsin Press, 1961.

————. *Patterns of Learning*. San Francisco: Jossey-Bass, 1984.

————, AND NELSON, CHARLES A. *The University, the Citizen, and World Affairs*. Washington, DC: American Council on Education, 1956.

ILLICH, IVAN. *Deschooling Society*. New York: Harper & Row, 1971.

IOWA STATE UNIVERSITY. "Iowa State University Alumni Survey: Preliminary Tabulations." Ames: Iowa State University, August 1980.

JOWETT, BENJAMIN, ed. *The Republic of Plato*, Third ed., 2 vols. Oxford: Clarendon Press, 1908.

KATCHADOURIAN, HERANT, AND BOLI, JOHN. *Careerism and Intellectualism Among College Students: Patterns of Academic and Career Choice in the Undergraduate Years*. San Francisco: Jossey-Bass, 1985.

KEATES, JON. "The Alumni Auditor Cometh." Washington, DC: CASE *Currents*, February 1980, p. 21.

KITZHABER, ALBERT R. *Themes, Theories, and Therapy: The Teaching of Writing in College*, Report of the Dartmouth Study of Student Writing. New York: McGraw-Hill, 1963.

KNOWLES, MALCOLM S. *The Adult Education Movement in the United States*. New York: Holt, Rinehart & Winston, 1962.

————. *The Adult Learner: A Neglected Species*, second ed. Houston, TX: Gulf Publishing Co., 1978.

————. "Adult Learning in the Next 20 Years." *Learning Connection*, vol. 3, no. 3 (Fall 1982), p. 3.

————. *Higher Adult Education in the United States: The Current Picture, Trends, and Issues*. Washington, DC: American Council on Education, 1969.

————, AND ASSOCIATES. *Andragogy in Action: Applying Modern Principles of Adult Learning*. San Francisco: Jossey-Bass, 1984.

KNOX, ALAN B. *Adult Development and Learning: A Handbook on Individual Growth and Competence in the Adult Years for Education and the Helping Professions*. San Francisco: Jossey-Bass, 1977.

LANGAS, ASPASIA. "Women's Careers Shift Gears." *CASE Currents*, July 1979, p. 17.

LENZ, ELINOR, *Creating and Marketing Programs in Continuing Education*. New York: McGraw-Hill, 1980.

LEVINSON, DANIEL J., WITH DARROW, CHARLOTTE N.; KLEIN, EDWARD B.; LEVINSON, MARIA H.; AND MCKEE, BRAXTON. *The Seasons of a Man's Life*. New York: Ballantine Books, 1978.

LOEVINGER, JANE. *Ego Development: Conceptions and Theories*. San Francisco: Jossey-Bass, 1976.

LOWE, JOHN. *The Education of Adults: A World Perspective*. Toronto: UNESCO, second ed., 1982.

MCHUGH, G. MICHAEL. "More Than a Sentimental Journey: Give Your Alumni Something to Think About with a Reunion Mini-College." *CASE Currents*, February 1984, pp. 26–27.

MCINTOSH, NAOMI E. *A Degree of Difference: The Open University of the United Kingdom*. New York: Praeger, 1977.

MCMAHON, ERNEST E. "New Directions for Alumni: Continuing Education for the College Graduate," Chicago: Center for the Study of Liberal Education for Adults, 1960.

————. "A Period of Economic Depression and Restructuring, 1929–1941." *The NUEA Spectactor*, June 1976, vol. XL, no. 24, pp. 13–15.

MALONE, VIOLET M., AND DILLER, MARY ANN. *The Guidance Function and Counseling Roles in an Adult Education Program*. Washington, DC: National Association for Public Continuing and Adult Education, 1978.

NEWMAN, JOHN HENRY CARDINAL. *The Idea of a University Defined and Illustrated*. New York: Longmans, Green, 1939.

NEWMAN, LAURA. "Summerweek: Plenty of 'Positive Fallout.' " *CASE Currents*, June 1979, pp. 30–32.

NOFFSINGER, JOHN S. *Correspondence Schools, Lyceums, Chautauquas*. New York: Macmillan, 1926.

PARKE, K. *The Folk College in America.* Rochester, NY: Cricket Press, 1977.

PENLAND, P. *Individual Self-Planned Learning in America.* Washington, DC: Office of Education, Department of Health, Education, and Welfare, 1977.

PERRY, SIR WALTER. "Locked into an Outdated Philosophy of Learning." *Chronicle of Higher Education,* 27 November 1978, p. 72.

PETERS, THOMAS J., AND WATERMAN, ROBERT H., JR. *In Search of Excellence: Lessons from America's Best-Run Companies.* New York: Harper & Row, 1982.

PETERSON, RICHARD E., AND ASSOCIATES. *Lifelong Learning in America.* San Francisco: Jossey-Bass, 1980.

PIRSIG, ROBERT M. *Zen and the Art of Motorcycle Maintenance: An Inquiry into Values.* New York: Bantam Books, 1974.

RICHBURG, KEITH B. "College Students' Average Age Rises." *Washington Post,* 14 August 1985.

RIGGS, SALLIE K. "Attracting 'New' Alumni through Continuing Education." CASE *Currents,* May 1979, pp. 20–22.

ROBERTSON, ADELLE F. "Profile Changes of Continuing Education Students in the 80s: External and Internal Forces," *Proceedings of the 43rd Annual Meeting.* Knoxville, TN: Association for Continuing Higher Education, 1981, pp. 33–41.

ROWLAND, A. WESTLEY. *Handbook of Institutional Advancement,* second ed. San Francisco: Jossey-Bass, 1986.

SHEATS, PAUL A. AND SMITH, LYNDA T. "A Period of Divergent Influences, 1941–1950." *The NUEA Spectator,* June 1976, vol. XL, no. 24, pp. 16–18.

SINGER, MARK. "Alumni Magazines: The Editors Reach Out." *The Nation,* 5 October 1974, pp. 306–308.

SMITH, HUSTON, "Teaching to a Camera." *Educational Record,* vol. 37, no. 1 (January 1956).

SMITH, R. M.; AKER, G. F.; AND KIDD, J. R. *Handbook of Adult Education.* New York: Macmillan, 1970.

————, AND HAVERKAMP, K. K. "Toward a Theory of Learning How to Learn." *Adult Education,* vol. 28 (Fall 1977), pp. 3–21.

STERN, MILTON. "At a Slight Angle to the University." Address to the NEH-NUEA Conference on Continuing Education in the Humanities, Memphis, TN, 1979.

THEODORE, EUSTACE D. Interviewed in "A Teacher Moves In at Alumni House," *Yale Alumni Magazine*, vol. 45, no. 1 (October 1981).

THOMPSON, JOHN C. "How to Plan an Alumni Week." CASE *Currents*, September 1975, pp. 12–14.

TOPOR, ROBERT. *Marketing Higher Education: A Practical Guide.* Washington, DC: Council for Advancement and Support of Education, 1983.

TRIPPETT, FRANK. "A New Distrust of the Experts." *Time*, 14 May 1979, pp. 54, 59.

TURNER, JUDITH AXLER. "Private Company to Offer 170 Courses by Computer in 'Electronic University.'" *Chronicle of Higher Education*, 21 September 1983, p. 18.

University of Michigan: An Encyclopedic Survey. Ann Arbor: University of Michigan Press, 1942.

VAILLANT, GEORGE E. *Adaptation to Life.* Boston: Little, Brown, 1977.

VINCENT, JOHN. *The Chautauqua Movement.* Boston: Chautauqua Press, 1886.

WEDEMEYER, CHARLES A. "Determinants of Educational Change: The Period 1915–1929. *The NUEA Spectator*, June 1976, vol. XL, no. 24, pp. 9–12.

WHITE, DANIEL N. "The Festival and Fantasy of Princeton Reunions." *Princeton Alumni Weekly*, 8 May 1978; pp. 26–33.

WIDMAYER, CHARLES, E. *Hopkins of Dartmouth.* Hanover, NH: University Press of New England, 1977.

WINTER, DAVID G.; MCCLELLAND, DAVID C.; AND STEWART, ABIGAIL J. *A New Case for the Liberal Arts: Assessing Institutional Goals and Student Development.* San Francisco: Jossey-Bass, 1981.

YALE UNIVERSITY COMMISSION ON ALUMNI AFFAIRS. *Report of the Commission on Alumni Affairs.* New Haven, CT: Yale University, 1970.

INDEX

INDEX